CBSP: Escape From Bitch Mountain

By Abi Bailey, Lauren Burke, Liana Buzska, Hannah K. Chapman, Amy Chase, Atla Hrafney, Nicole Miles, Jenny Mure, Ahmara Smith, April Szafranski, Becca Tobin, Léa Vera Toro, Mathilde Van Gheluwe, Korinna Veropoulou and Jenn Woodall

Published by Avery Hill Publishing

First Printing October 2018

ISBN: 978-1-910395-44-8

ESCAPE FROM BITCH MOUNTAIN

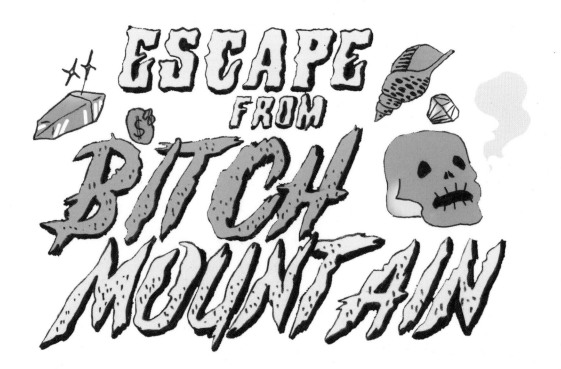

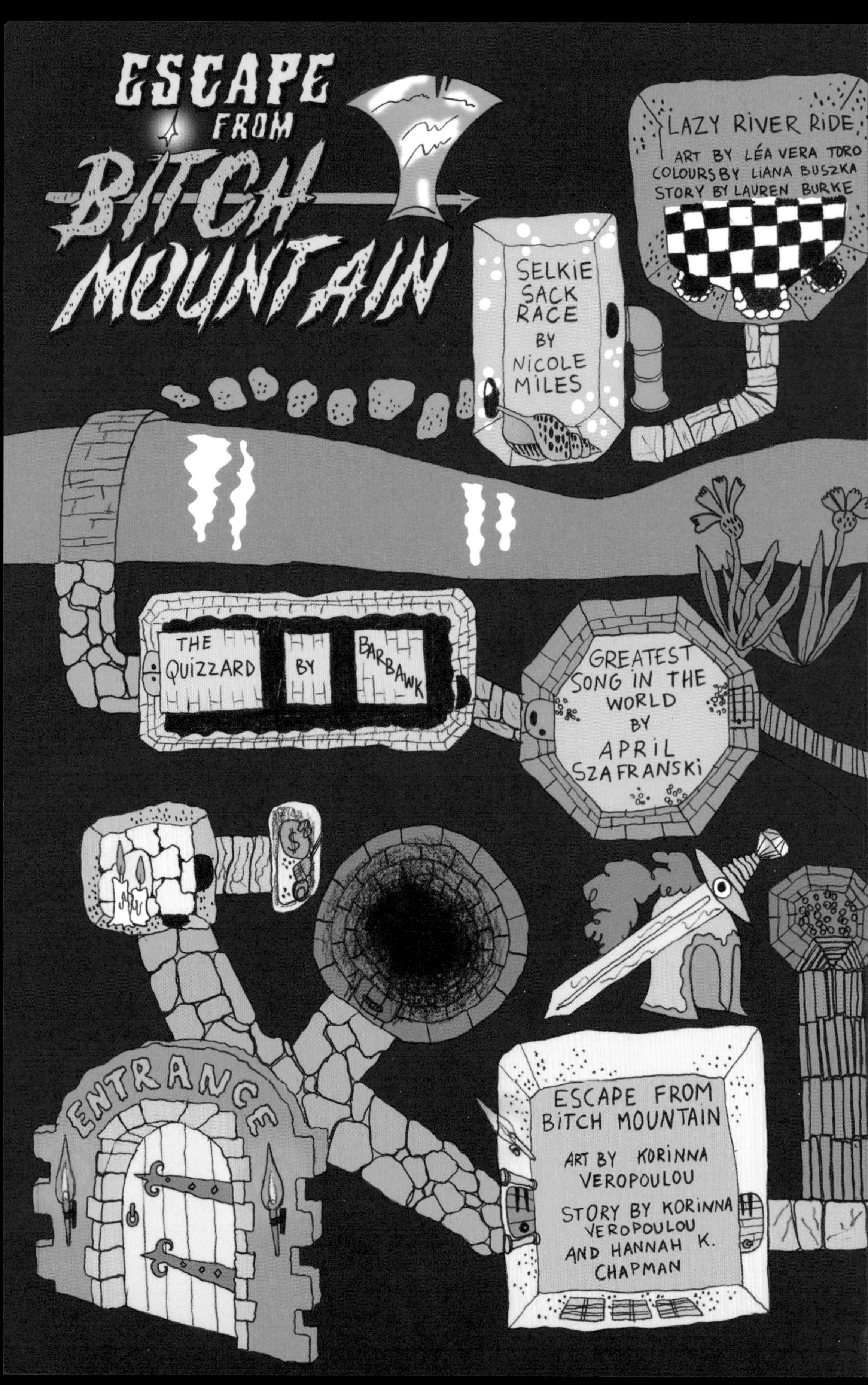
ESCAPE FROM BITCH MOUNTAIN
LAZY RIVER RIDE
ART BY LÉA VERA TORO
COLOURS BY LIANA BUSZKA
STORY BY LAUREN BURKE
SELKIE SACK RACE BY NICOLE MILES
THE QUIZZARD BY BARBAWK
GREATEST SONG IN THE WORLD BY APRIL SZAFRANSKI
ENTRANCE
ESCAPE FROM BITCH MOUNTAIN
ART BY KORINNA VEROPOULOU
STORY BY KORINNA VEROPOULOU AND HANNAH K. CHAPMAN

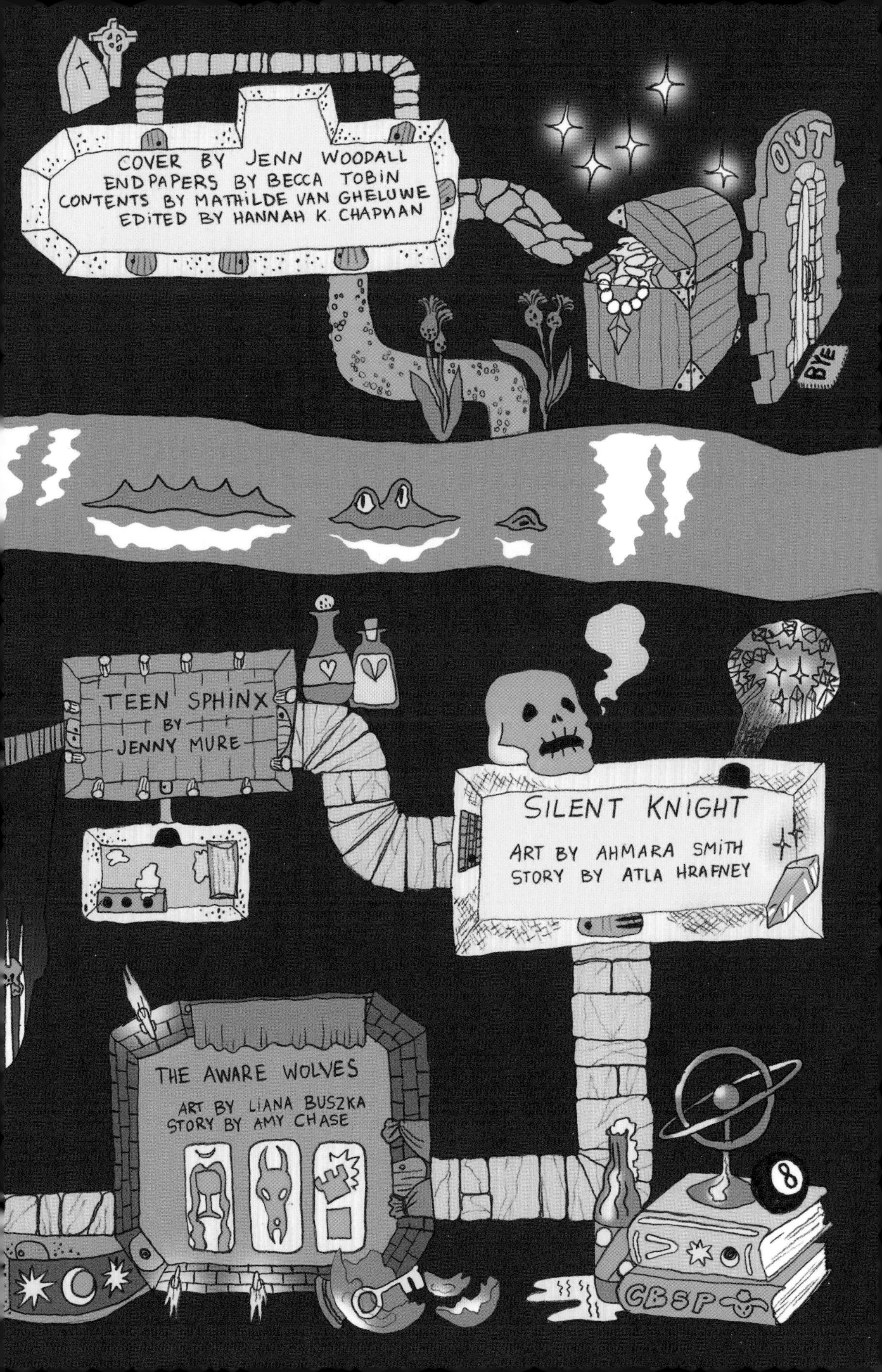
COVER BY JENN WOODALL
ENDPAPERS BY BECCA TOBIN
CONTENTS BY MATHILDE VAN GHELUWE
EDITED BY HANNAH K. CHAPMAN
OUT
BYE
TEEN SPHINX
BY
JENNY MURE
SILENT KNIGHT
ART BY AHMARA SMITH
STORY BY ATLA HRAFNEY
THE AWARE WOLVES
ART BY LIANA BUSZKA
STORY BY AMY CHASE
8
CBSP

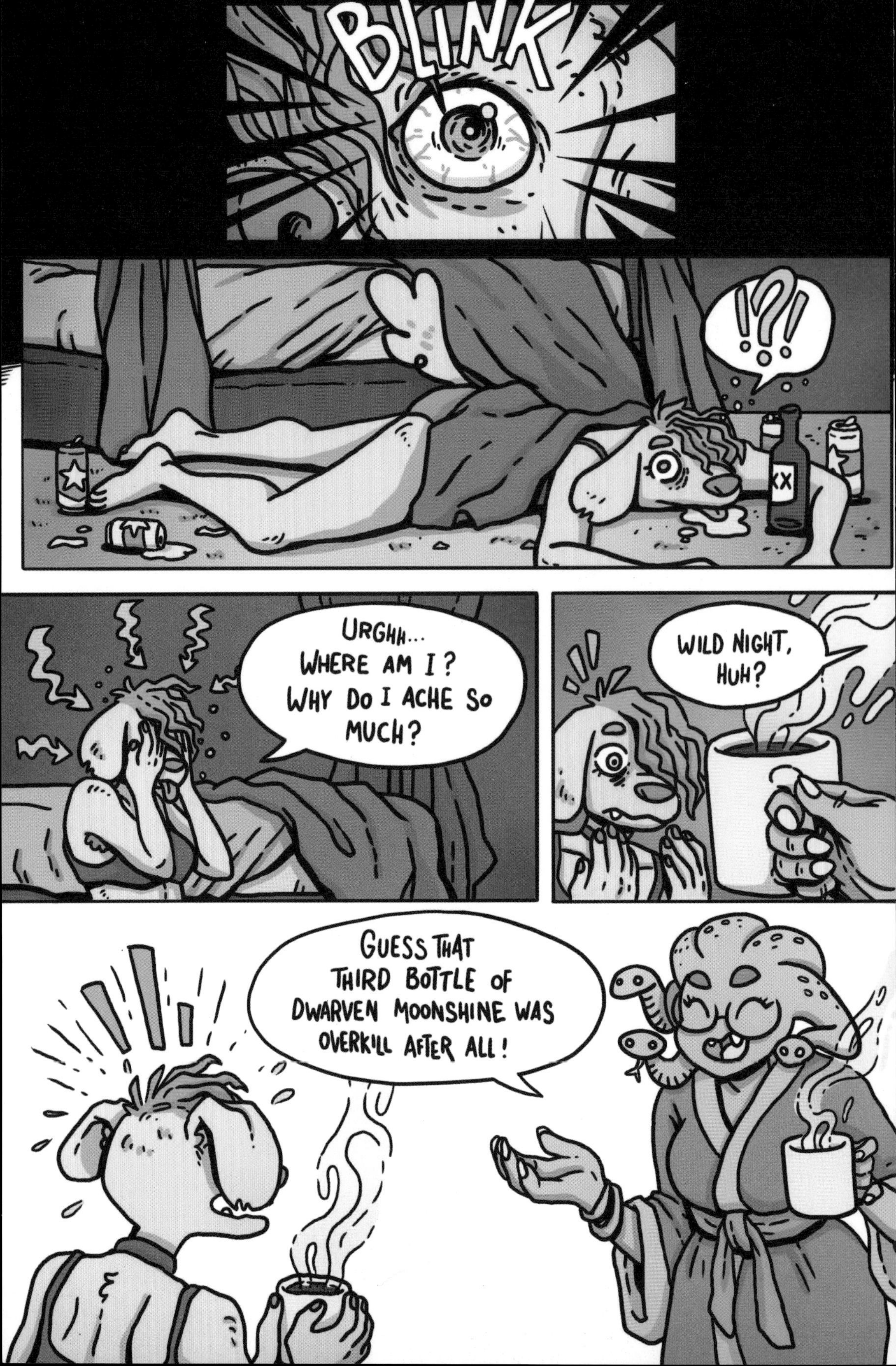
BLINK
!?!
URGHH...
WHERE AM I?
WHY DO I ACHE SO MUCH?
WILD NIGHT, HUH?
GUESS THAT THIRD BOTTLE OF DWARVEN MOONSHINE WAS OVERKILL AFTER ALL!

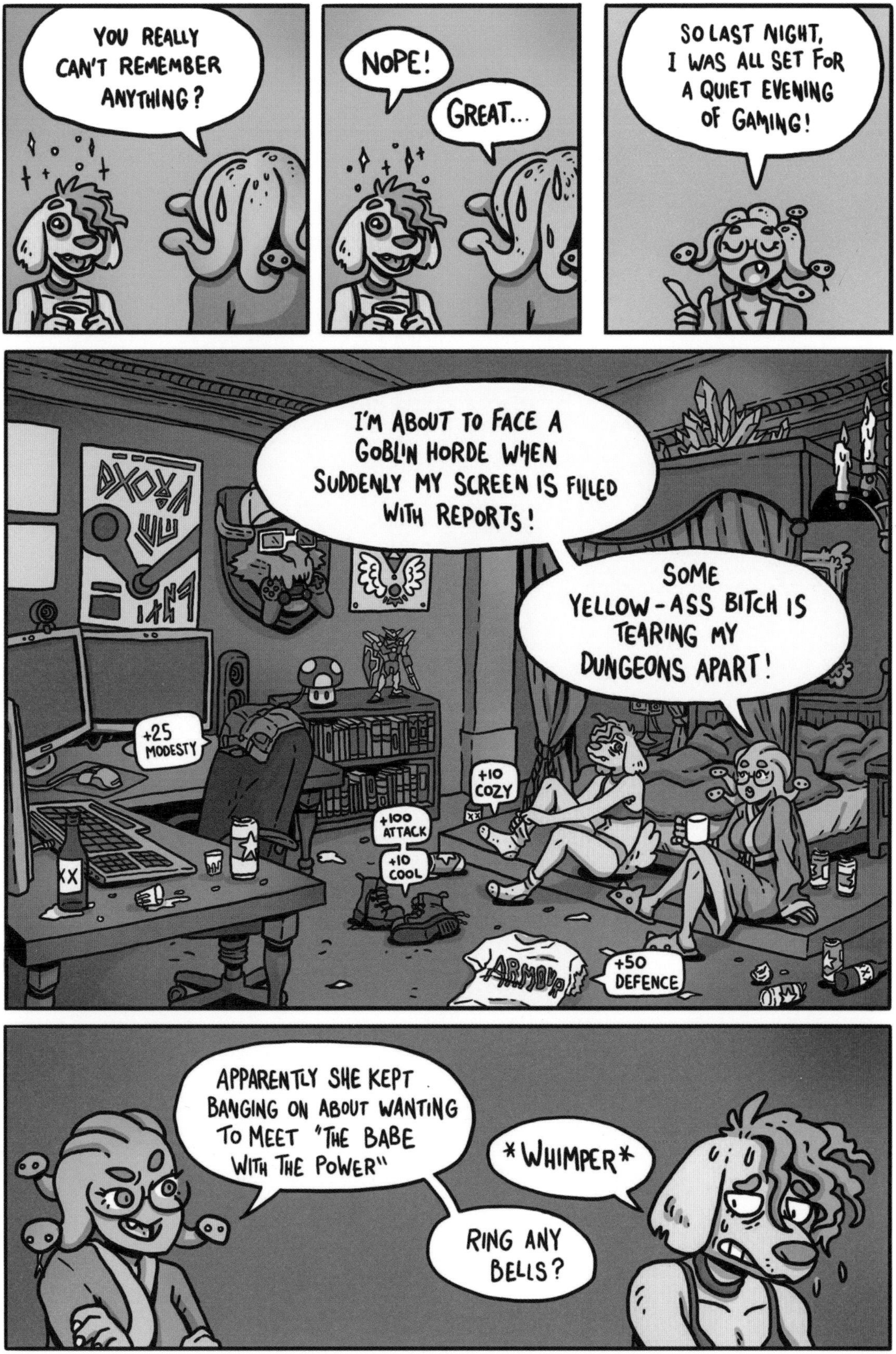

YOU REALLY CAN'T REMEMBER ANYTHING?
NOPE!
GREAT...
SO LAST NIGHT, I WAS ALL SET FOR A QUIET EVENING OF GAMING!
I'M ABOUT TO FACE A GOBLIN HORDE WHEN SUDDENLY MY SCREEN IS FILLED WITH REPORTS!
SOME YELLOW-ASS BITCH IS TEARING MY DUNGEONS APART!
+25 MODESTY
+10 COZY
+100 ATTACK
+10 COOL
ARMOUR
+50 DEFENCE
APPARENTLY SHE KEPT BANGING ON ABOUT WANTING TO MEET "THE BABE WITH THE POWER"
WHIMPER
RING ANY BELLS?

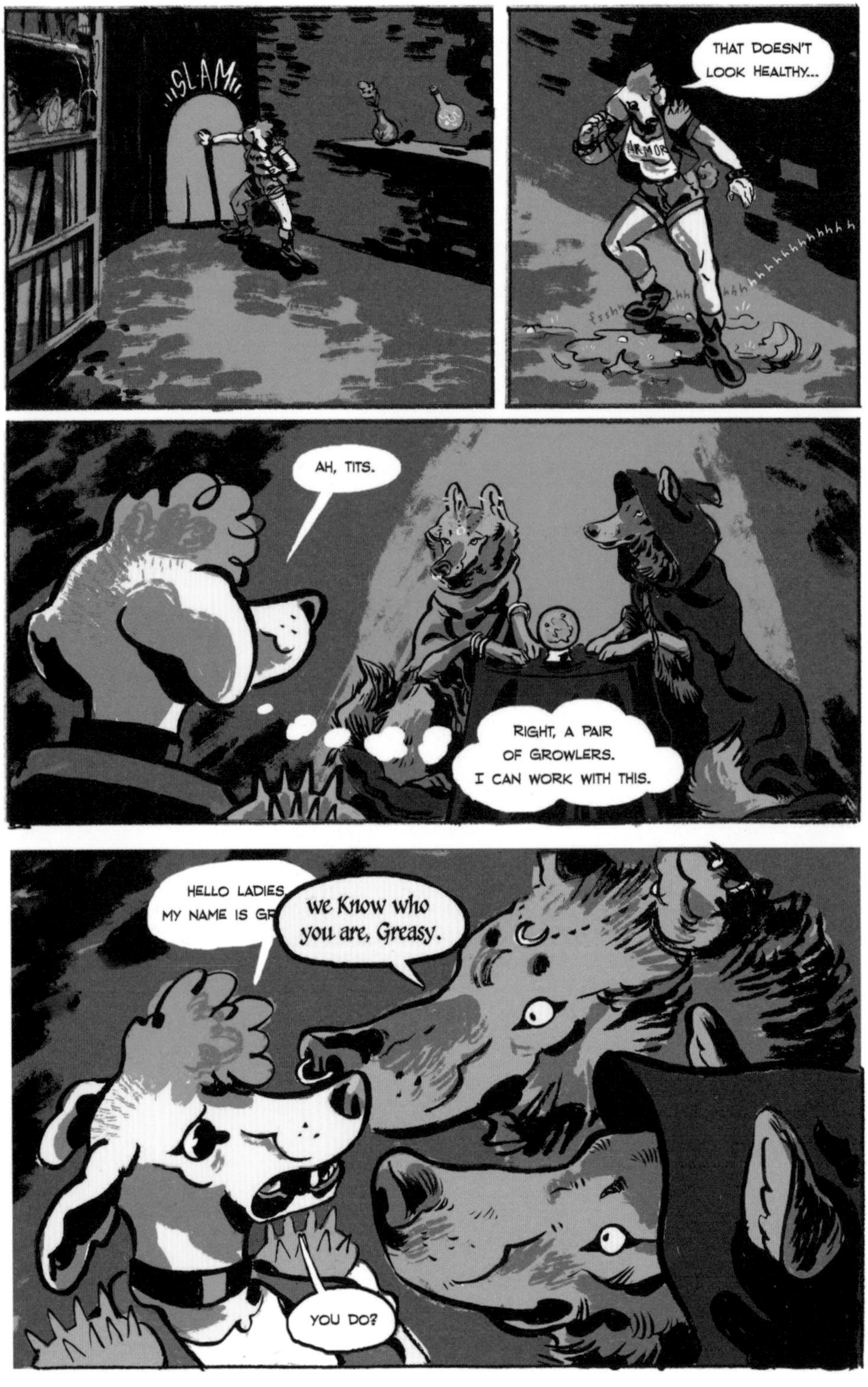
SLAM
THAT DOESN'T LOOK HEALTHY...
fsshh
hhhhhhhhhhh
AH, TITS.
RIGHT, A PAIR OF GROWLERS. I CAN WORK WITH THIS.
HELLO LADIES MY NAME IS GR
we Know who you are, Greasy.
YOU DO?

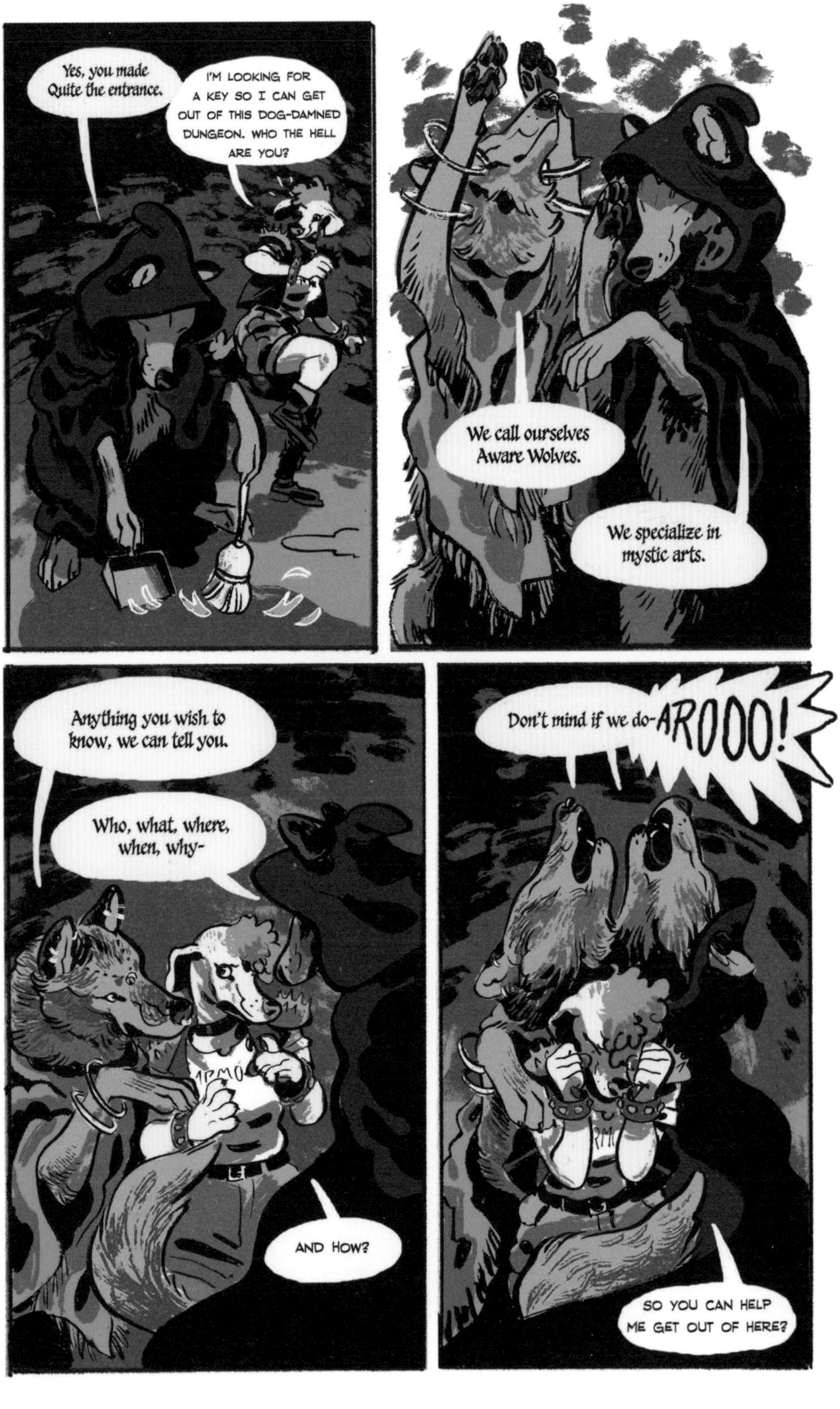
Yes, you made Quite the entrance.
I'M LOOKING FOR A KEY SO I CAN GET OUT OF THIS DOG-DAMNED DUNGEON. WHO THE HELL ARE YOU?
We call ourselves Aware Wolves.
We specialize in mystic arts.
Anything you wish to know, we can tell you.
Who, what, where, when, why-
AND HOW?
Don't mind if we do-AROOO!
SO YOU CAN HELP ME GET OUT OF HERE?

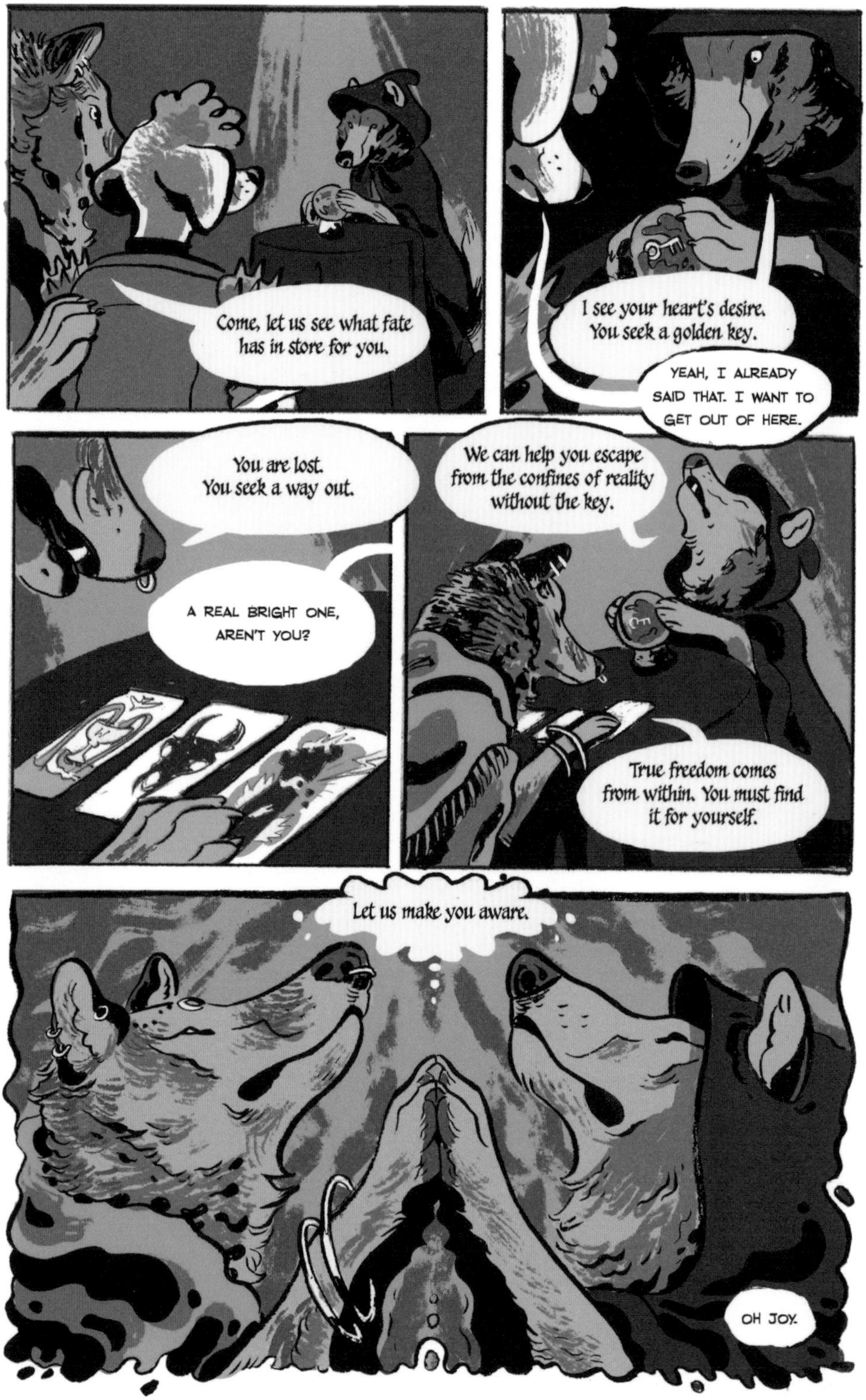
Come, let us see what fate has in store for you.
I see your heart's desire. You seek a golden key.
YEAH, I ALREADY SAID THAT. I WANT TO GET OUT OF HERE.
You are lost. You seek a way out.
A REAL BRIGHT ONE, AREN'T YOU?
We can help you escape from the confines of reality without the key.
True freedom comes from within. You must find it for yourself.
Let us make you aware.
OH JOY.

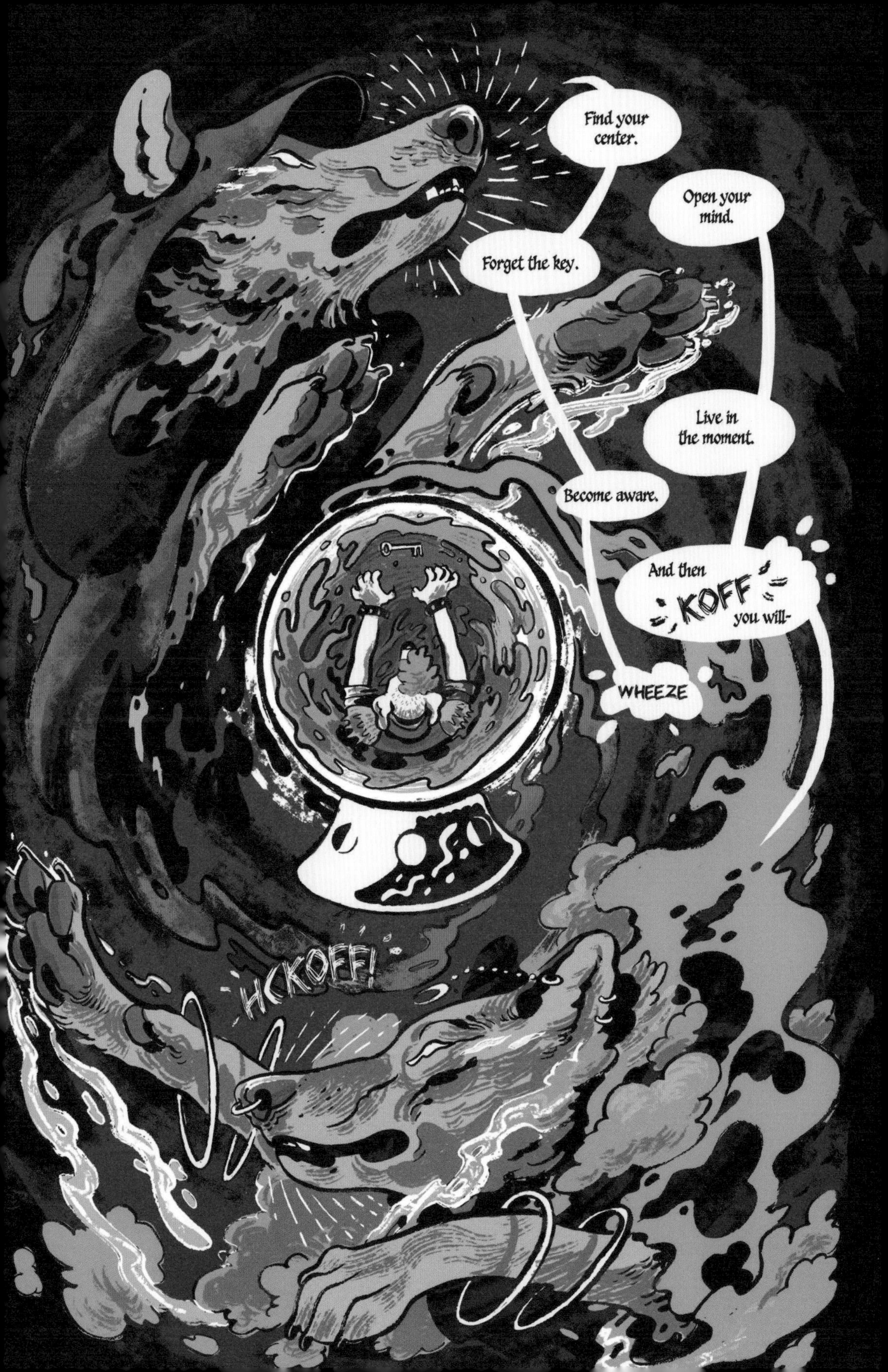

Find your center.
Forget the key.
Open your mind.
Live in the moment.
Become aware.
And then KOFF you will-
WHEEZE
HCKOFF!

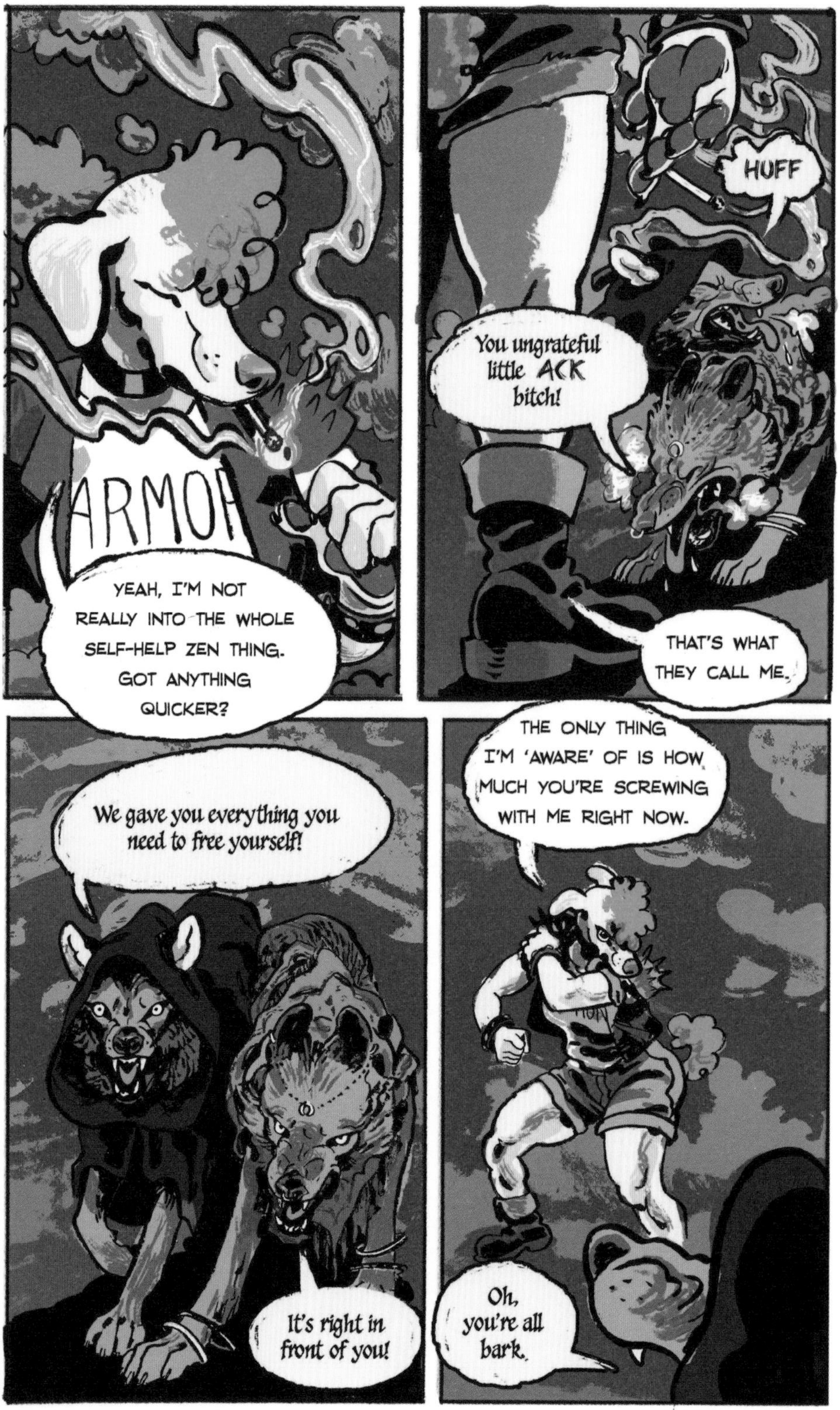
ARMOR
YEAH, I'M NOT REALLY INTO THE WHOLE SELF-HELP ZEN THING. GOT ANYTHING QUICKER?
HUFF
You ungrateful little ACK bitch!
THAT'S WHAT THEY CALL ME.
We gave you everything you need to free yourself!
It's right in front of you!
THE ONLY THING I'M 'AWARE' OF IS HOW MUCH YOU'RE SCREWING WITH ME RIGHT NOW.
Oh, you're all bark.

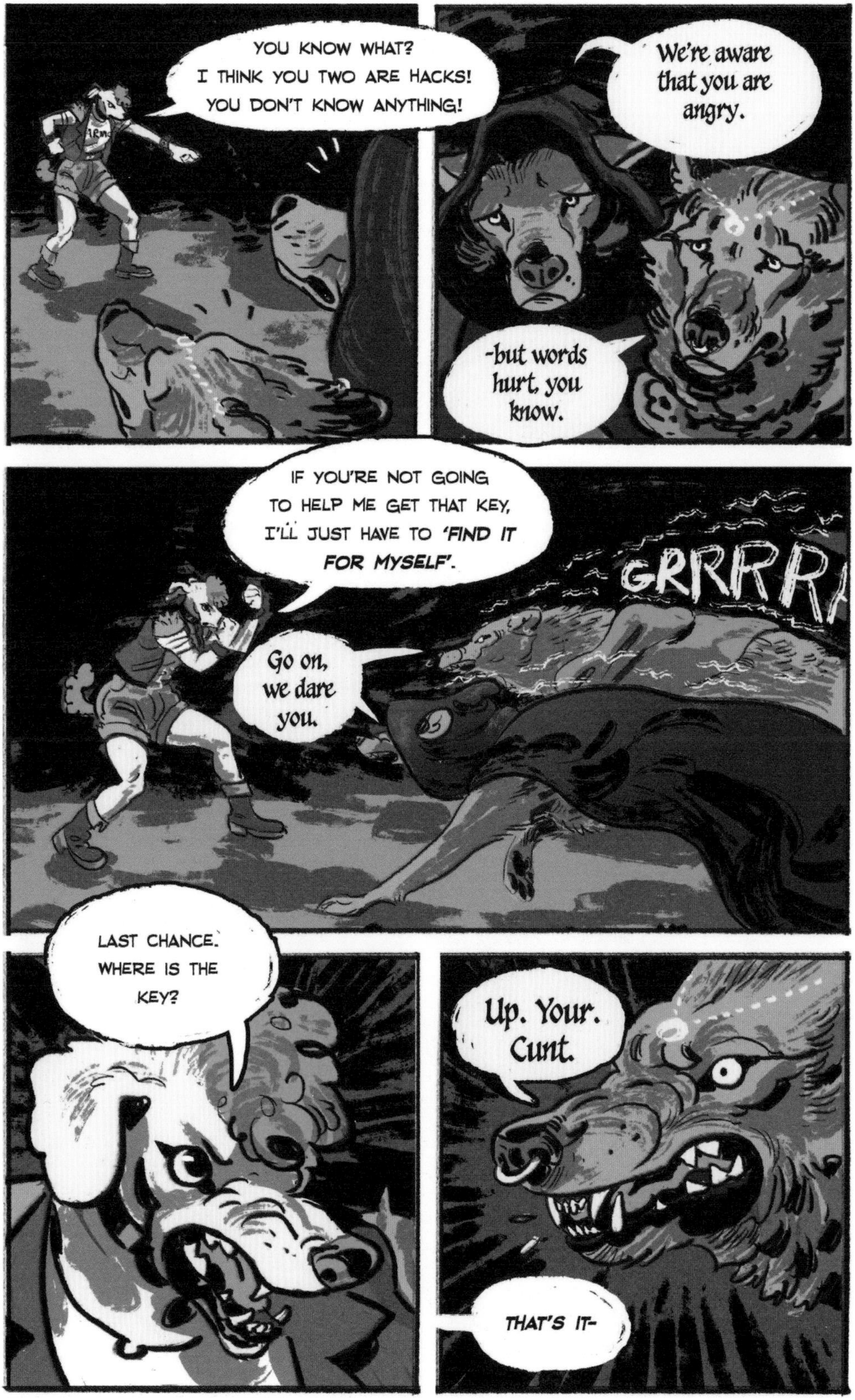
YOU KNOW WHAT? I THINK YOU TWO ARE HACKS! YOU DON'T KNOW ANYTHING!
We're aware that you are angry.
-but words hurt, you know.
IF YOU'RE NOT GOING TO HELP ME GET THAT KEY, I'LL JUST HAVE TO *'FIND IT FOR MYSELF'*.
GRRRRA
Go on, we dare you.
LAST CHANCE. WHERE IS THE KEY?
Up. Your. Cunt.
THAT'S IT-

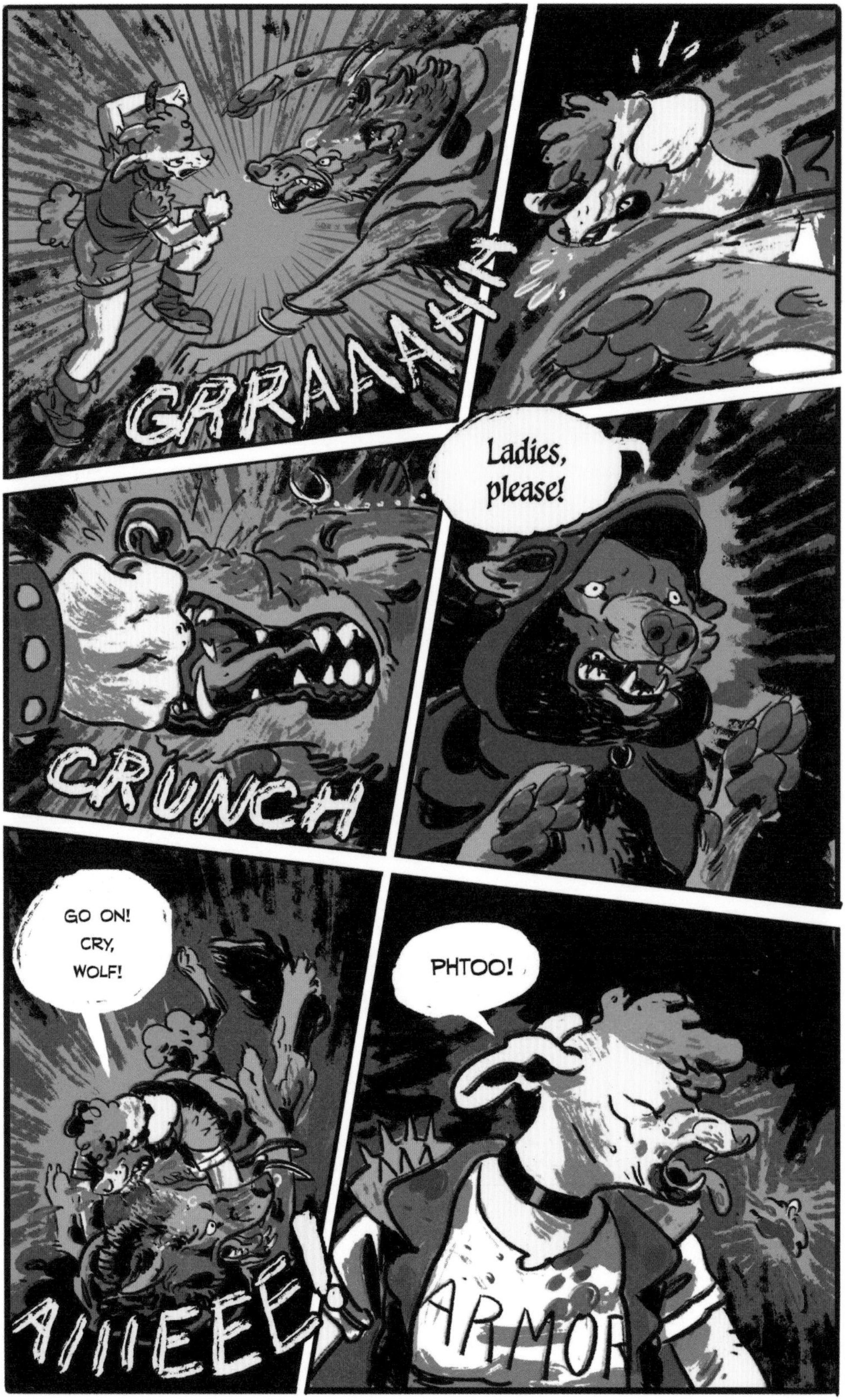
GRRAAAAHH
Ladies, please!
CRUNCH
GO ON! CRY, WOLF!
AIIEEE!
PHTOO!
ARMOR

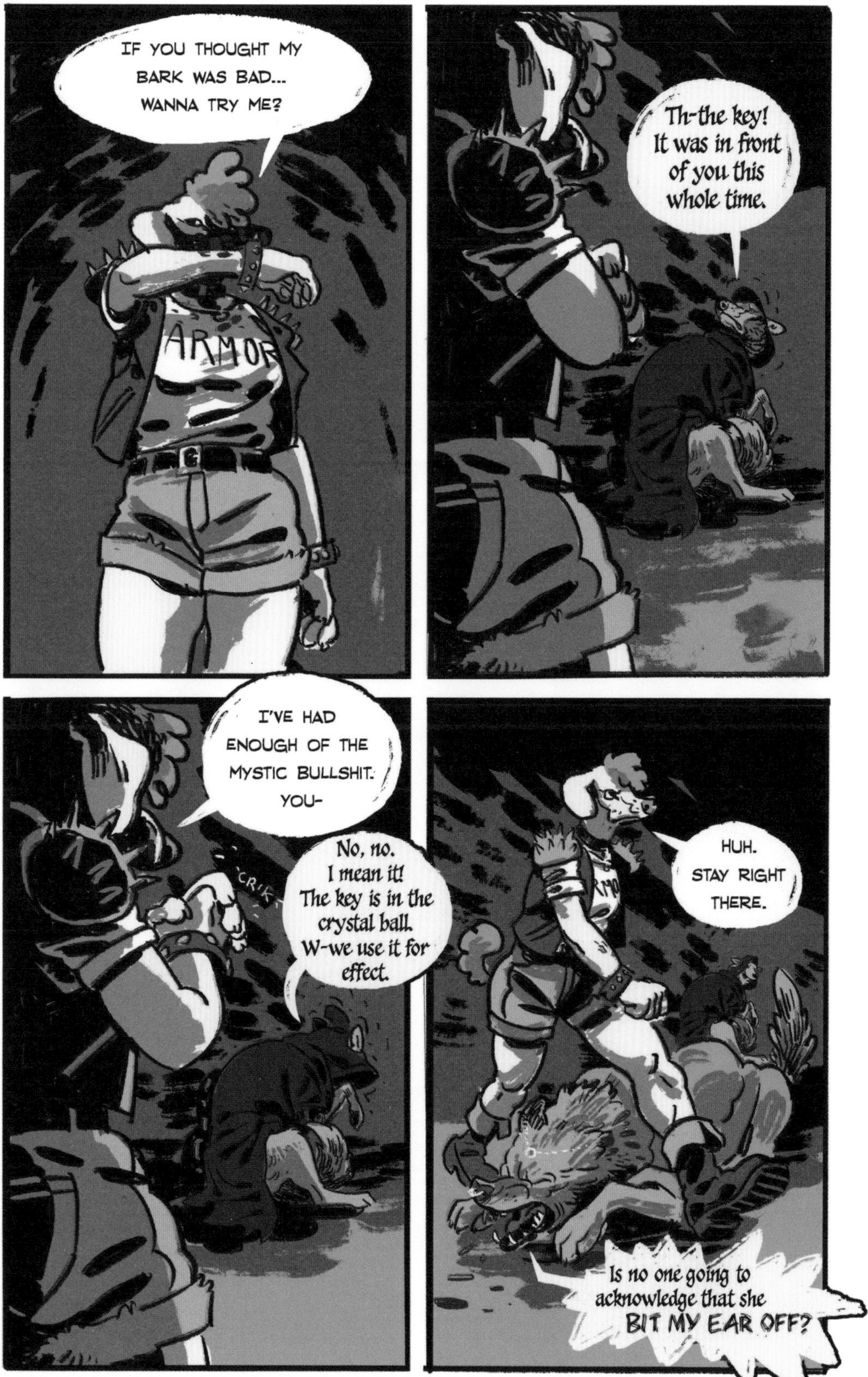
IF YOU THOUGHT MY BARK WAS BAD... WANNA TRY ME?
ARMOR
Th-the key! It was in front of you this whole time.
I'VE HAD ENOUGH OF THE MYSTIC BULLSHIT. YOU-
CRIK
No, no. I mean it! The key is in the crystal ball. W-we use it for effect.
HUH. STAY RIGHT THERE.
Is no one going to acknowledge that she BIT MY EAR OFF?

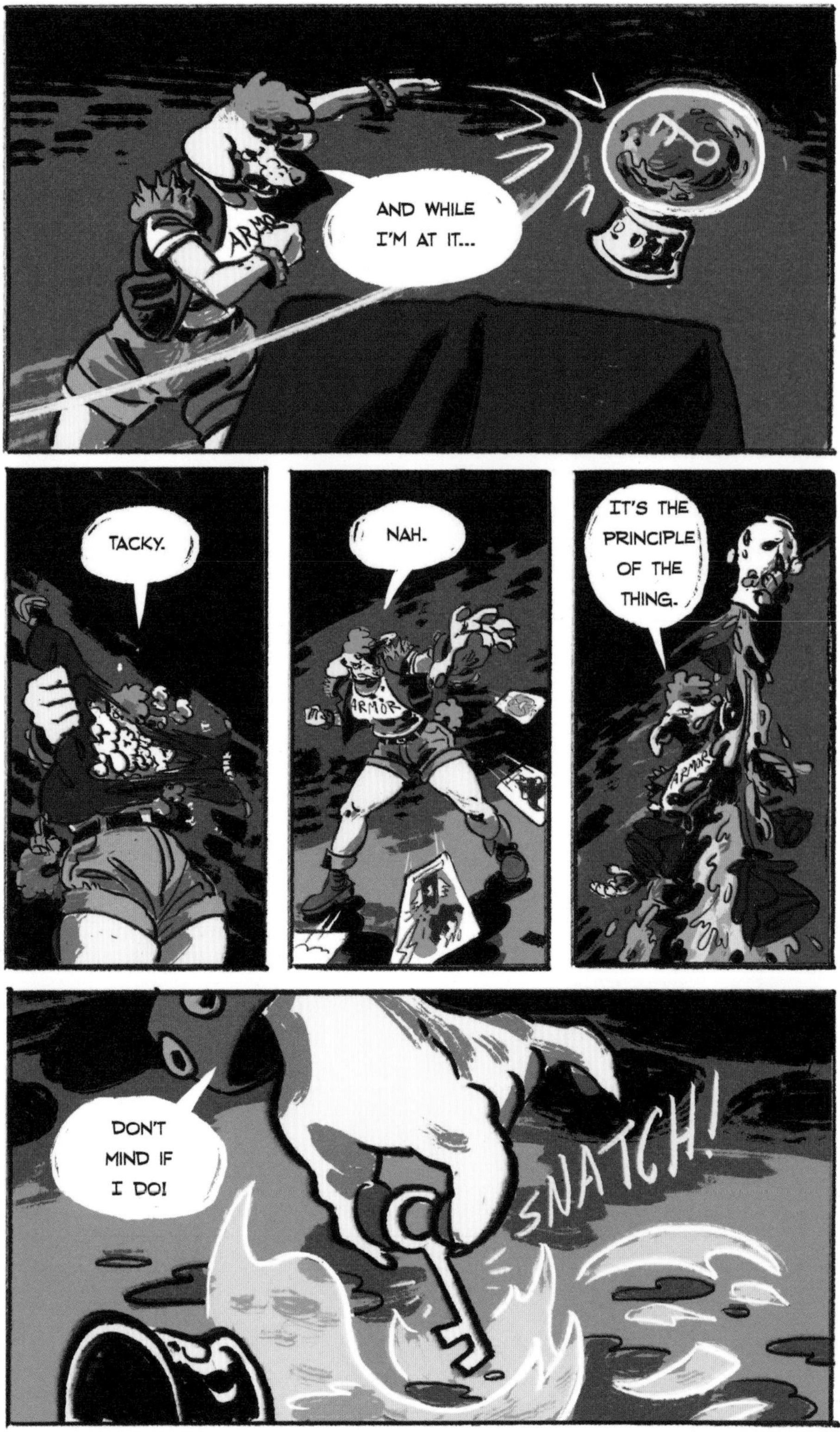
AND WHILE I'M AT IT...
ARMOR
TACKY.
NAH.
ARMOR
IT'S THE PRINCIPLE OF THE THING.
ARMOR
DON'T MIND IF I DO!
SNATCH!

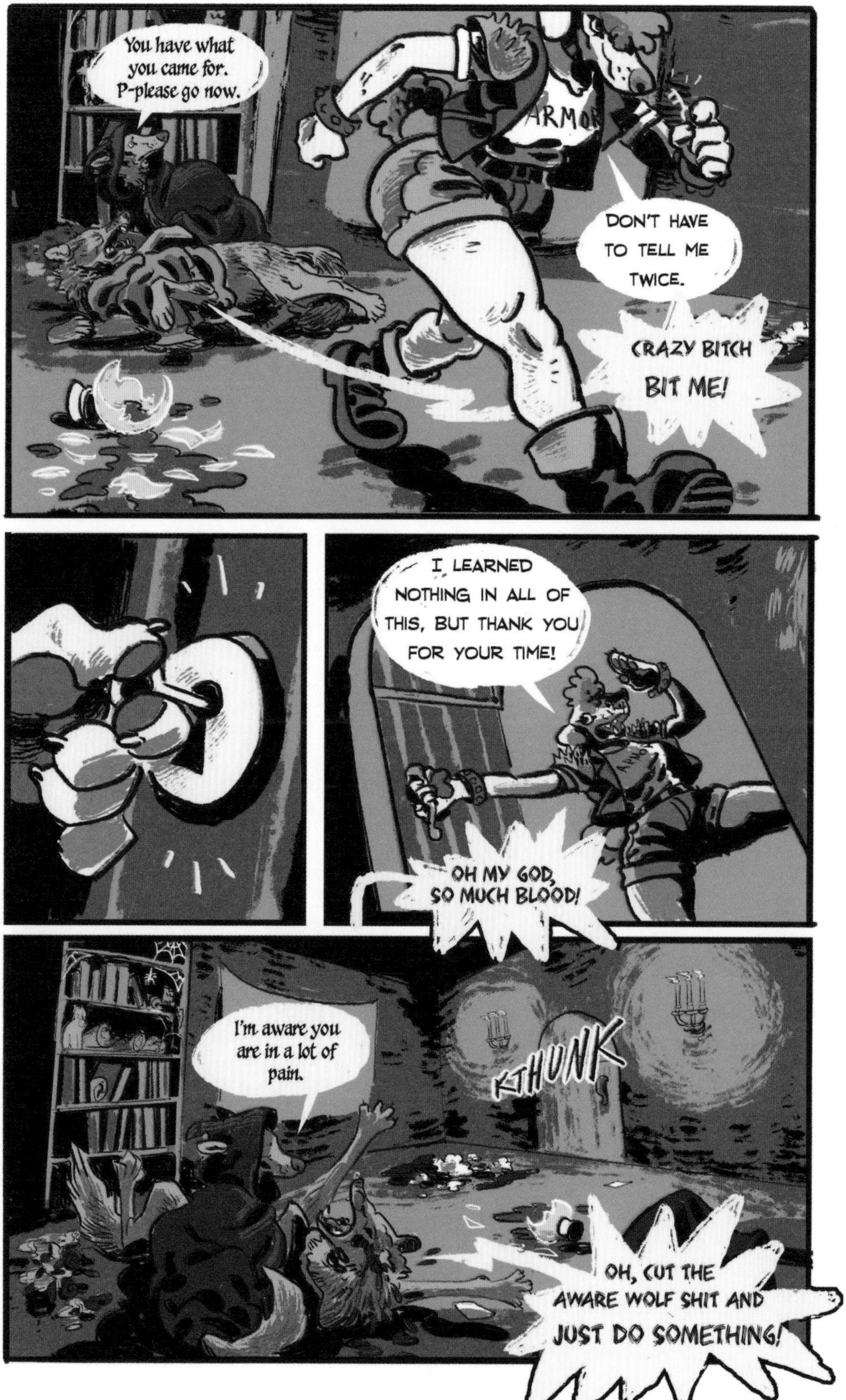
You have what you came for. P-please go now.
DON'T HAVE TO TELL ME TWICE.
CRAZY BITCH BIT ME!
I LEARNED NOTHING IN ALL OF THIS, BUT THANK YOU FOR YOUR TIME!
OH MY GOD, SO MUCH BLOOD!
KTHUNK
I'm aware you are in a lot of pain.
OH, CUT THE AWARE WOLF SHIT AND JUST DO SOMETHING!

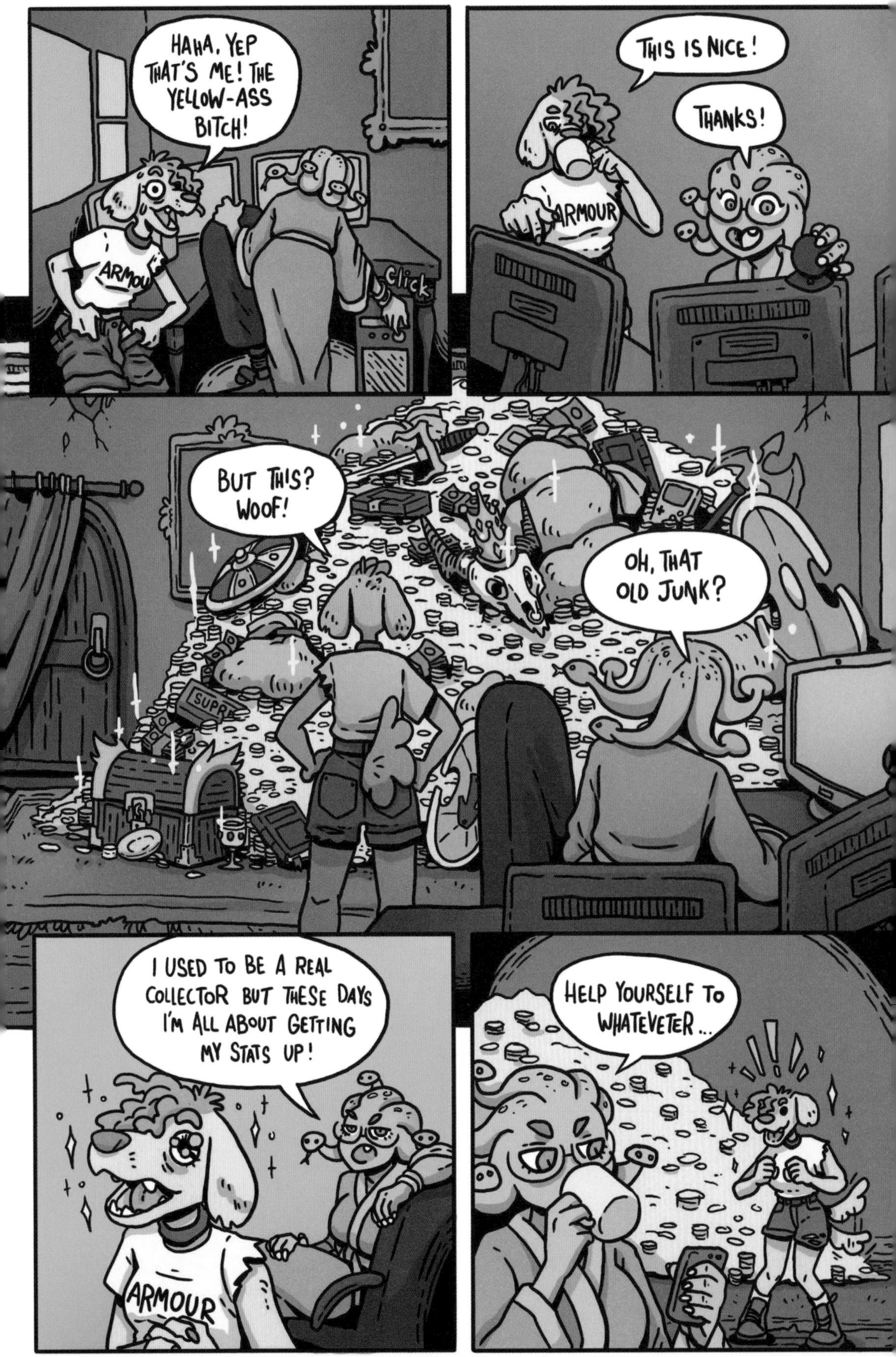
HAHA. YEP THAT'S ME! THE YELLOW-ASS BITCH!
CLICK
THIS IS NICE!
THANKS!
ARMOUR
BUT THIS? WOOF!
OH, THAT OLD JUNK?
I USED TO BE A REAL COLLECTOR BUT THESE DAYS I'M ALL ABOUT GETTING MY STATS UP!
HELP YOURSELF TO WHATEVETER...

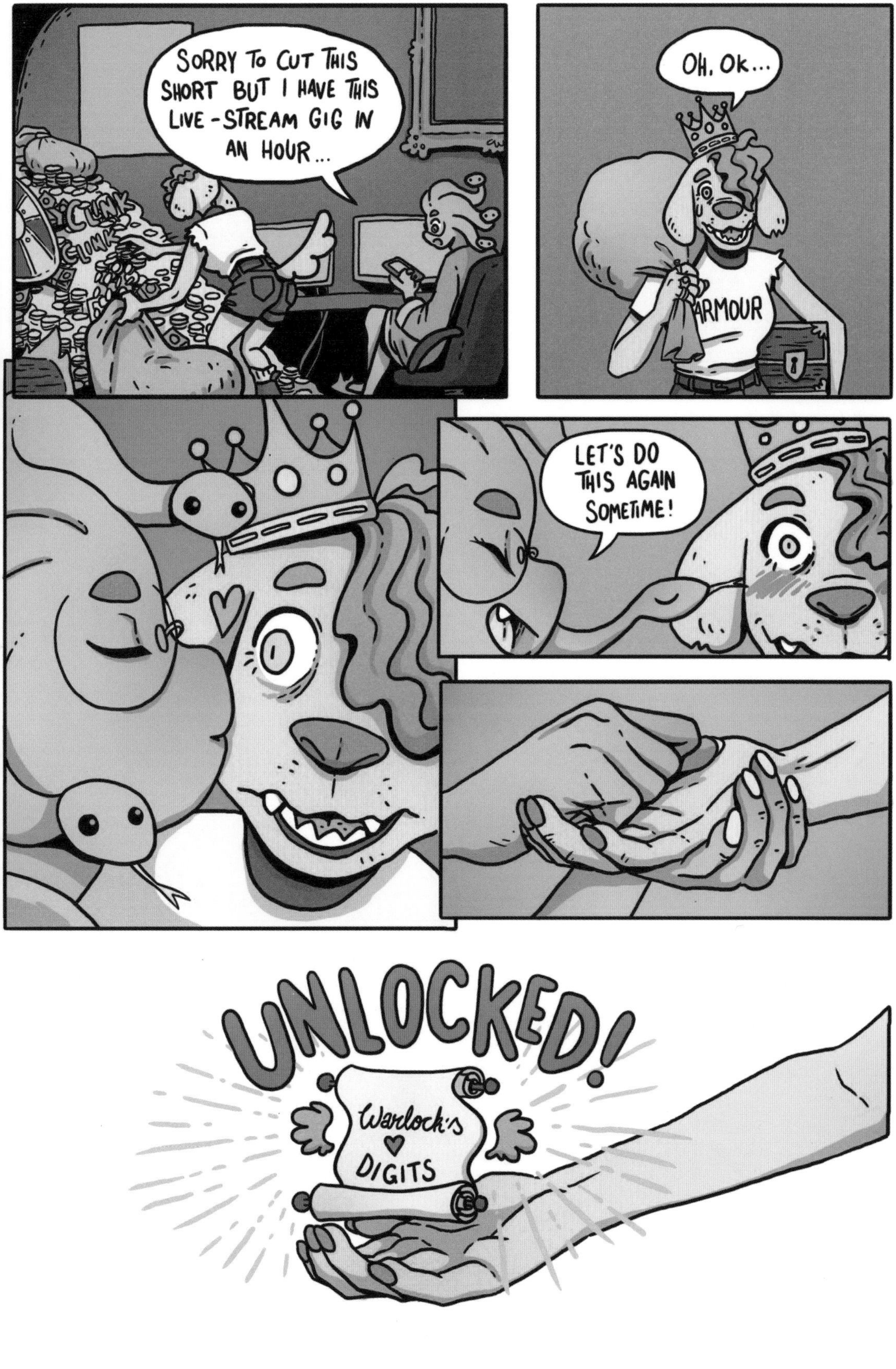

SORRY TO CUT THIS SHORT BUT I HAVE THIS LIVE-STREAM GIG IN AN HOUR...
CLINK
CLINK
OH, OK...
ARMOUR
LET'S DO THIS AGAIN SOMETIME!
UNLOCKED!
Warlock's ♥ DIGITS

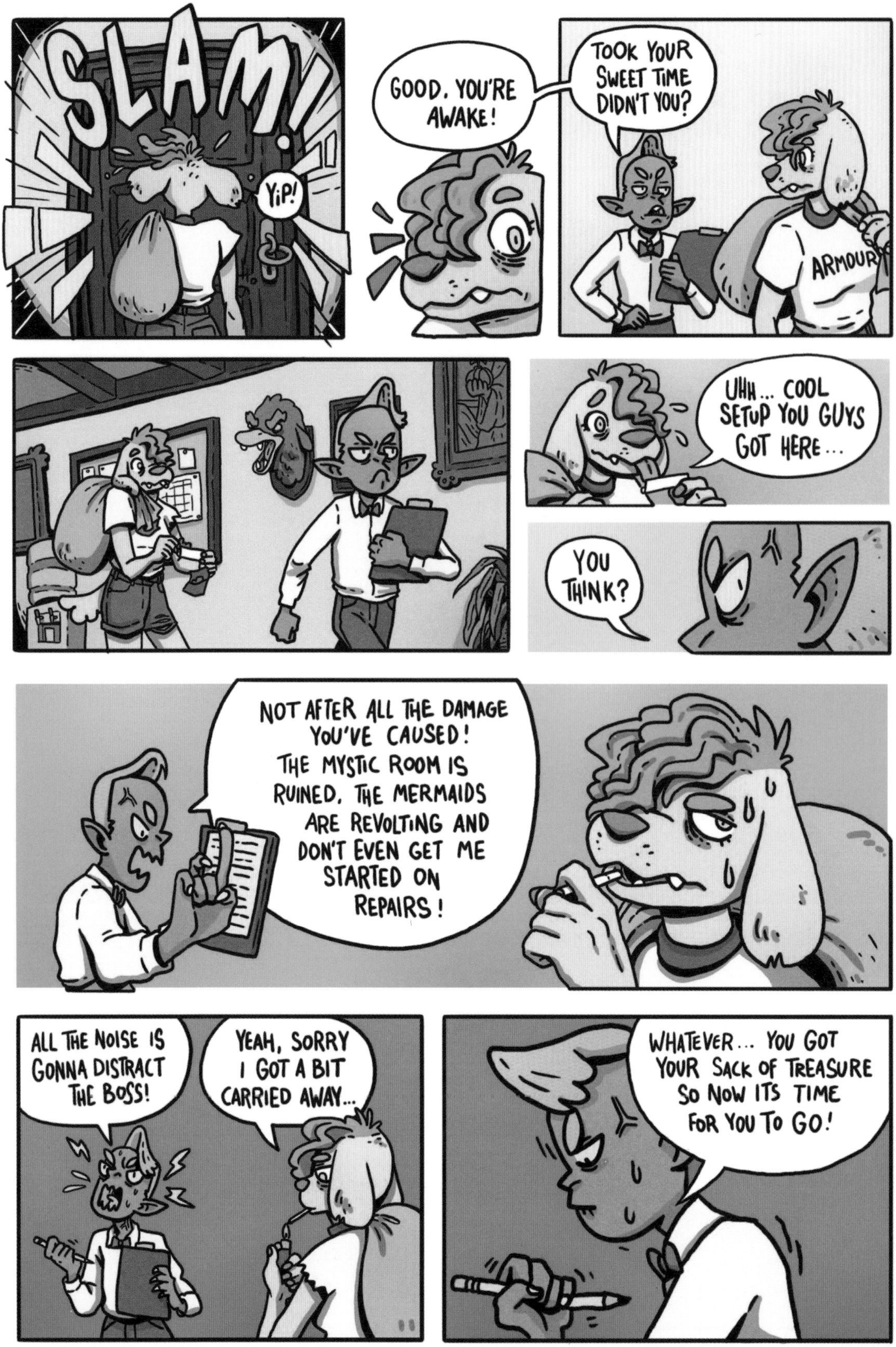
SLAM!!
YIP!
GOOD. YOU'RE AWAKE!
TOOK YOUR SWEET TIME DIDN'T YOU?
ARMOUR
UHH... COOL SETUP YOU GUYS GOT HERE...
YOU THINK?
NOT AFTER ALL THE DAMAGE YOU'VE CAUSED! THE MYSTIC ROOM IS RUINED. THE MERMAIDS ARE REVOLTING AND DON'T EVEN GET ME STARTED ON REPAIRS!
ALL THE NOISE IS GONNA DISTRACT THE BOSS!
YEAH, SORRY I GOT A BIT CARRIED AWAY...
WHATEVER... YOU GOT YOUR SACK OF TREASURE SO NOW ITS TIME FOR YOU TO GO!

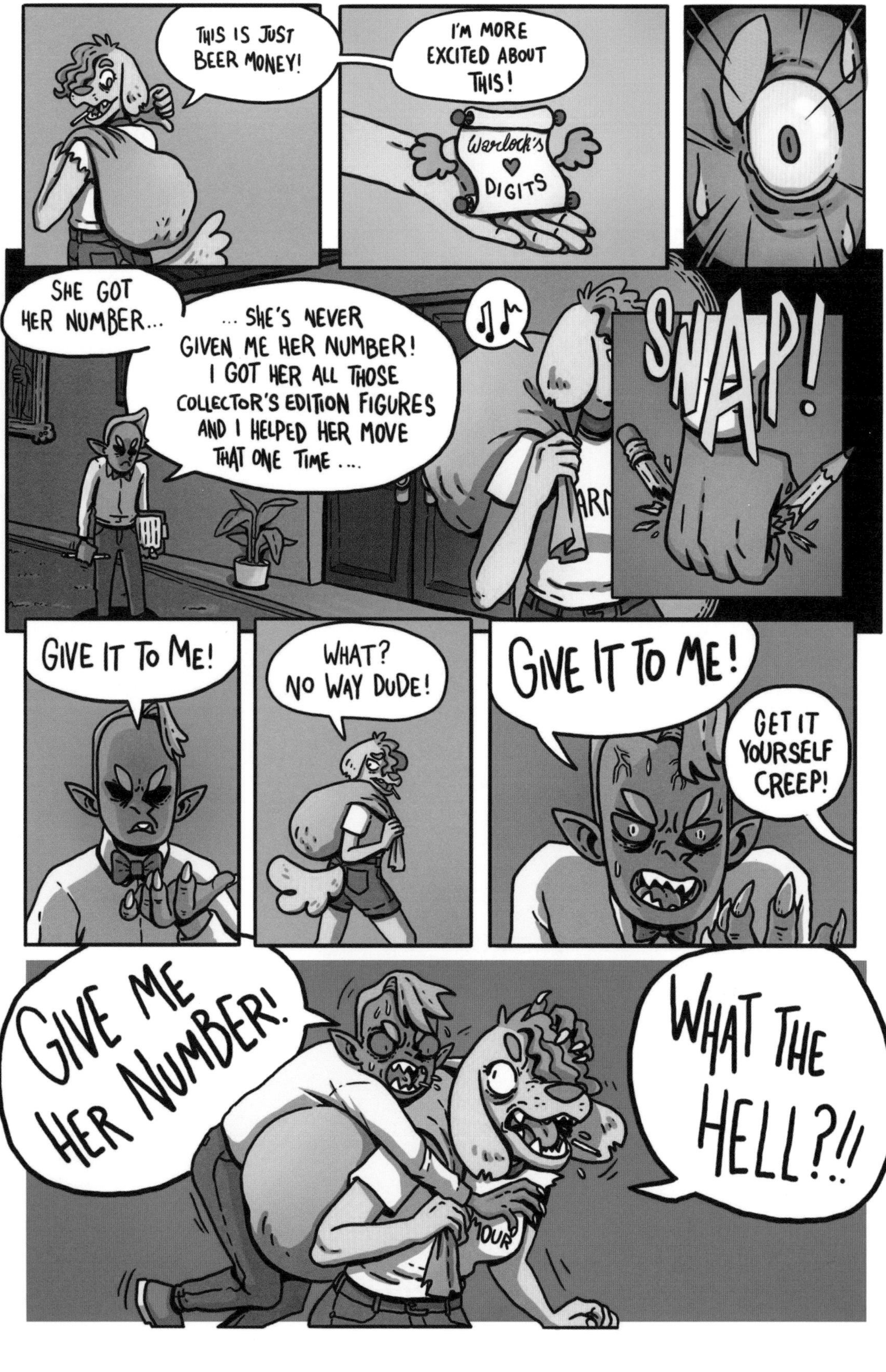
THIS IS JUST BEER MONEY!
I'M MORE EXCITED ABOUT THIS!
Warlock's ♥ DIGITS
SHE GOT HER NUMBER...
... SHE'S NEVER GIVEN ME HER NUMBER! I GOT HER ALL THOSE COLLECTOR'S EDITION FIGURES AND I HELPED HER MOVE THAT ONE TIME ....
SNAP!
GIVE IT TO ME!
WHAT? NO WAY DUDE!
GIVE IT TO ME!
GET IT YOURSELF CREEP!
GIVE ME HER NUMBER!
WHAT THE HELL?!!

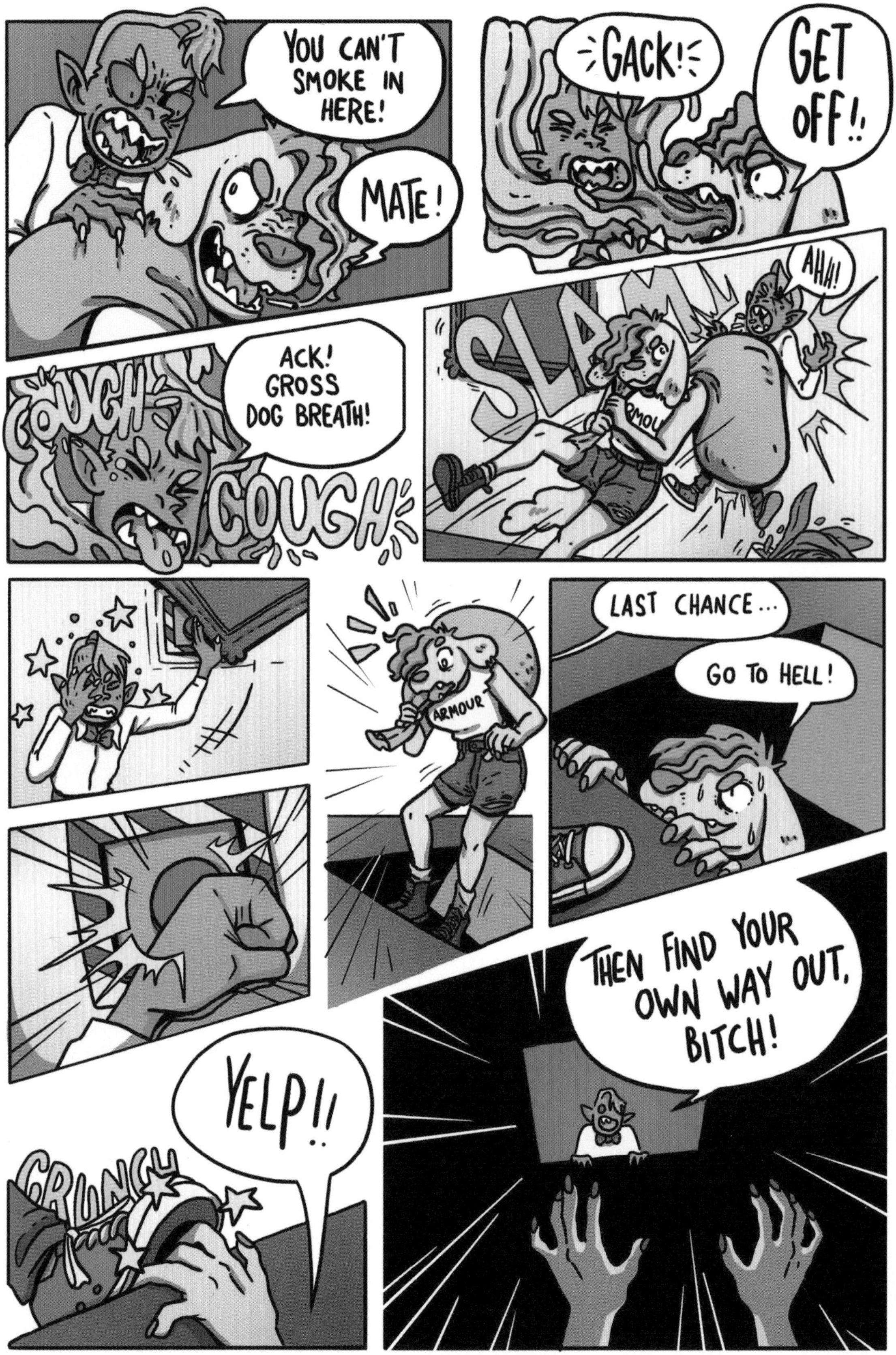
YOU CAN'T SMOKE IN HERE!
MATE!
GACK!
GET OFF!!
ACK! GROSS DOG BREATH!
COUGH
COUGH
SLAM
AHA!
ARMOUR
LAST CHANCE...
GO TO HELL!
THEN FIND YOUR OWN WAY OUT, BITCH!
YELP!!
CRUNCH

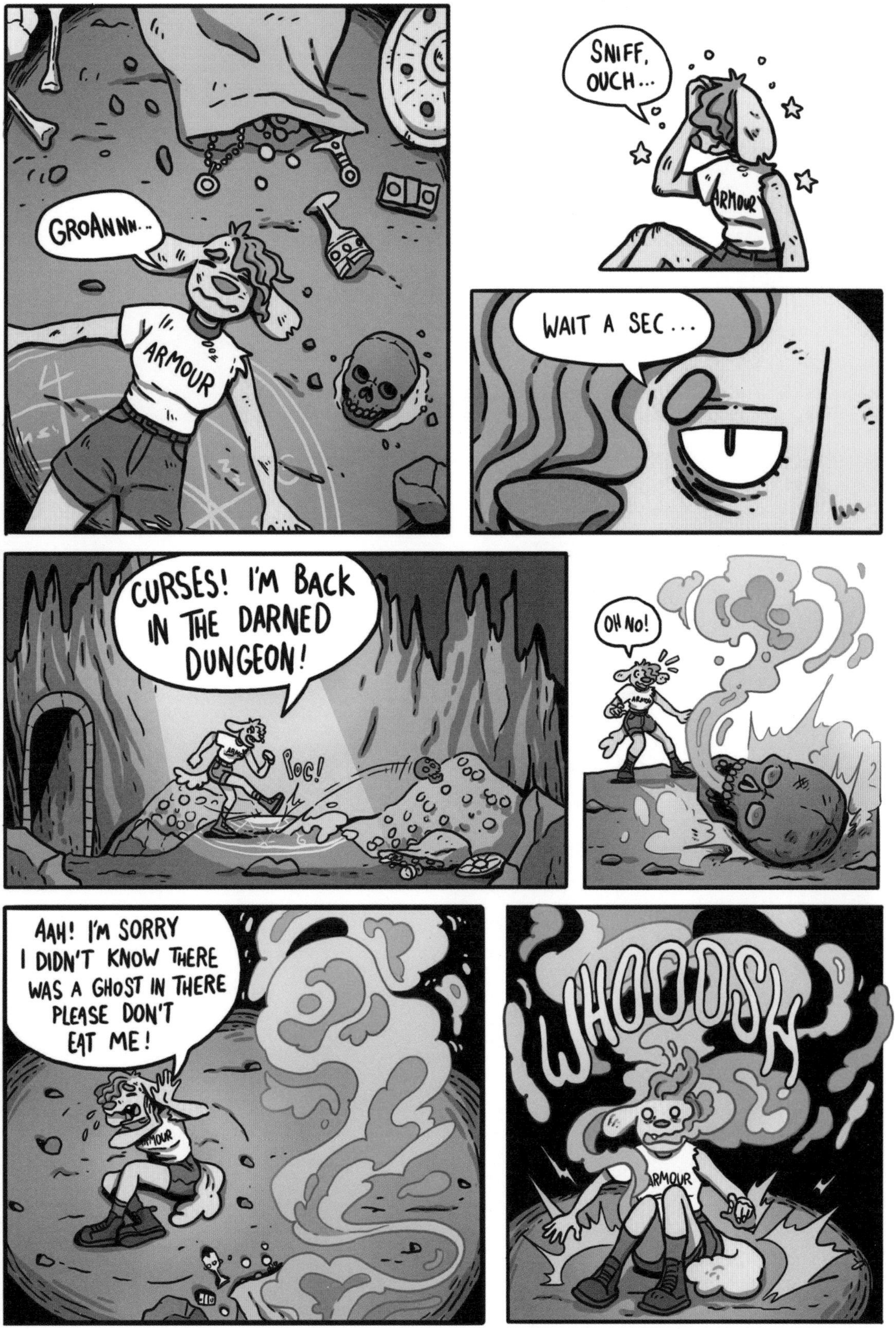
GROANNN...
ARMOUR
SNIFF, OUCH...
ARMOUR
WAIT A SEC...
CURSES! I'M BACK IN THE DARNED DUNGEON!
POC!
OH NO!
AAH! I'M SORRY I DIDN'T KNOW THERE WAS A GHOST IN THERE PLEASE DON'T EAT ME!
WHOOOSH
ARMOUR

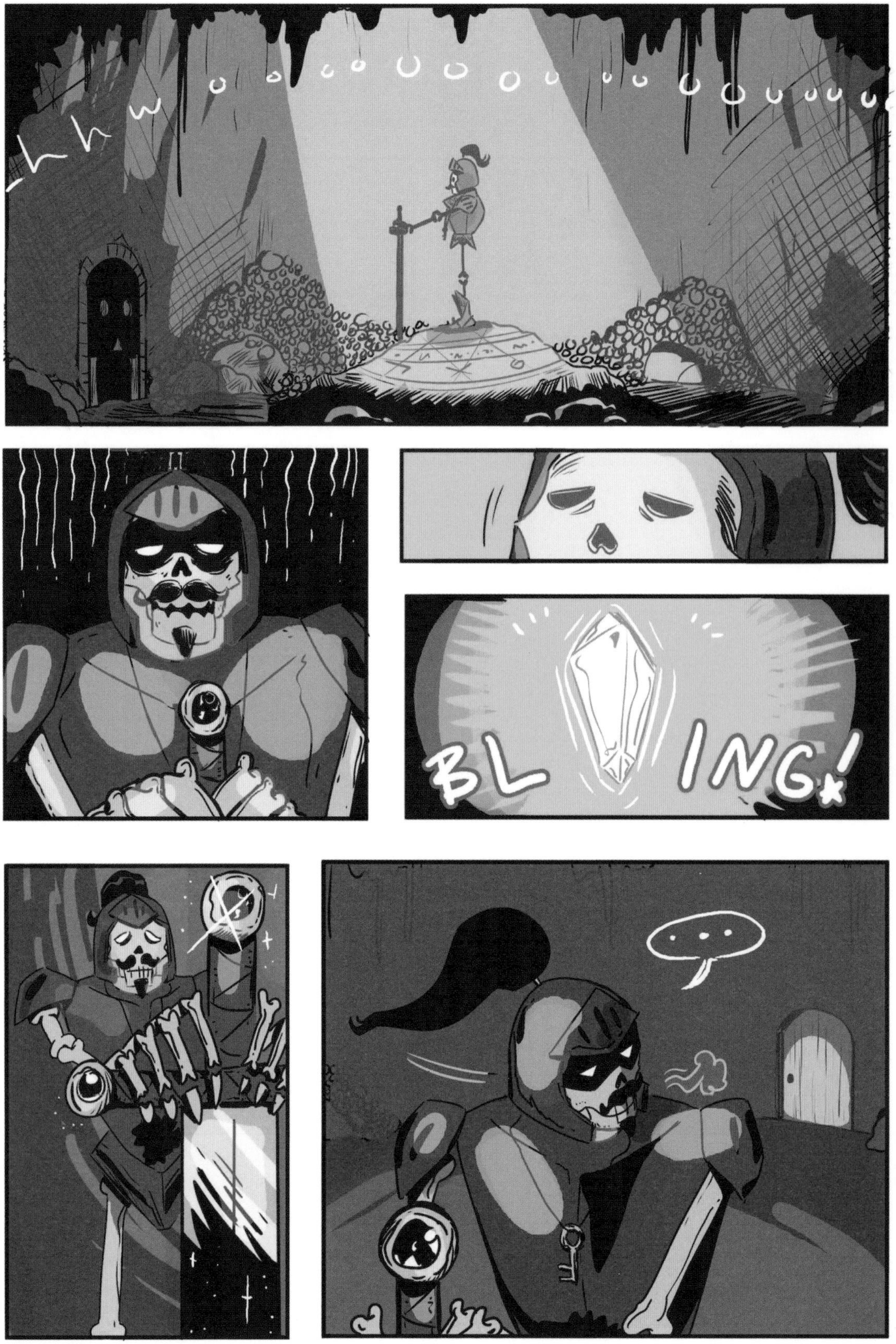

-hhwooooUUOOooooOOuuuuu
BL ING!
...

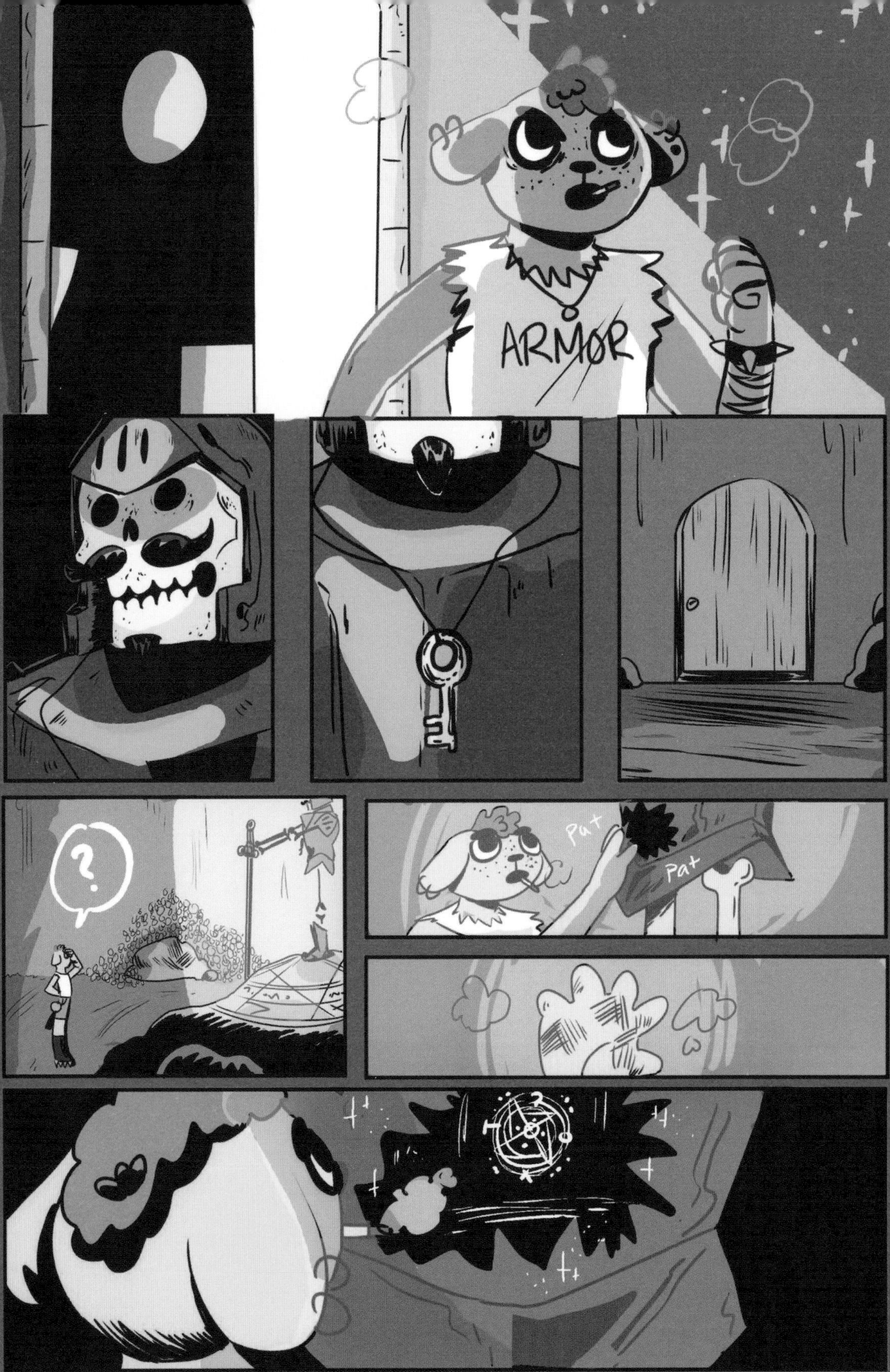
ARMOR
?
Pat
Pat

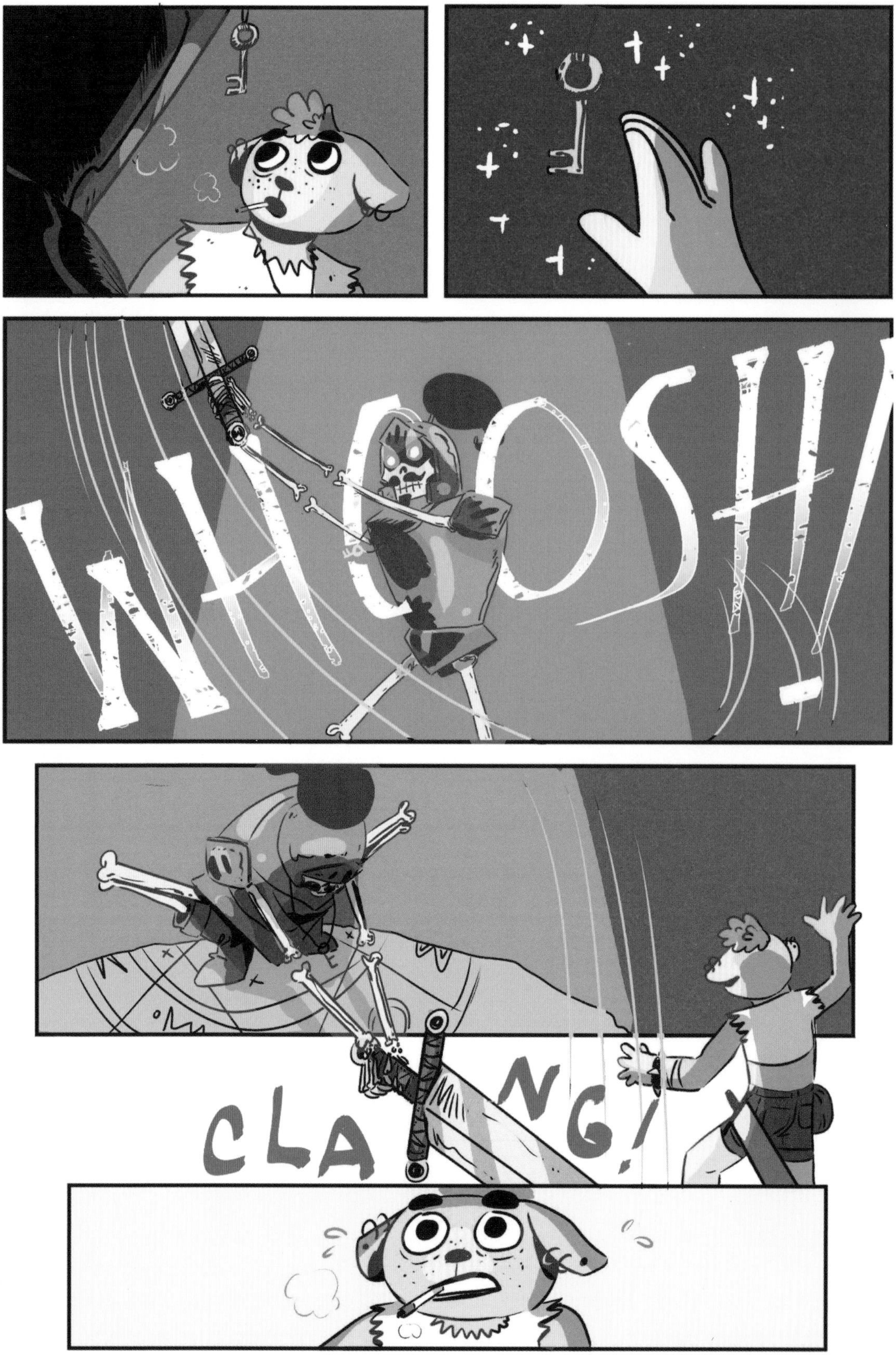
WHOOSH-
CLANG!

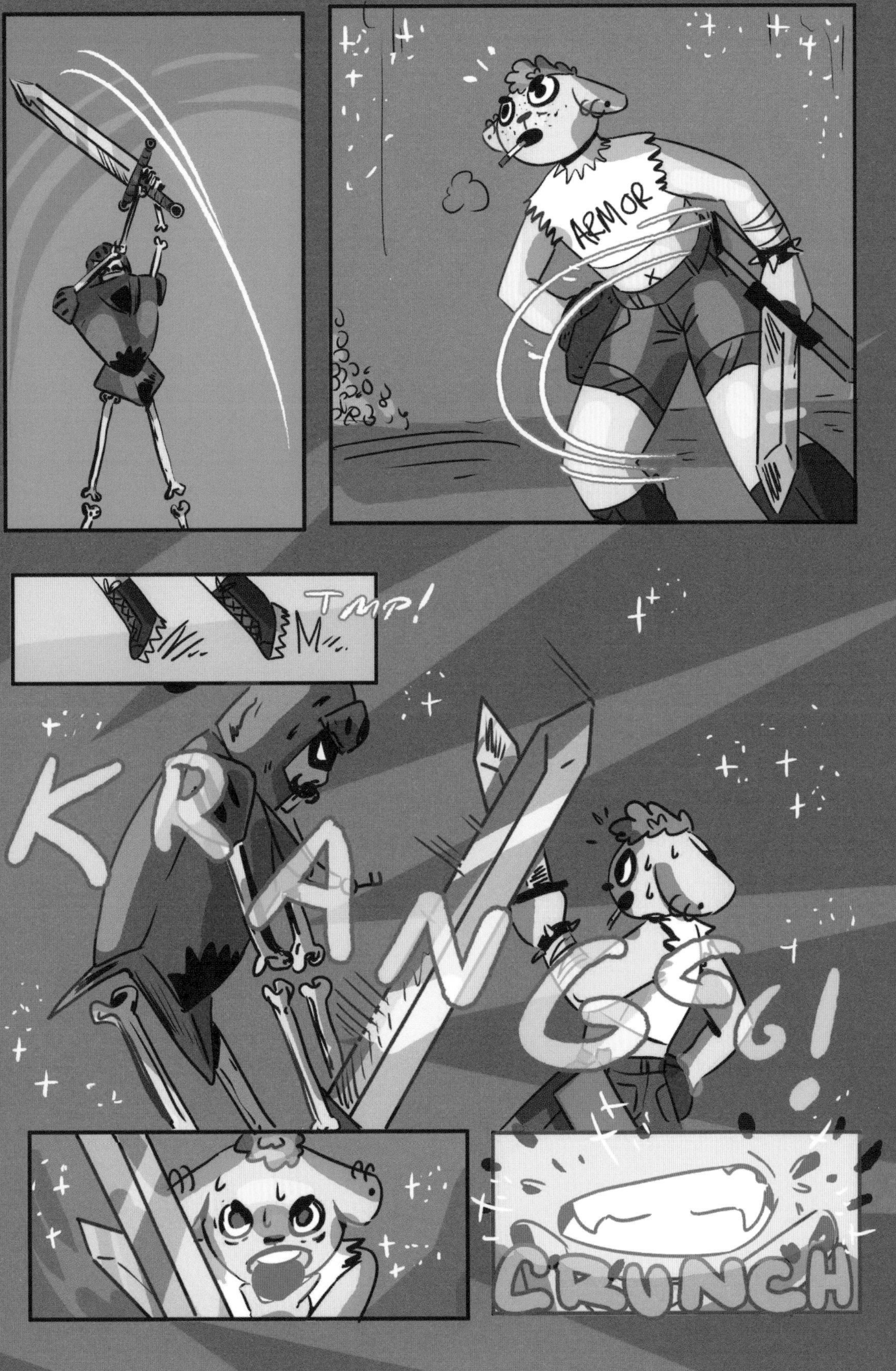
ARMOR
TMP!
KRANG!
CRUNCH

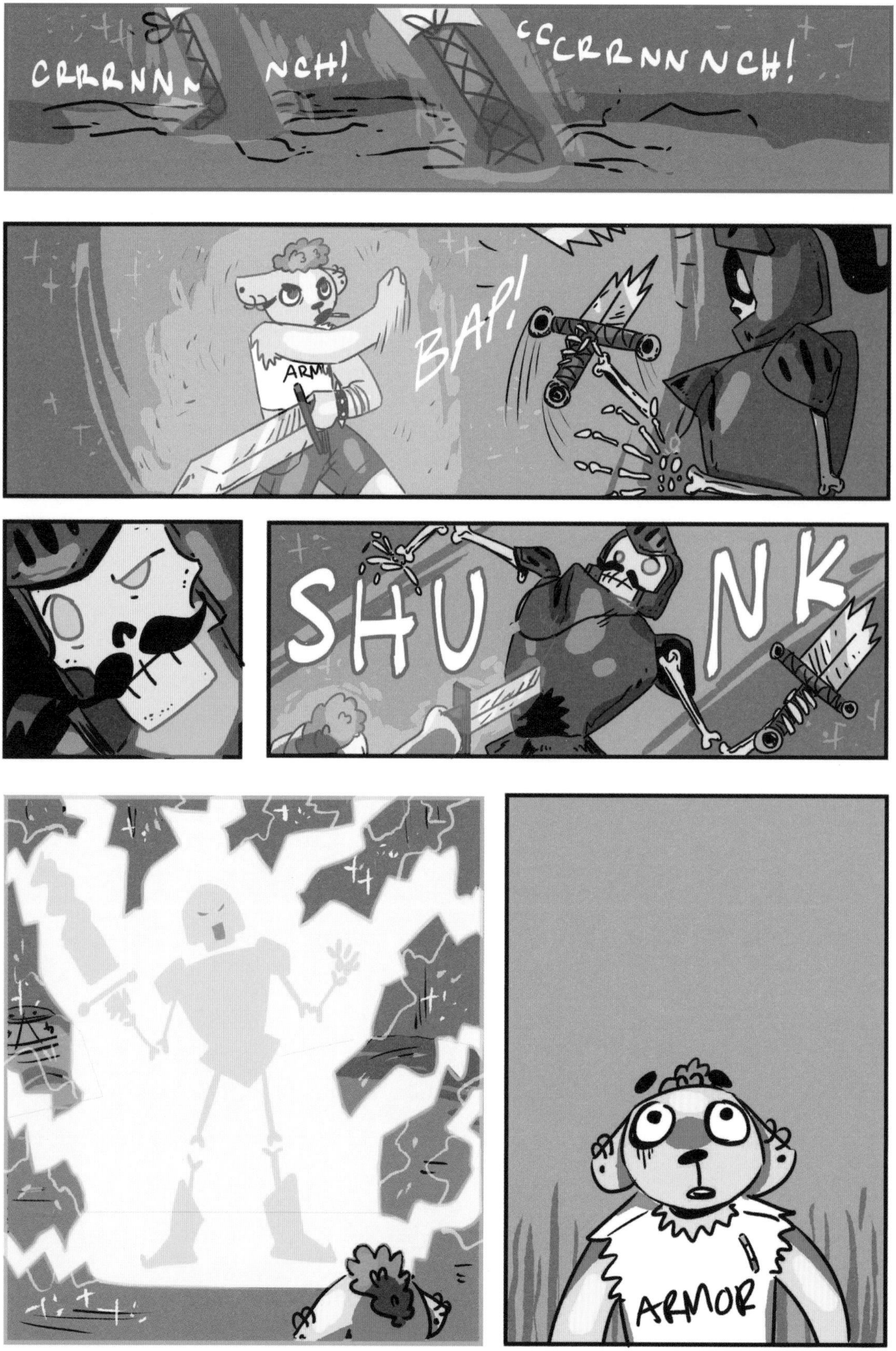
CRRRNNN NCH!
CCCRRNNNCH!
BAP!
ARM
SHU NK
ARMOR

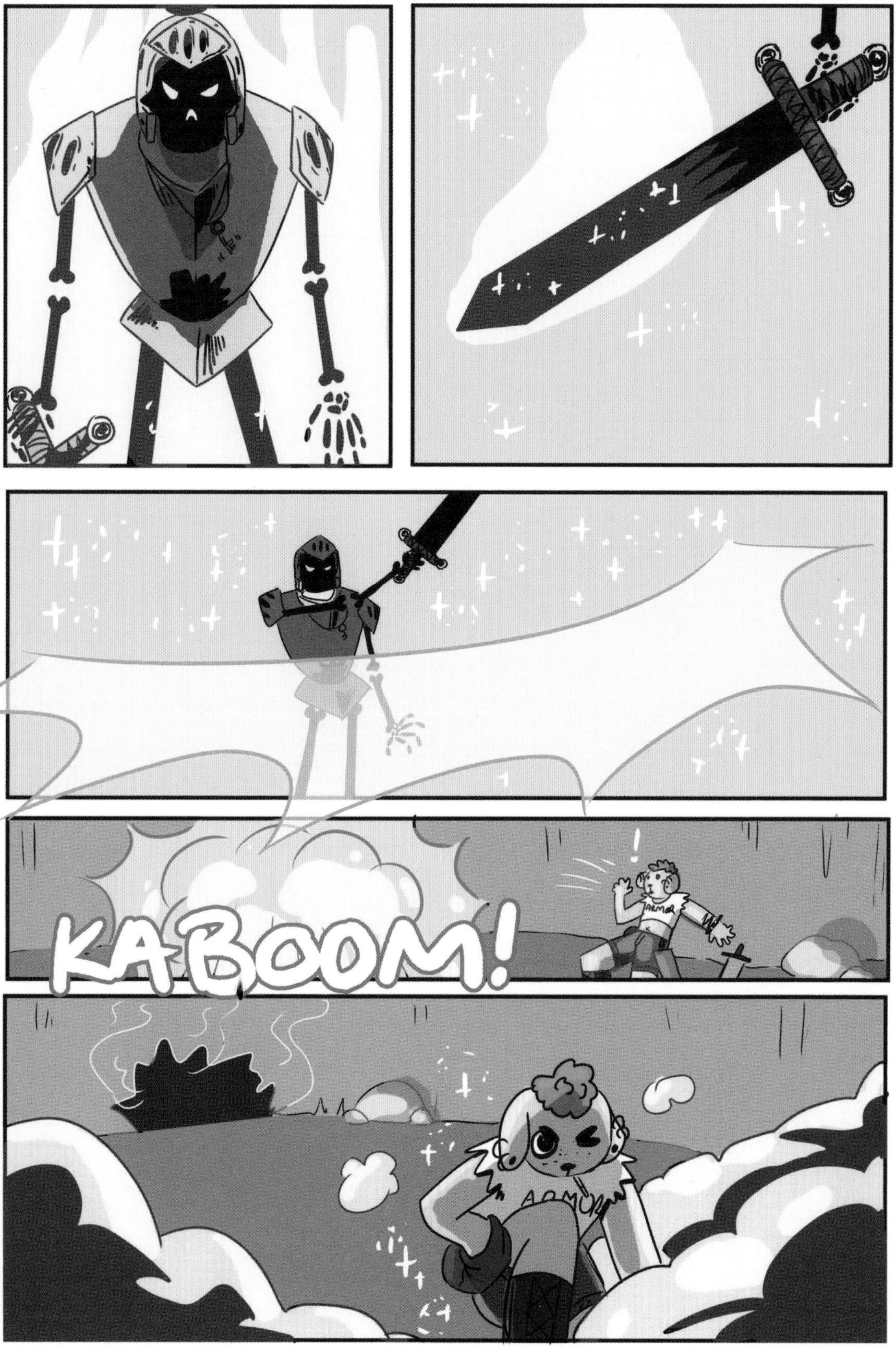
KABOOM!

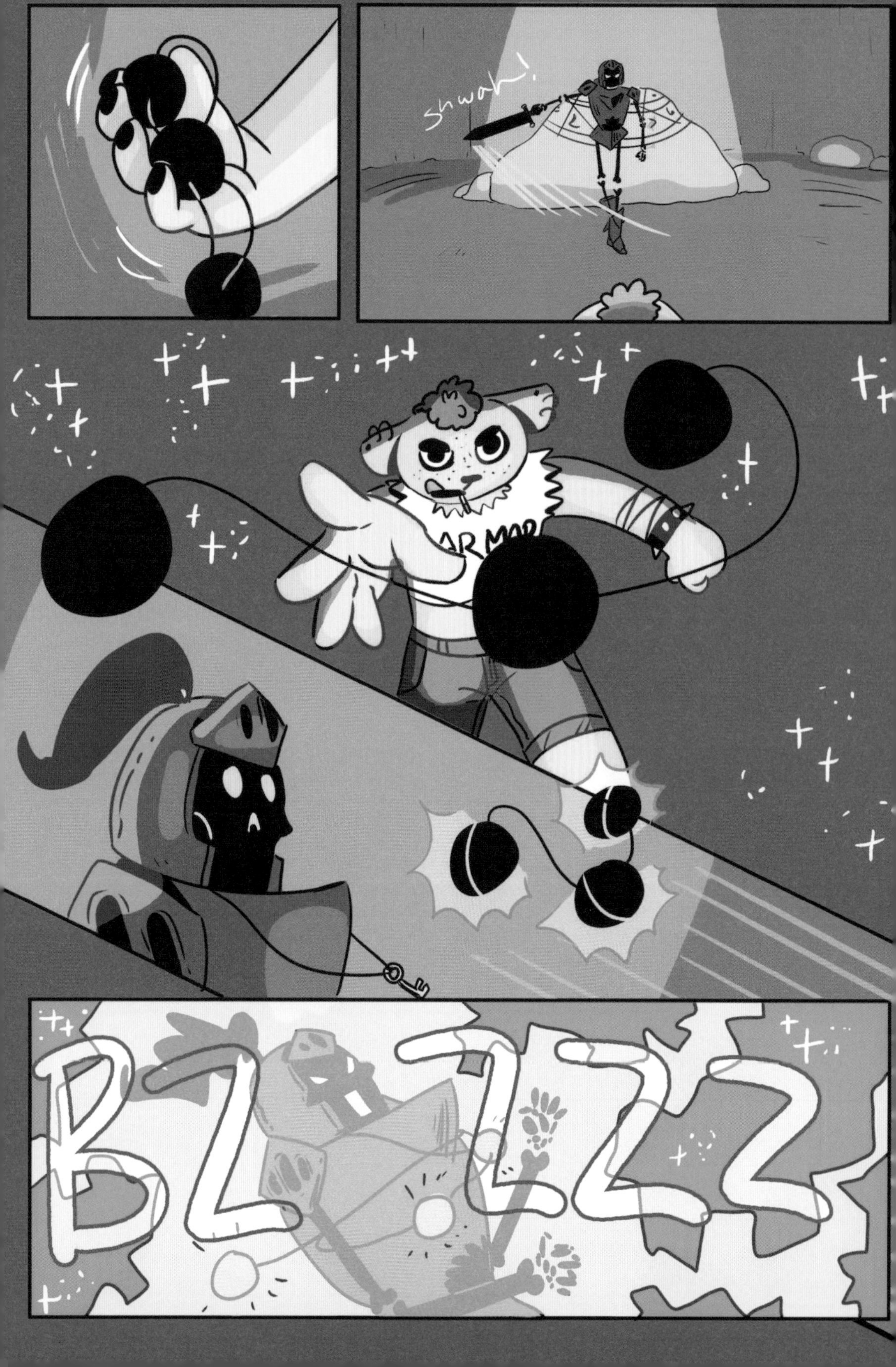
shwah!
ARMOR
BZZZZ

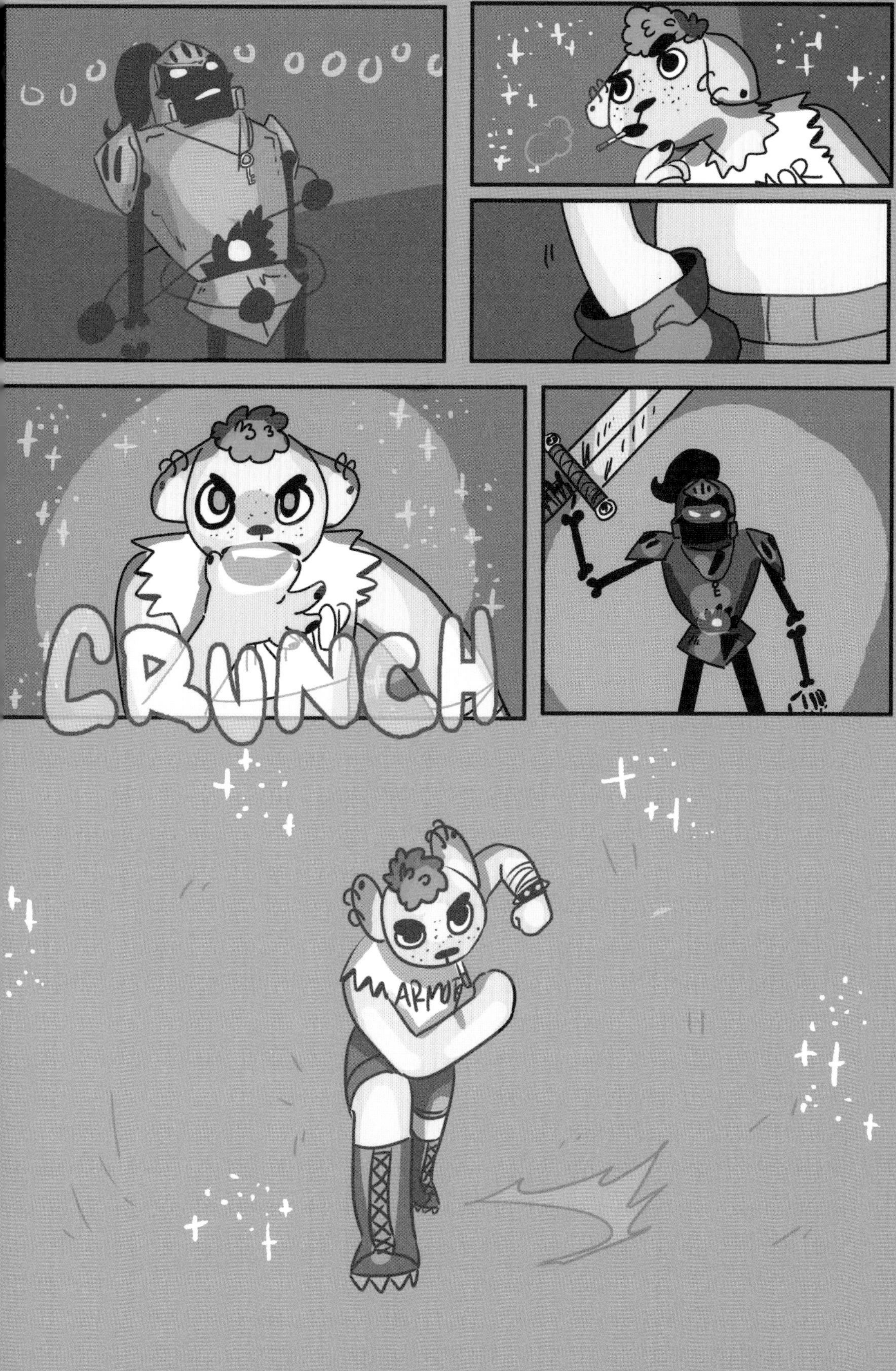
CRUNCH

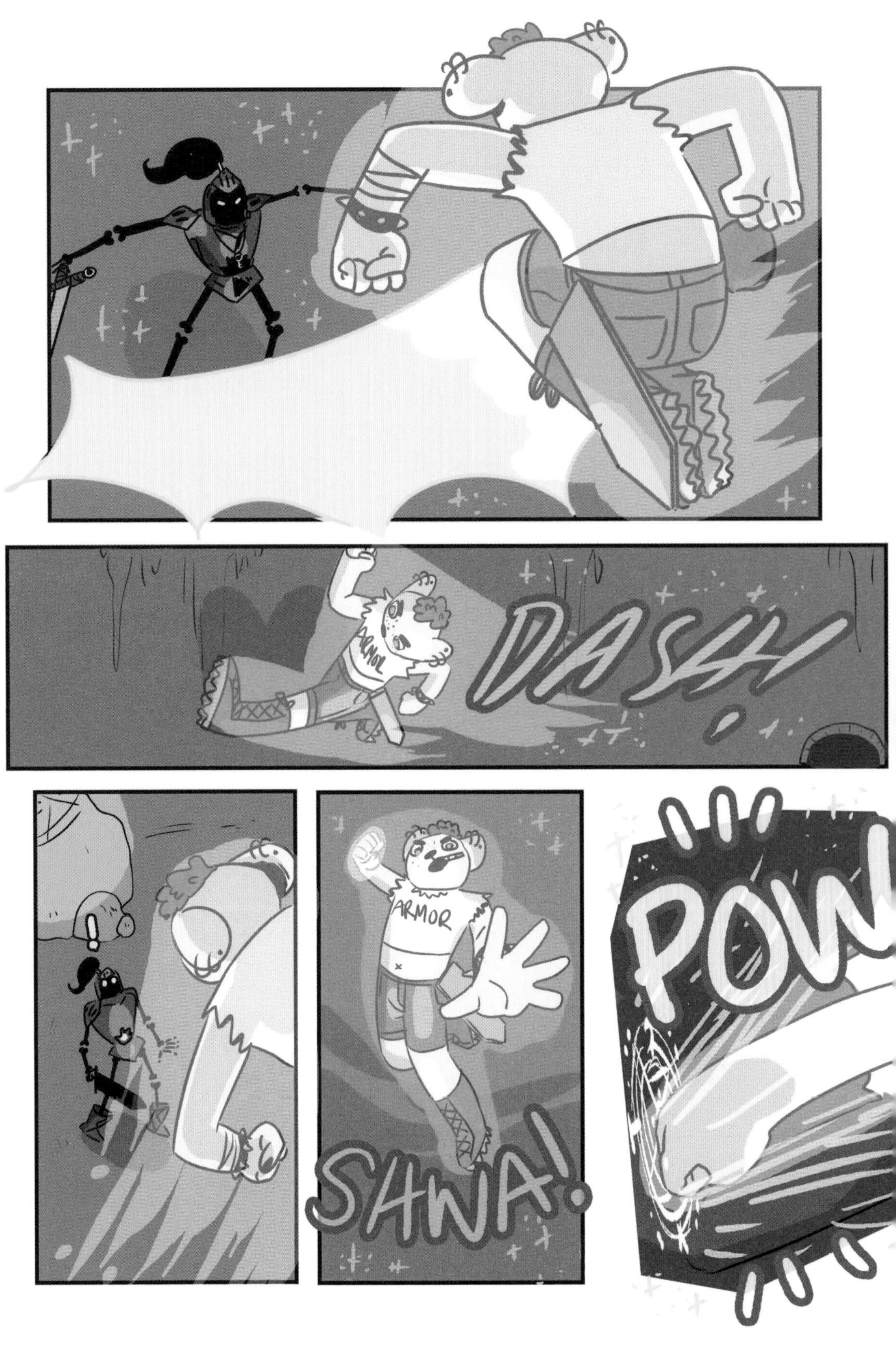
DASH!
ARMOR
!
ARMOR
SAWA!
POW

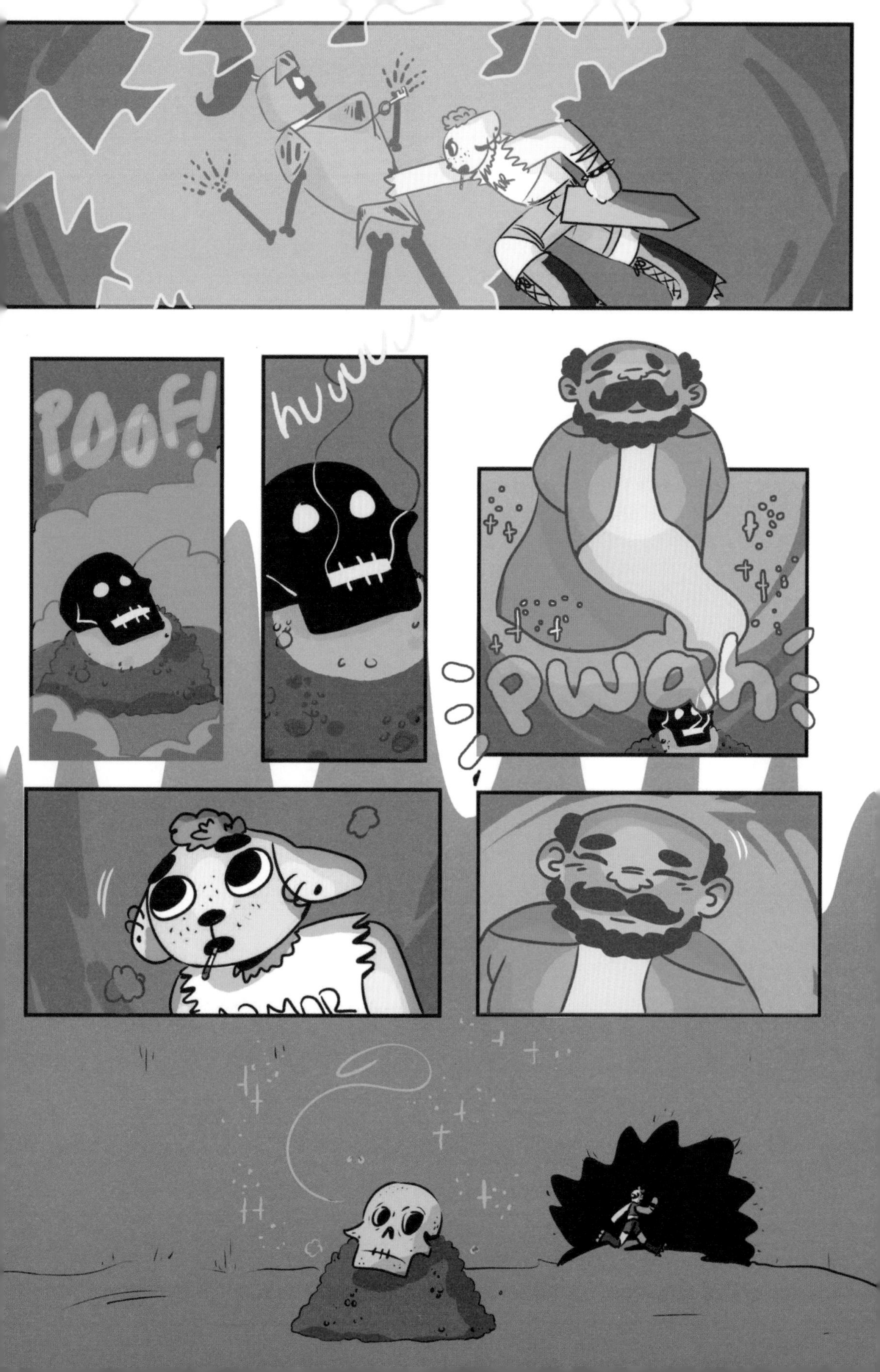

POOF!
huwwu
pwah!

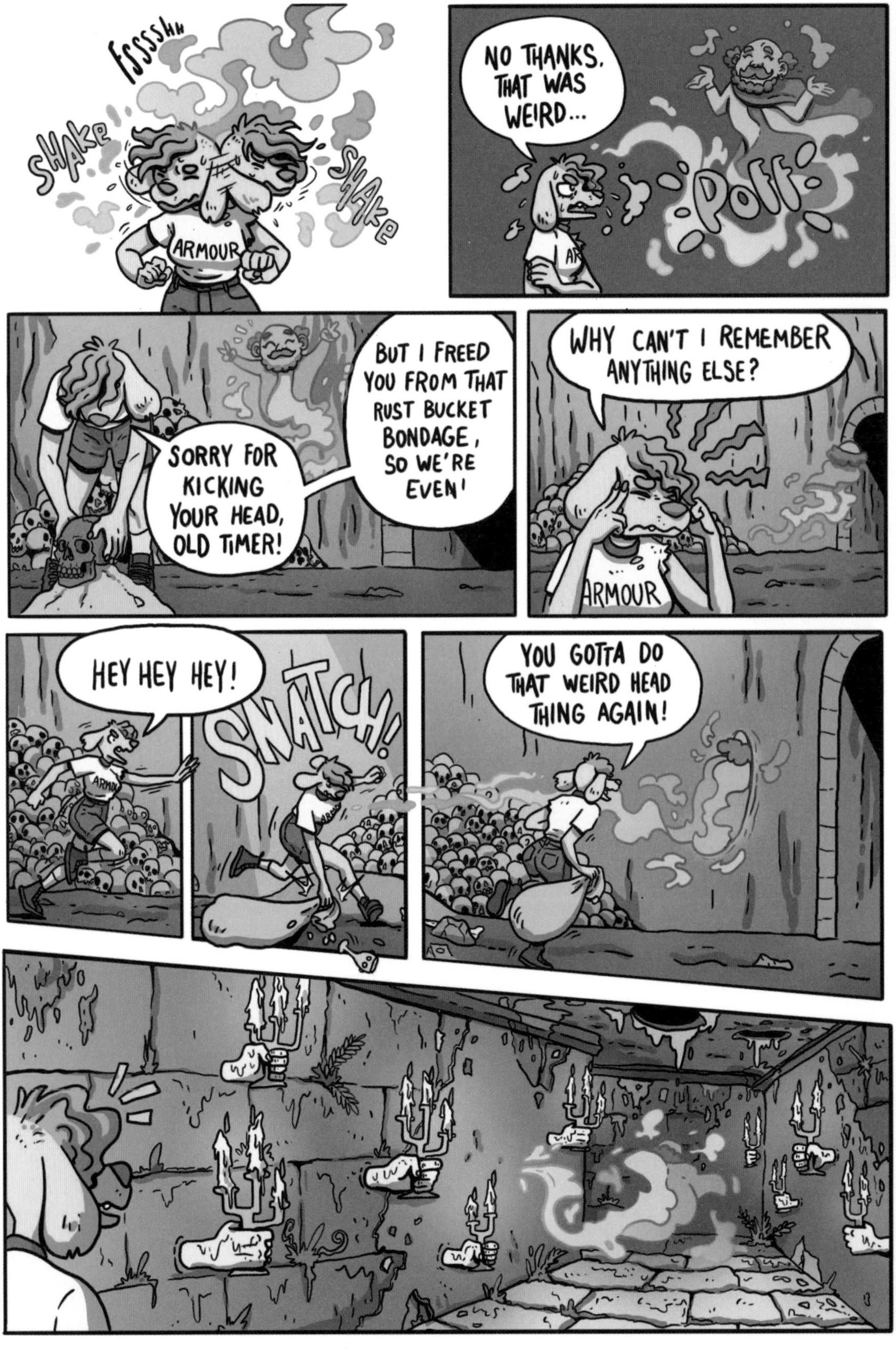
FSSSHH
SHAKE
SHAKE
ARMOUR
NO THANKS. THAT WAS WEIRD...
POFF
BUT I FREED YOU FROM THAT RUST BUCKET BONDAGE, SO WE'RE EVEN!
SORRY FOR KICKING YOUR HEAD, OLD TIMER!
WHY CAN'T I REMEMBER ANYTHING ELSE?
ARMOUR
HEY HEY HEY!
SNATCH!
YOU GOTTA DO THAT WEIRD HEAD THING AGAIN!

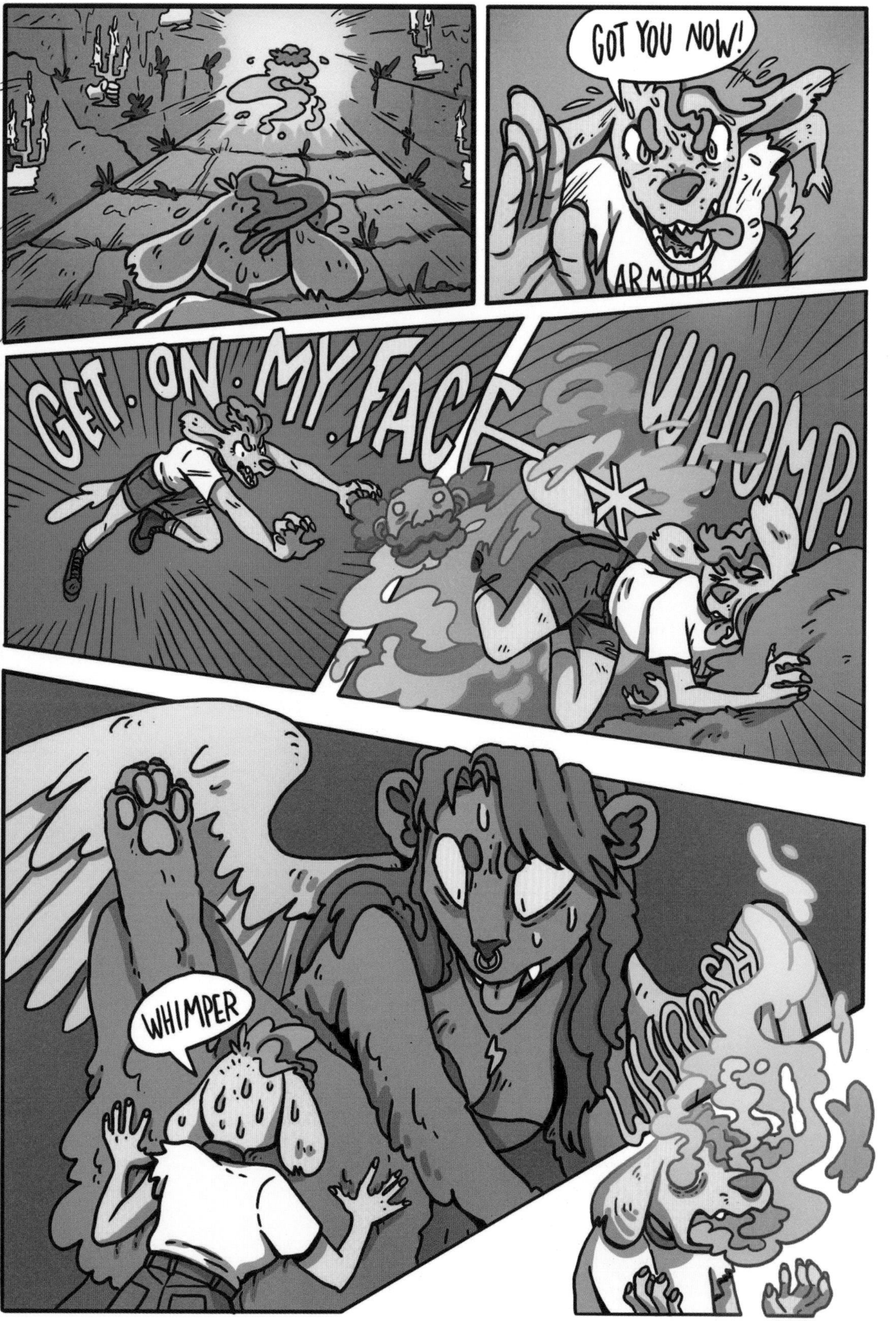
GOT YOU NOW!
ARMOUR
GET. ON. MY. FACE
WHOMP.
WHIMPER
WHOOOSH

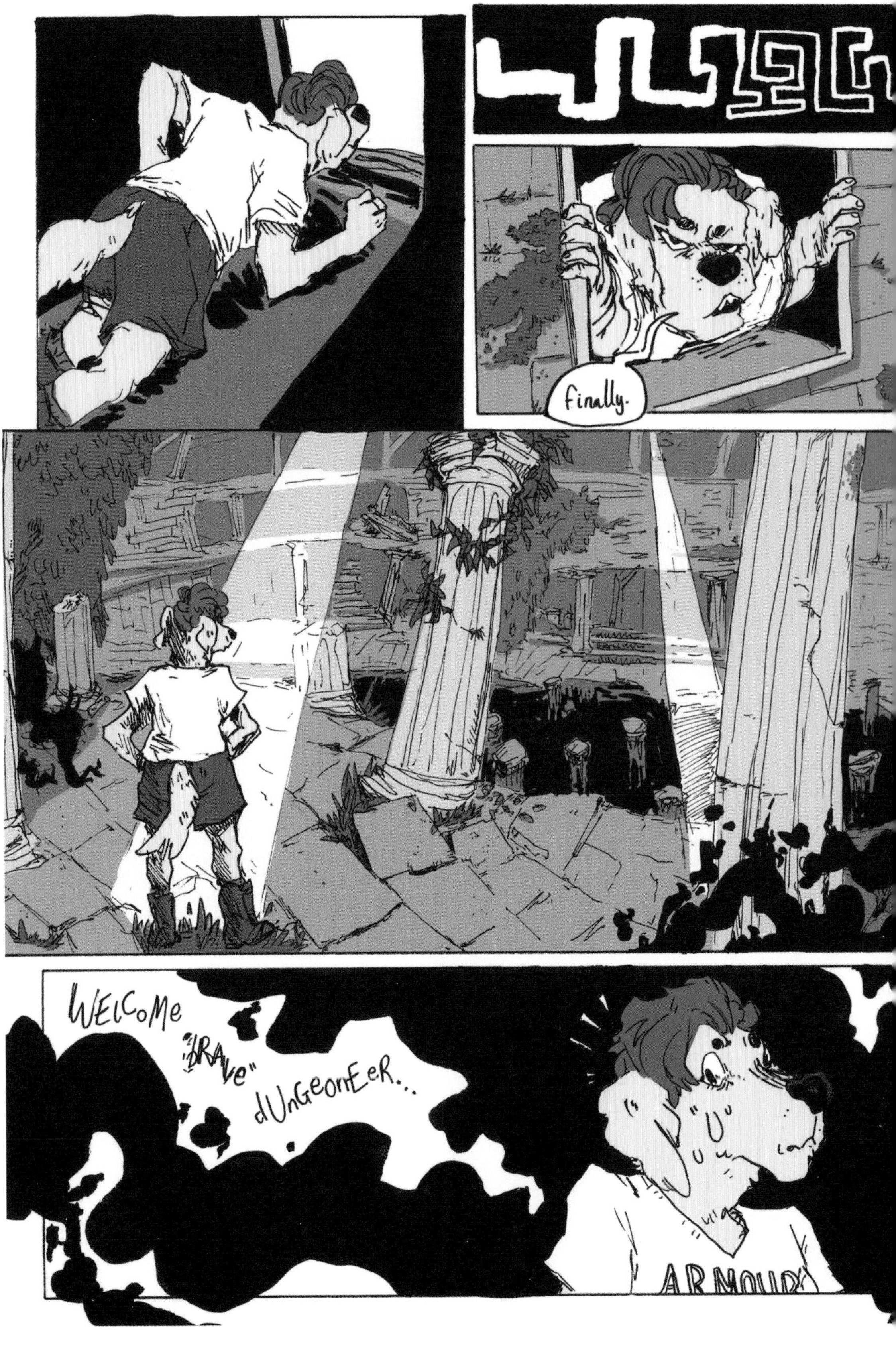
finally.
WELCOME "BRAVE" DUNGEONEER...
ARMOUR

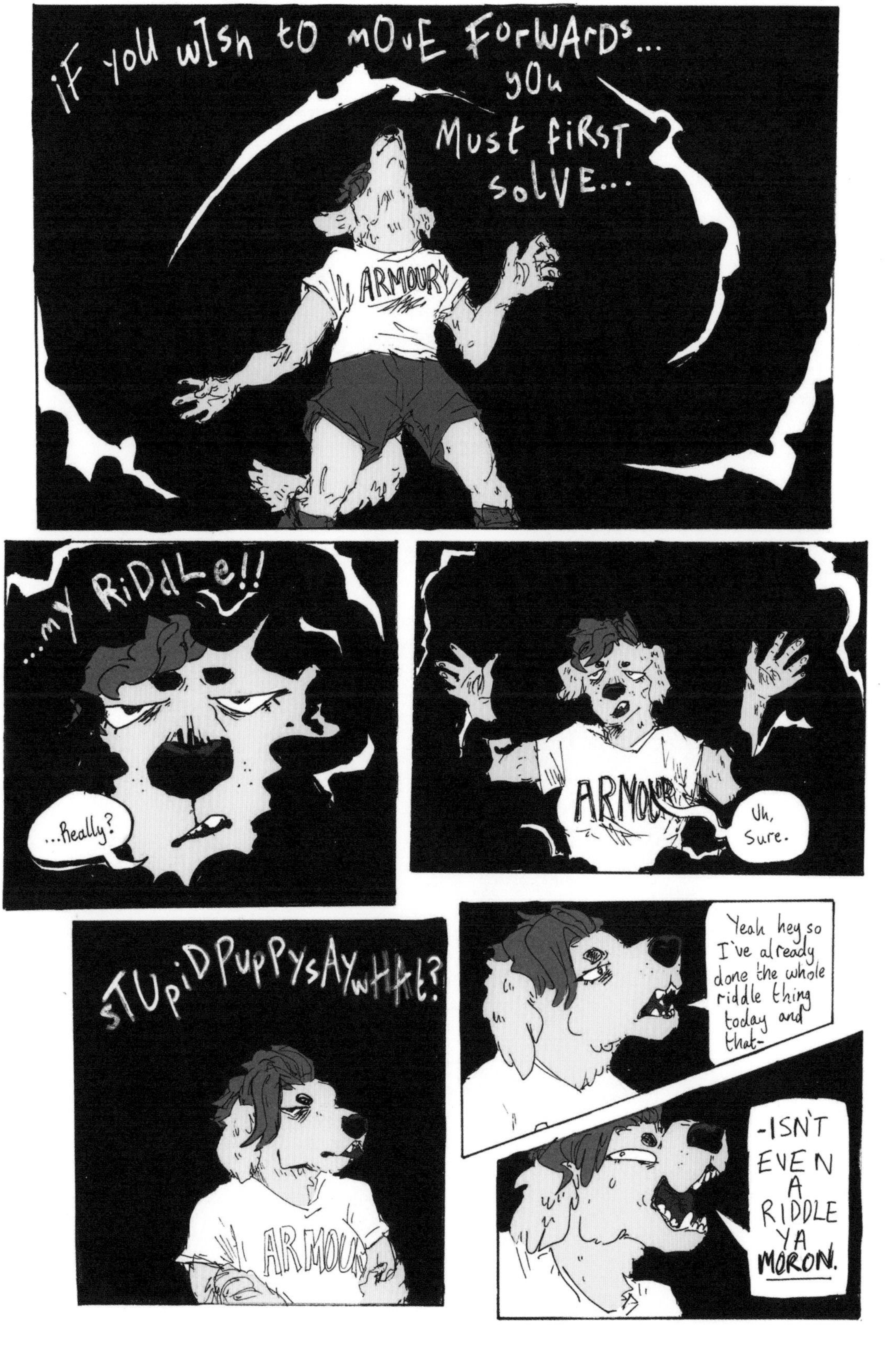

if you wish to move forwards... you must first solve...
...my RiDdLe!!
...Really?
Uh, sure.
STUPiD PUPPY SAY WHAT?
Yeah hey so I've already done the whole riddle thing today and that-
-ISN'T EVEN A RIDDLE YA MORON.

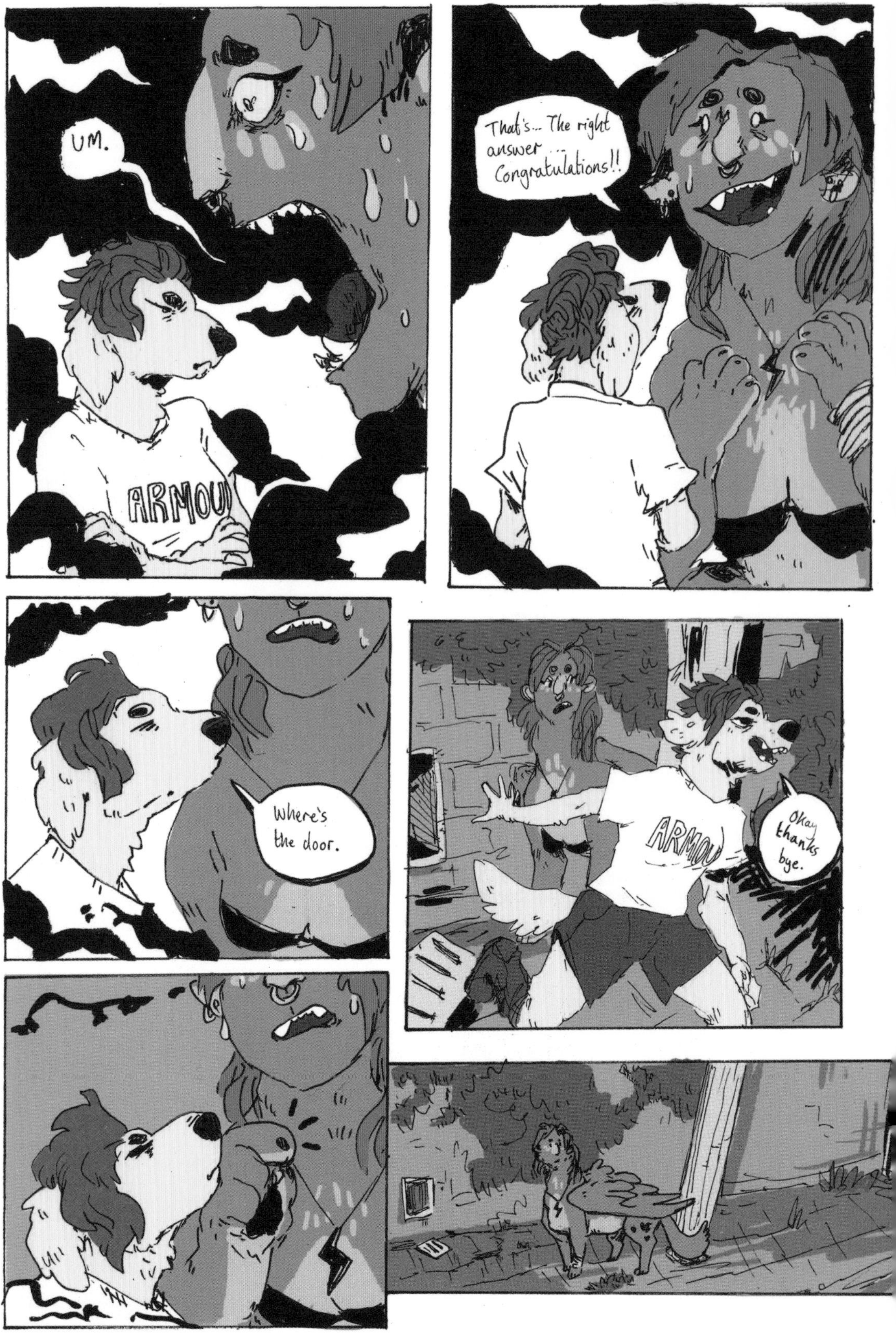
UM.
That's... The right answer... Congratulations!!
ARMOU
Where's the door.
ARMOU
Okay thanks bye.

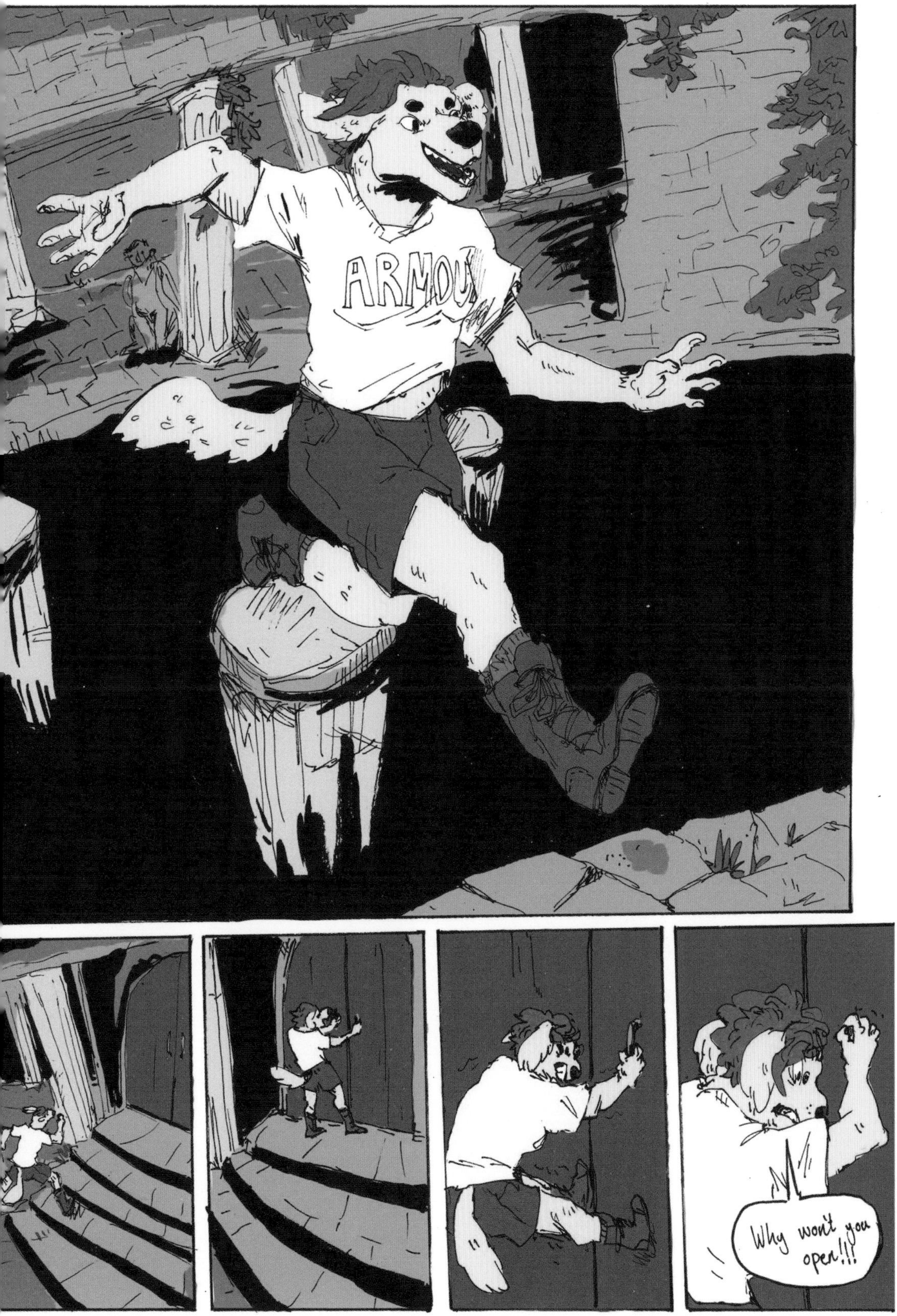
ARMOU
Why won't you open!!!

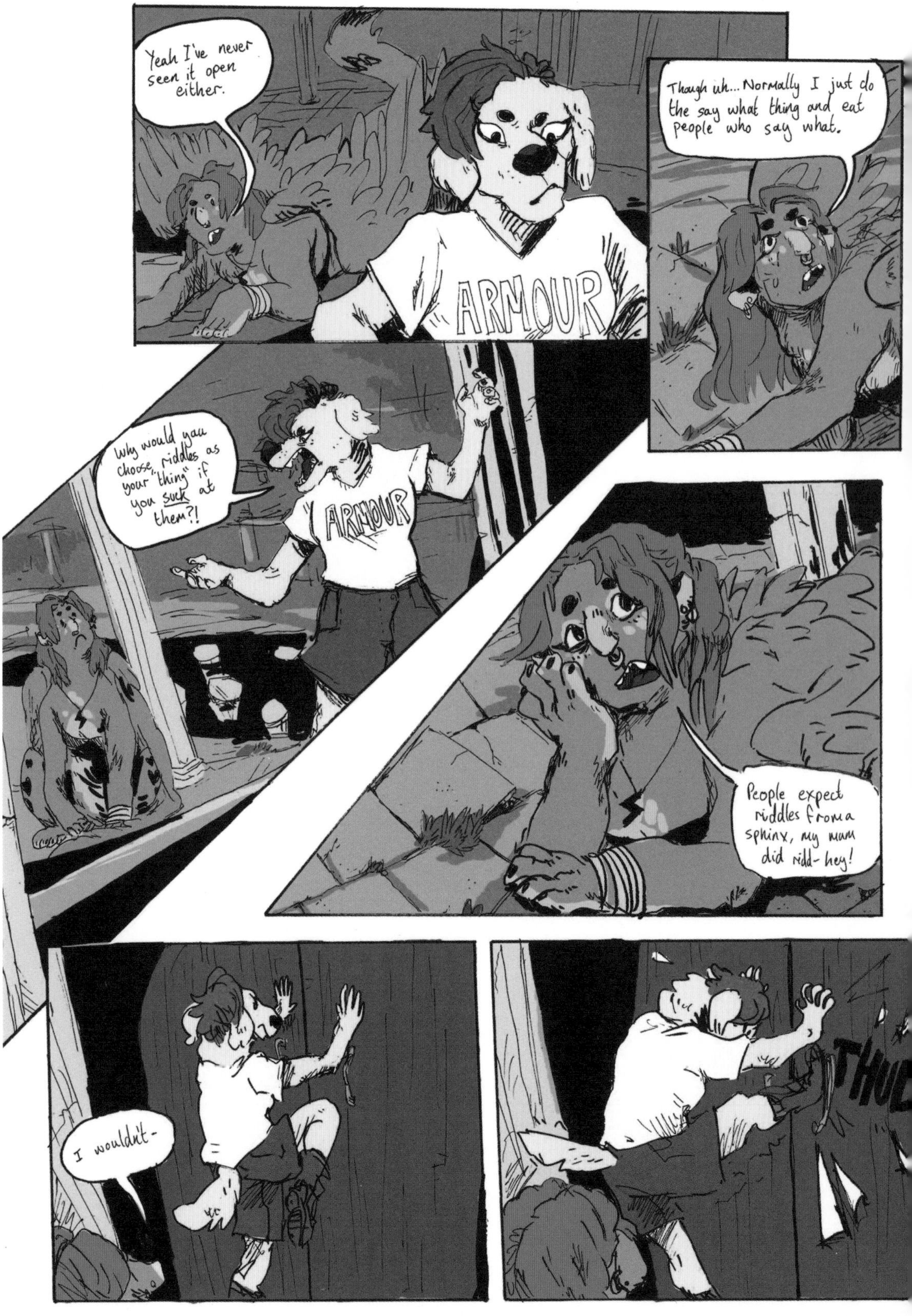
Yeah I've never seen it open either.
Though uh... Normally I just do the say what thing and eat people who say what.
ARMOUR
Why would you choose riddles as your "thing" if you suck at them?!
ARMOUR
People expect riddles from a sphinx, my mum did ridd- hey!
I wouldn't-
THUD

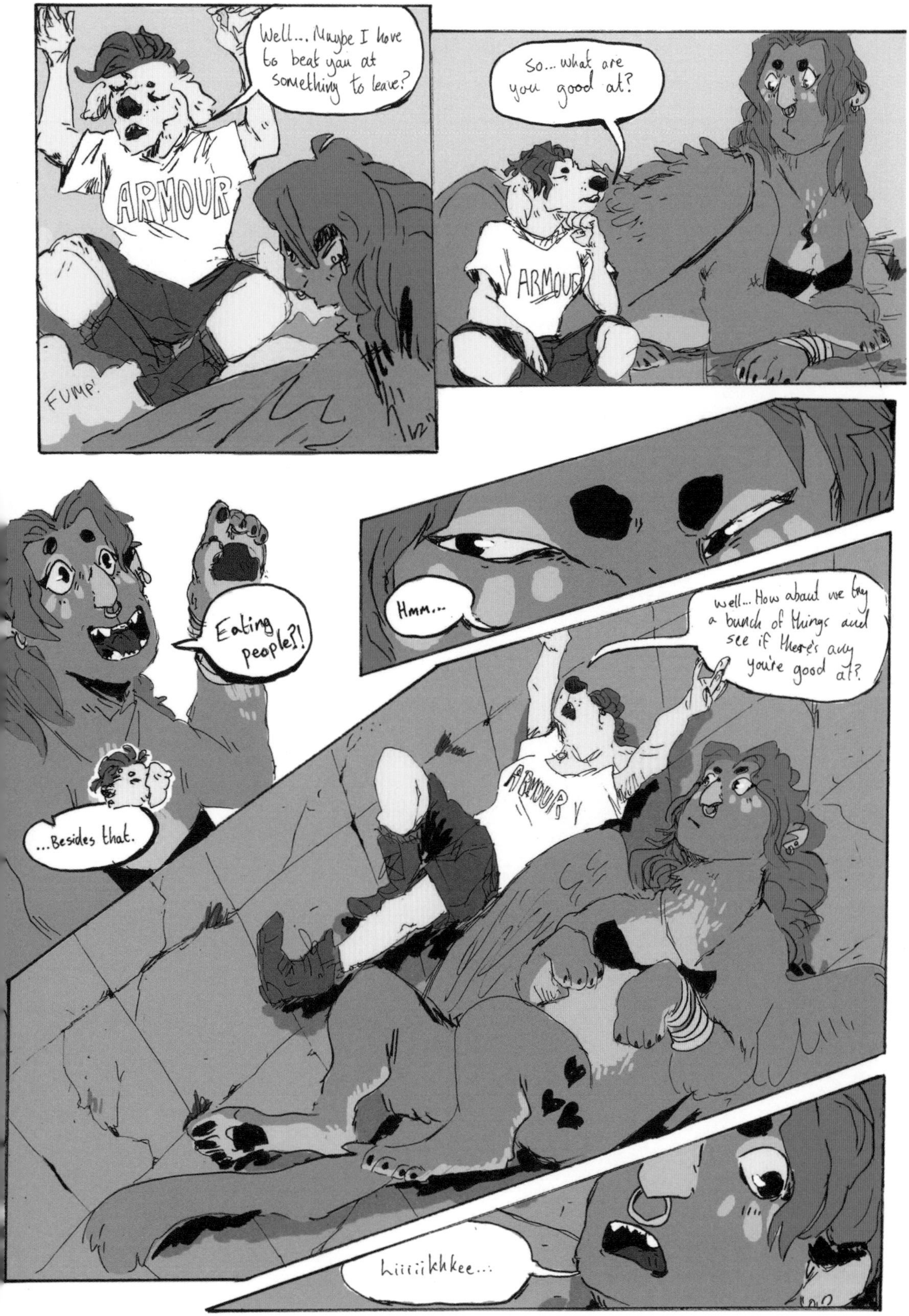
Well... Maybe I have to beat you at something to leave?
FUMP!
So... what are you good at?
Hmm...
Eating people?!
...Besides that.
well... How about we try a bunch of things and see if there's any you're good at?
Liiiiikhkee...

BALANCING CONTEST!

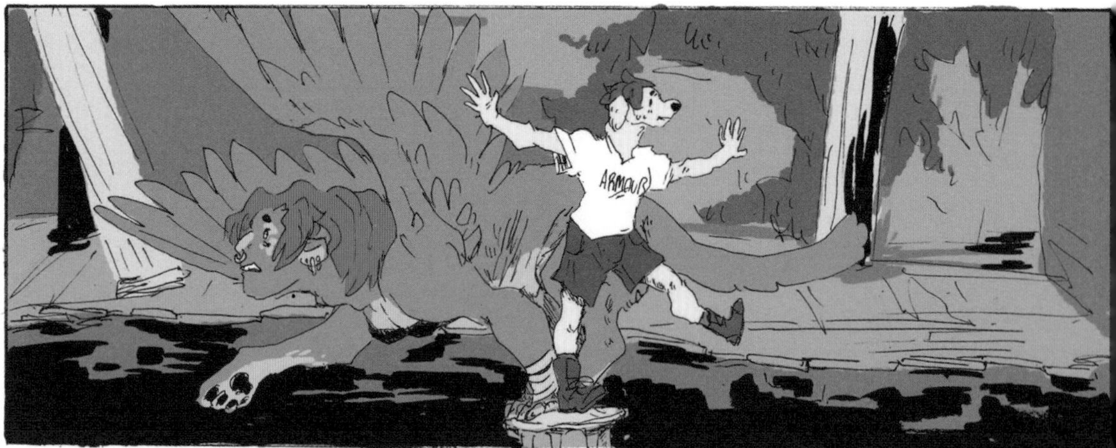

BADMINTON MATCH!

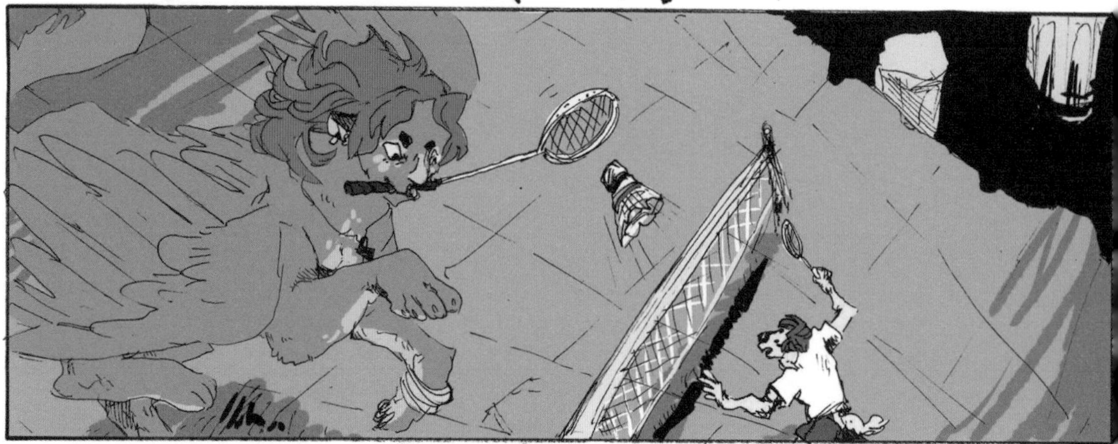

FASHION SHOW!!

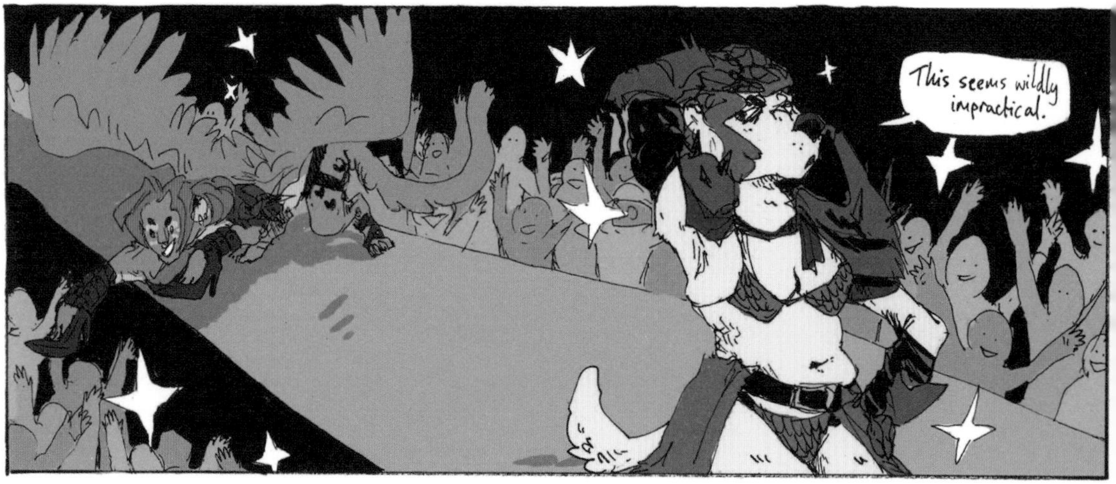
This seems wildly impractical.

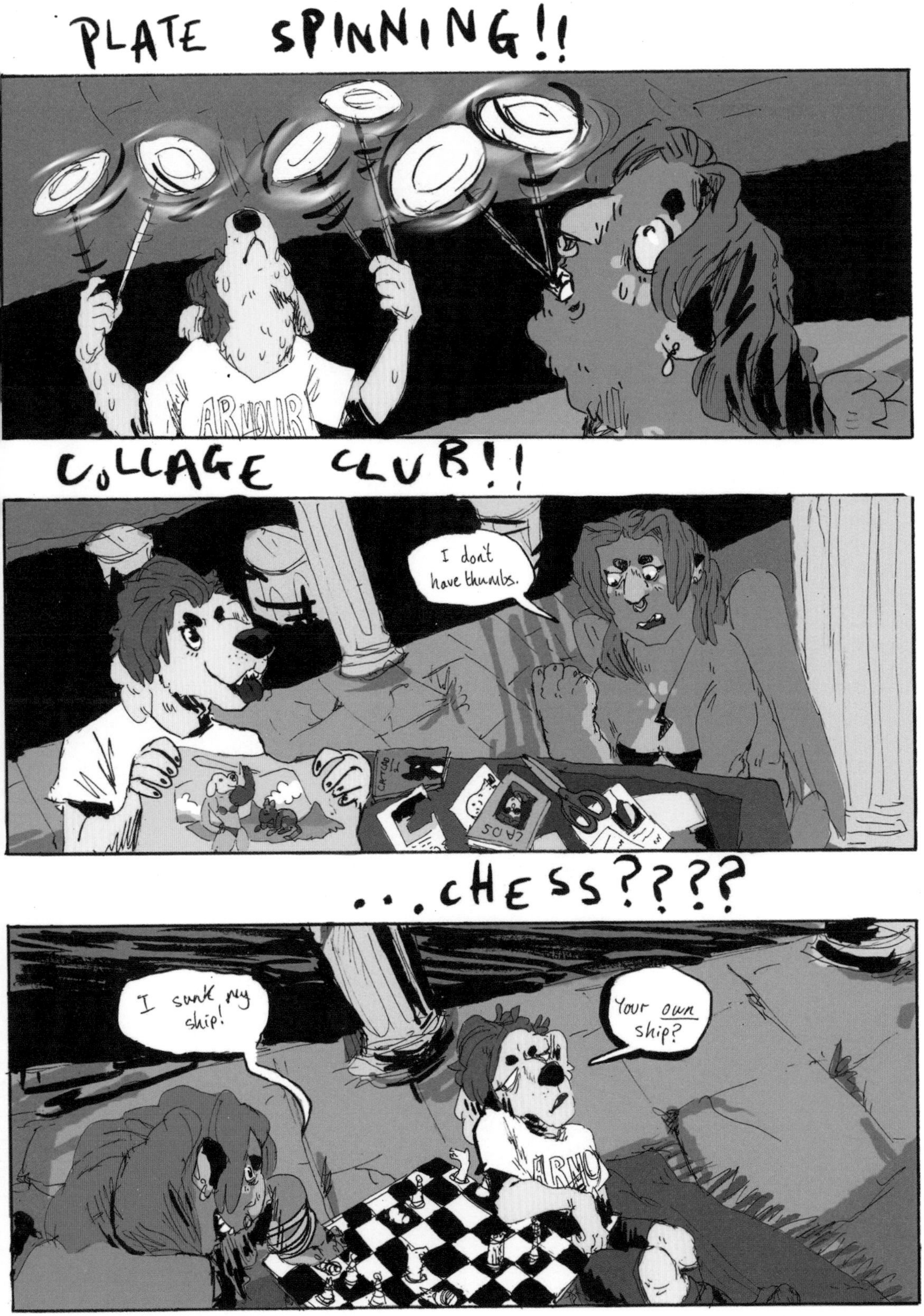
PLATE SPINNING!!
COLLAGE CLUB!!
I don't have thumbs.
...CHESS????
I sunk my ship!
Your own ship?

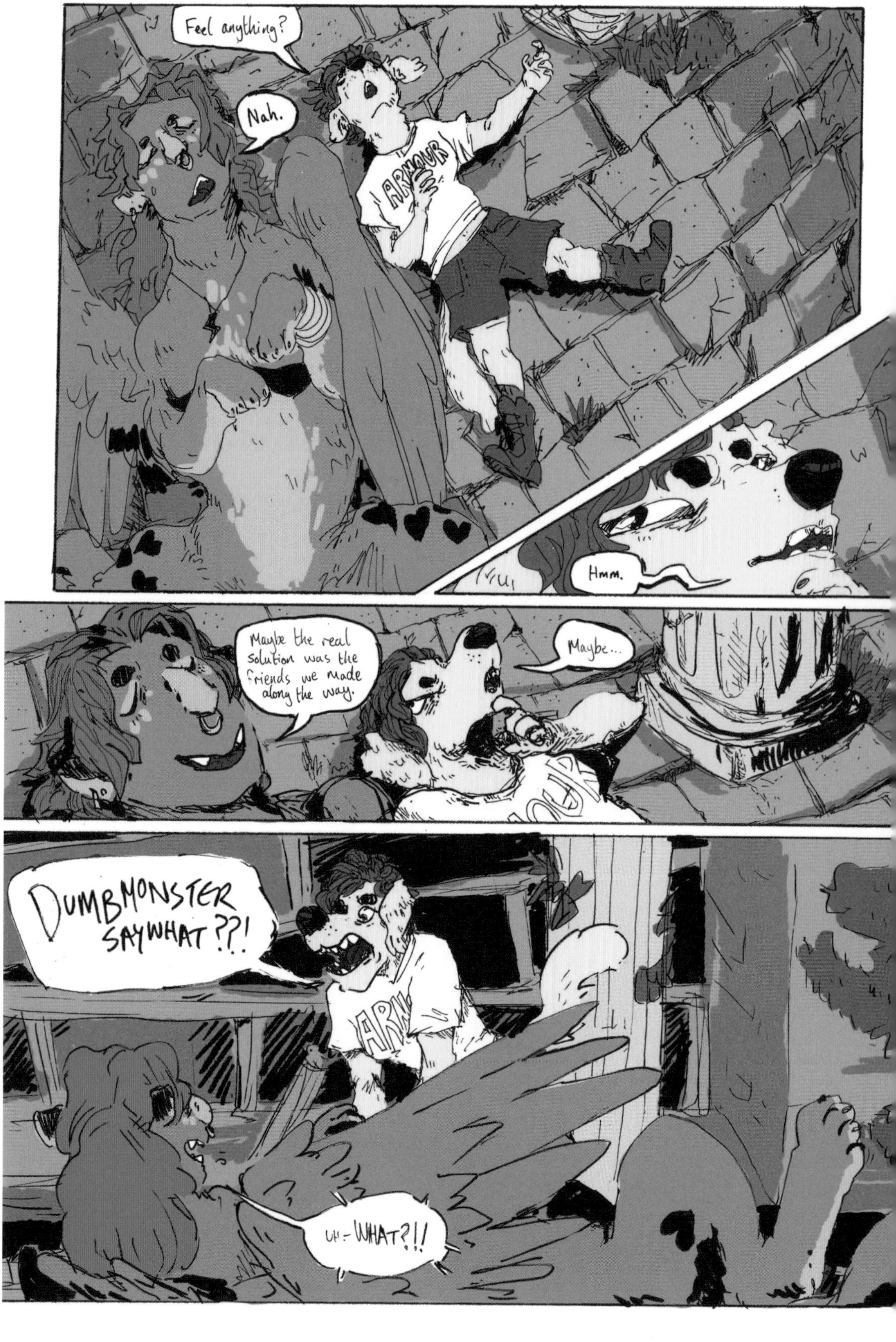
Feel anything?
Nah.
Hmm.
Maybe the real solution was the friends we made along the way.
Maybe...
DUMBMONSTER SAYWHAT ??!
Uh- WHAT?!!

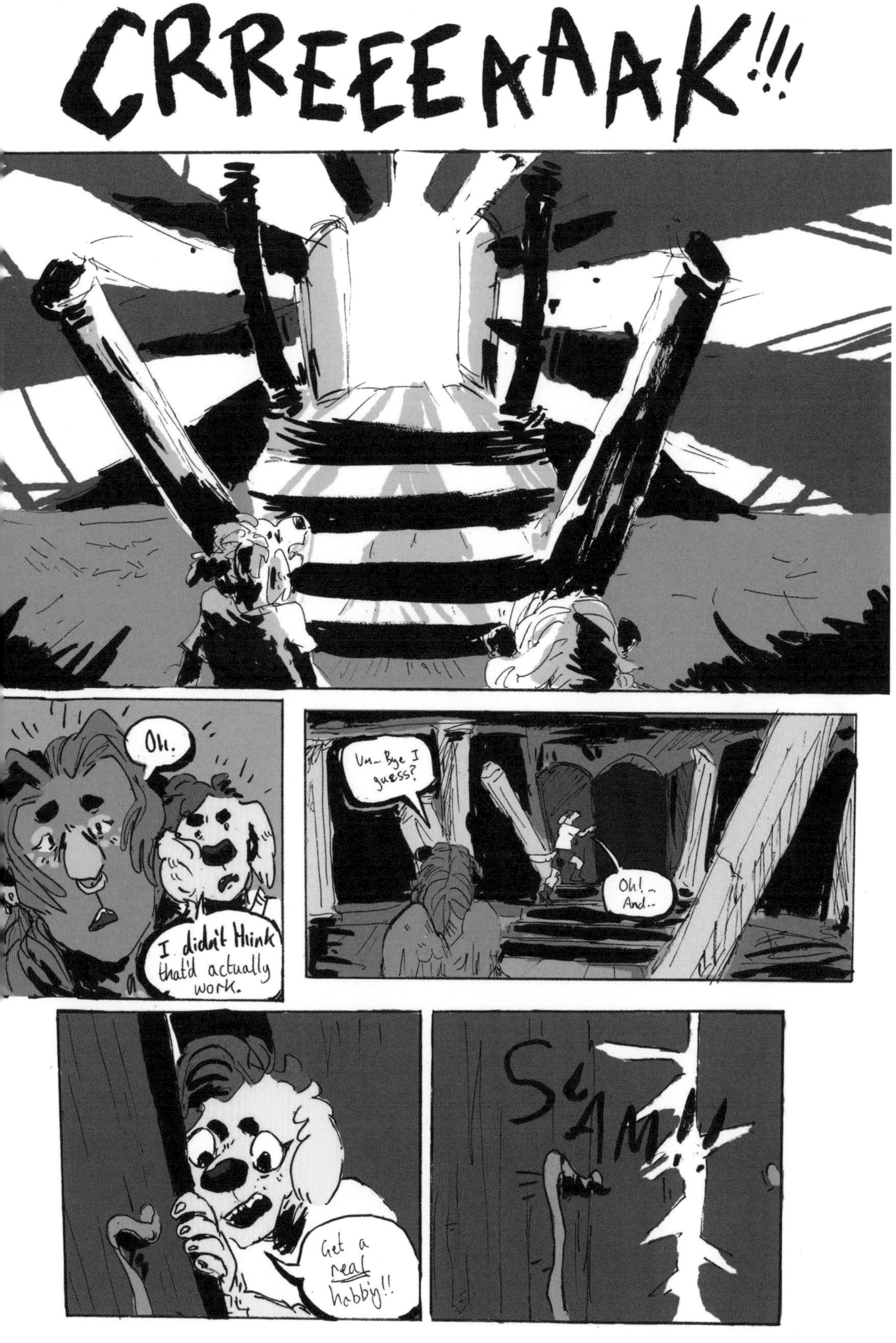
CRREEEAAAK!!!
Oh.
I didn't think that'd actually work.
Um... Bye I guess?
Oh!... And...
Get a real hobby!!
SLAM

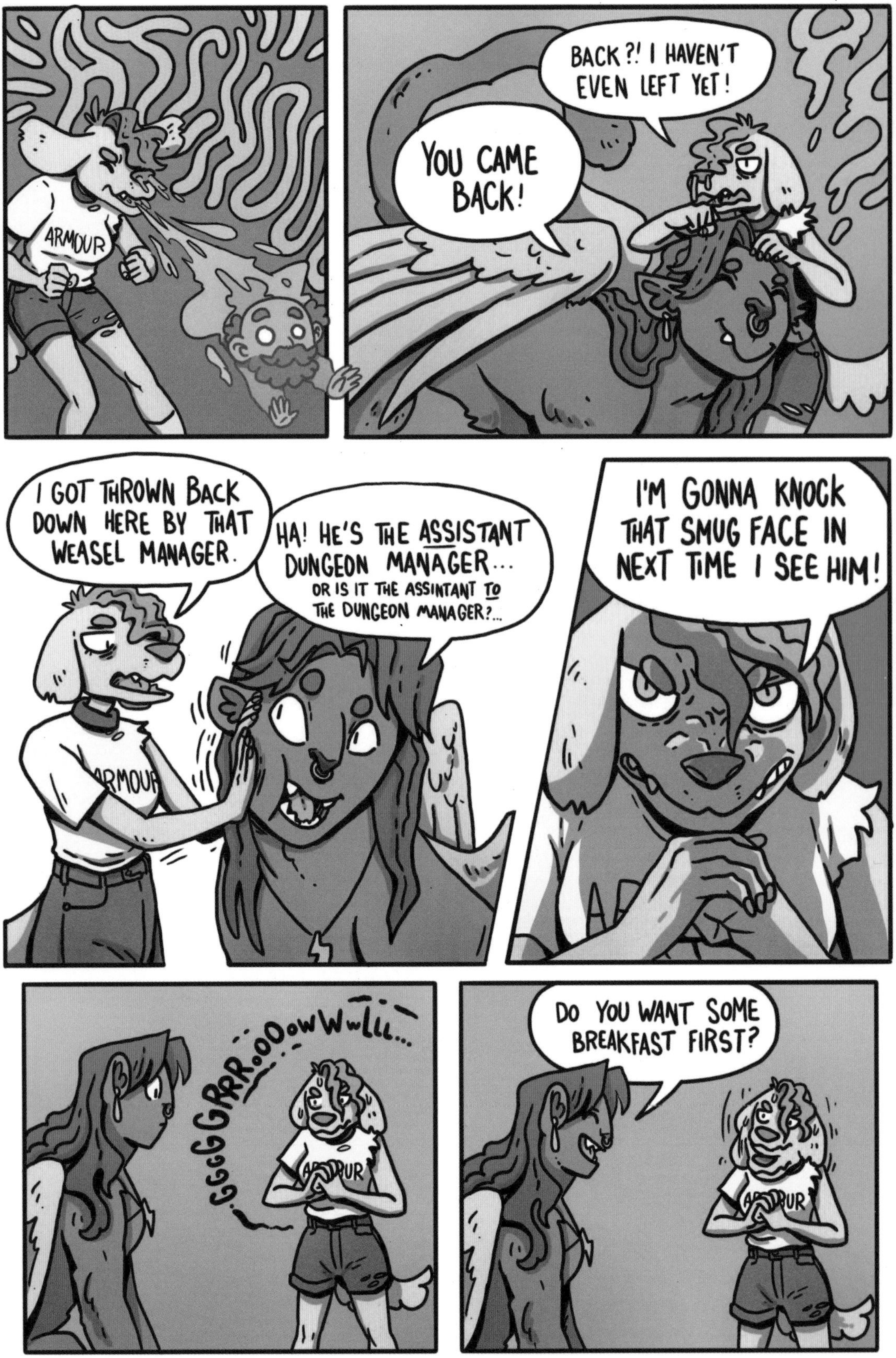
BACK?! I HAVEN'T EVEN LEFT YET!
YOU CAME BACK!
I GOT THROWN BACK DOWN HERE BY THAT WEASEL MANAGER.
HA! HE'S THE ASSISTANT DUNGEON MANAGER... OR IS IT THE ASSINTANT TO THE DUNGEON MANAGER?...
I'M GONNA KNOCK THAT SMUG FACE IN NEXT TIME I SEE HIM!
GGGGGRRR..OOowWwLLL...
DO YOU WANT SOME BREAKFAST FIRST?

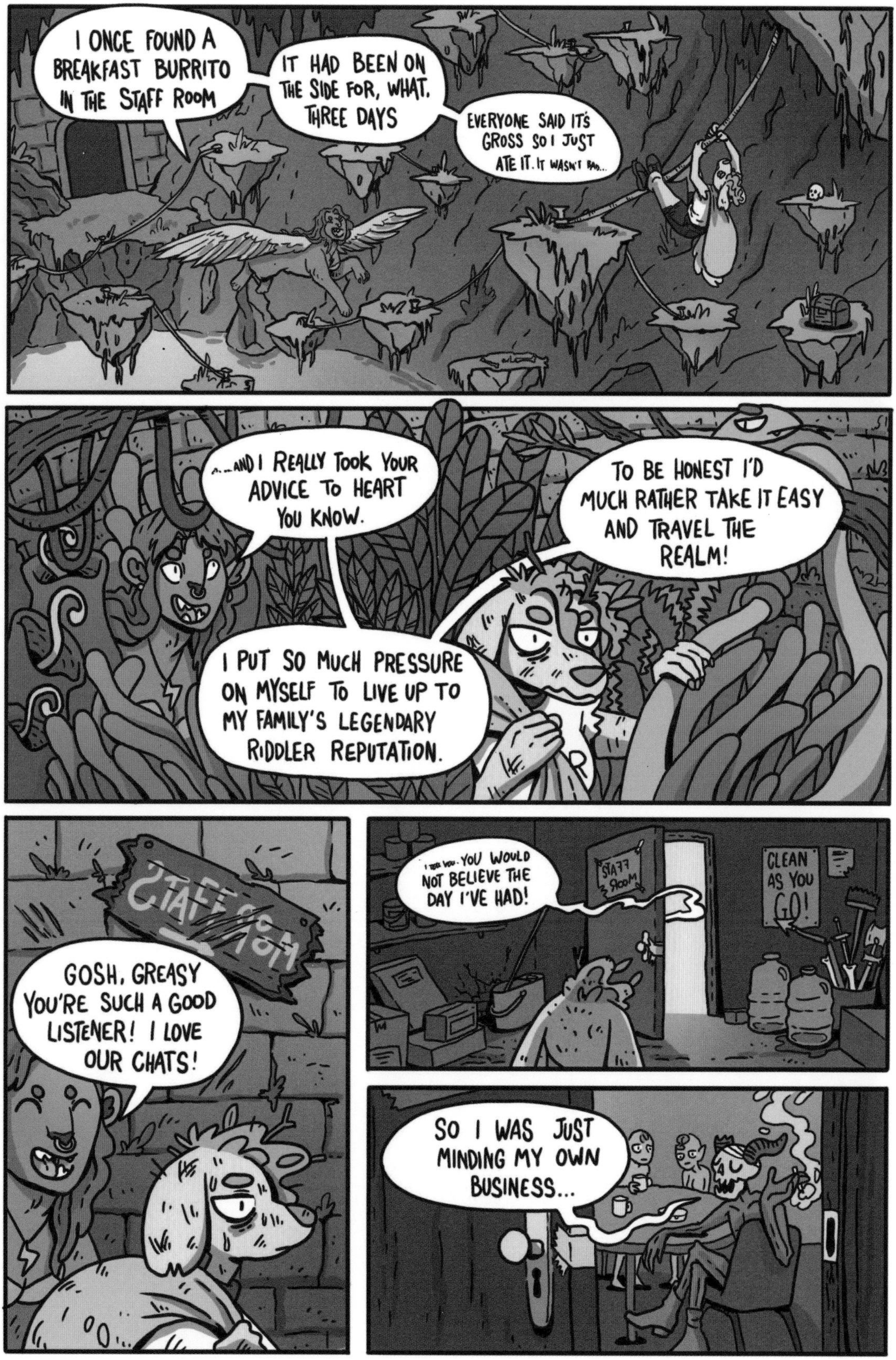
I ONCE FOUND A BREAKFAST BURRITO IN THE STAFF ROOM
IT HAD BEEN ON THE SIDE FOR, WHAT, THREE DAYS
EVERYONE SAID IT'S GROSS SO I JUST ATE IT. IT WASN'T BAD...
...AND I REALLY TOOK YOUR ADVICE TO HEART YOU KNOW.
TO BE HONEST I'D MUCH RATHER TAKE IT EASY AND TRAVEL THE REALM!
I PUT SO MUCH PRESSURE ON MYSELF TO LIVE UP TO MY FAMILY'S LEGENDARY RIDDLER REPUTATION.
GOSH, GREASY YOU'RE SUCH A GOOD LISTENER! I LOVE OUR CHATS!
YOU WOULD NOT BELIEVE THE DAY I'VE HAD!
STAFF ROOM
CLEAN AS YOU GO!
SO I WAS JUST MINDING MY OWN BUSINESS...

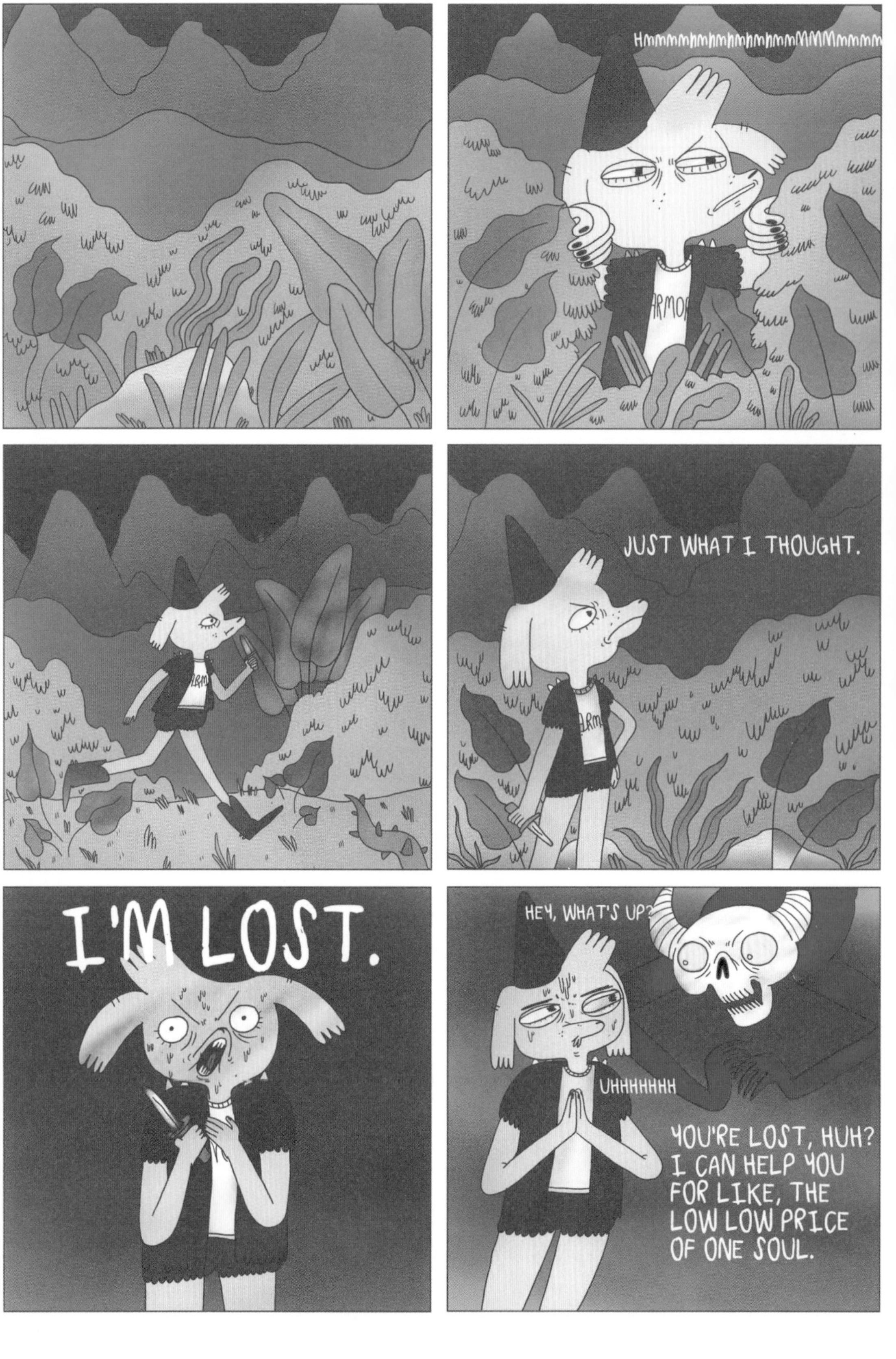
Hmmmmhmhmhmhmhmmmmmmmmm
JUST WHAT I THOUGHT.
I'M LOST.
HEY, WHAT'S UP?
UHHHHHHH
YOU'RE LOST, HUH? I CAN HELP YOU FOR LIKE, THE LOW LOW PRICE OF ONE SOUL.

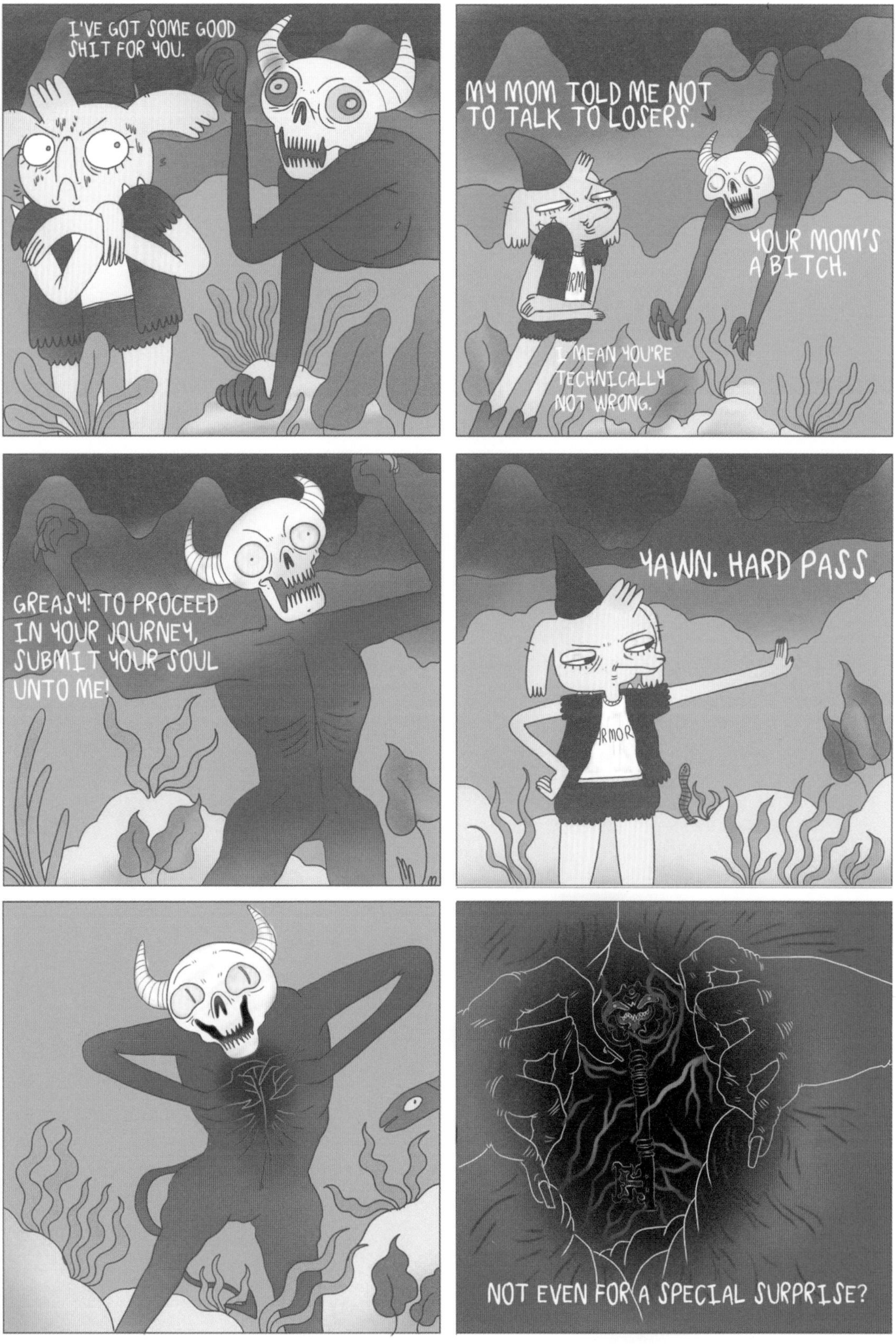
I'VE GOT SOME GOOD SHIT FOR YOU.
MY MOM TOLD ME NOT TO TALK TO LOSERS.
YOUR MOM'S A BITCH.
I MEAN YOU'RE TECHNICALLY NOT WRONG.
GREASY! TO PROCEED IN YOUR JOURNEY, SUBMIT YOUR SOUL UNTO ME!
YAWN. HARD PASS.
ARMOR
NOT EVEN FOR A SPECIAL SURPRISE?

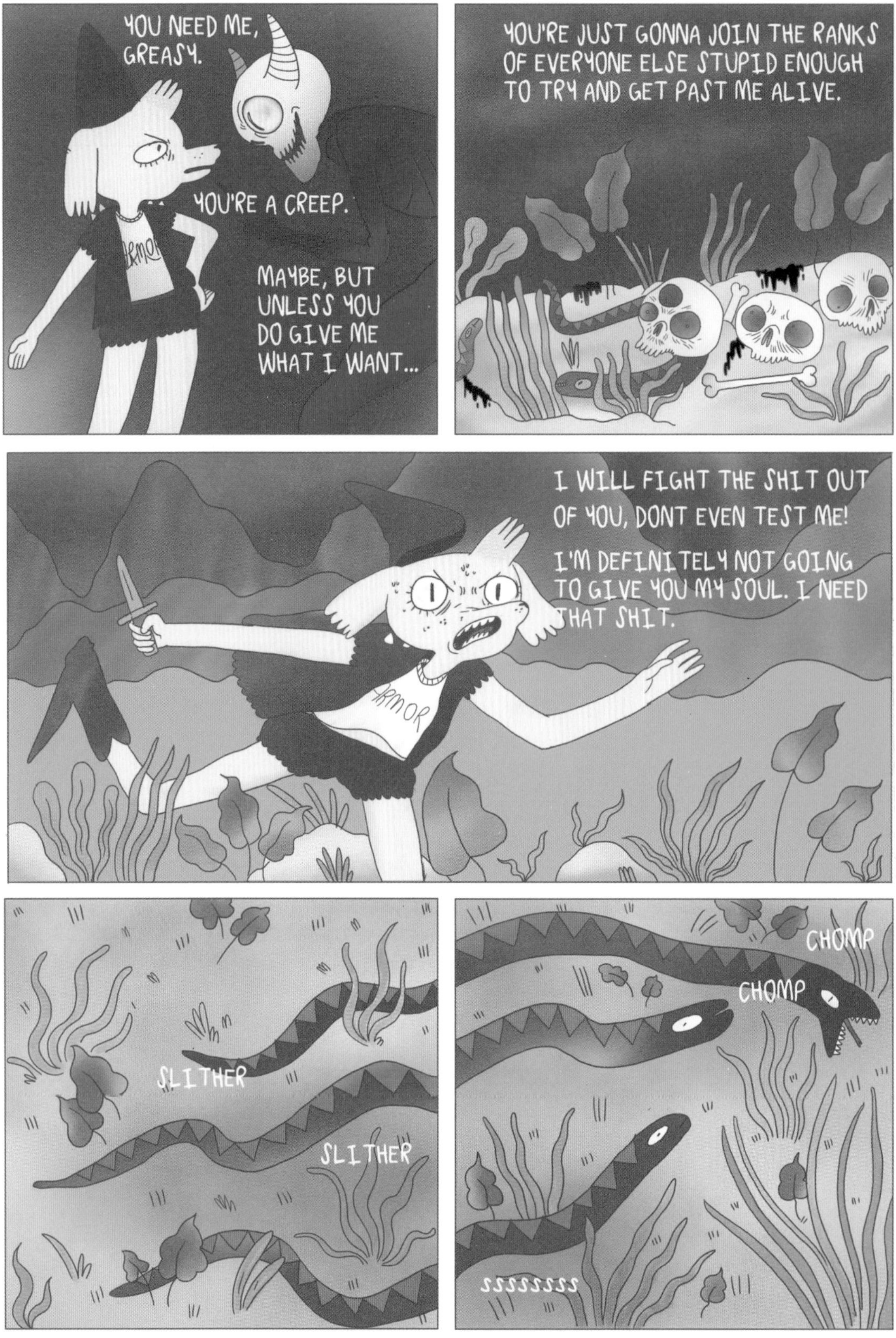

YOU NEED ME, GREASY.
YOU'RE A CREEP.
MAYBE, BUT UNLESS YOU DO GIVE ME WHAT I WANT...
YOU'RE JUST GONNA JOIN THE RANKS OF EVERYONE ELSE STUPID ENOUGH TO TRY AND GET PAST ME ALIVE.
I WILL FIGHT THE SHIT OUT OF YOU, DONT EVEN TEST ME!
I'M DEFINITELY NOT GOING TO GIVE YOU MY SOUL. I NEED THAT SHIT.
SLITHER
SLITHER
CHOMP
CHOMP
SSSSSSSS

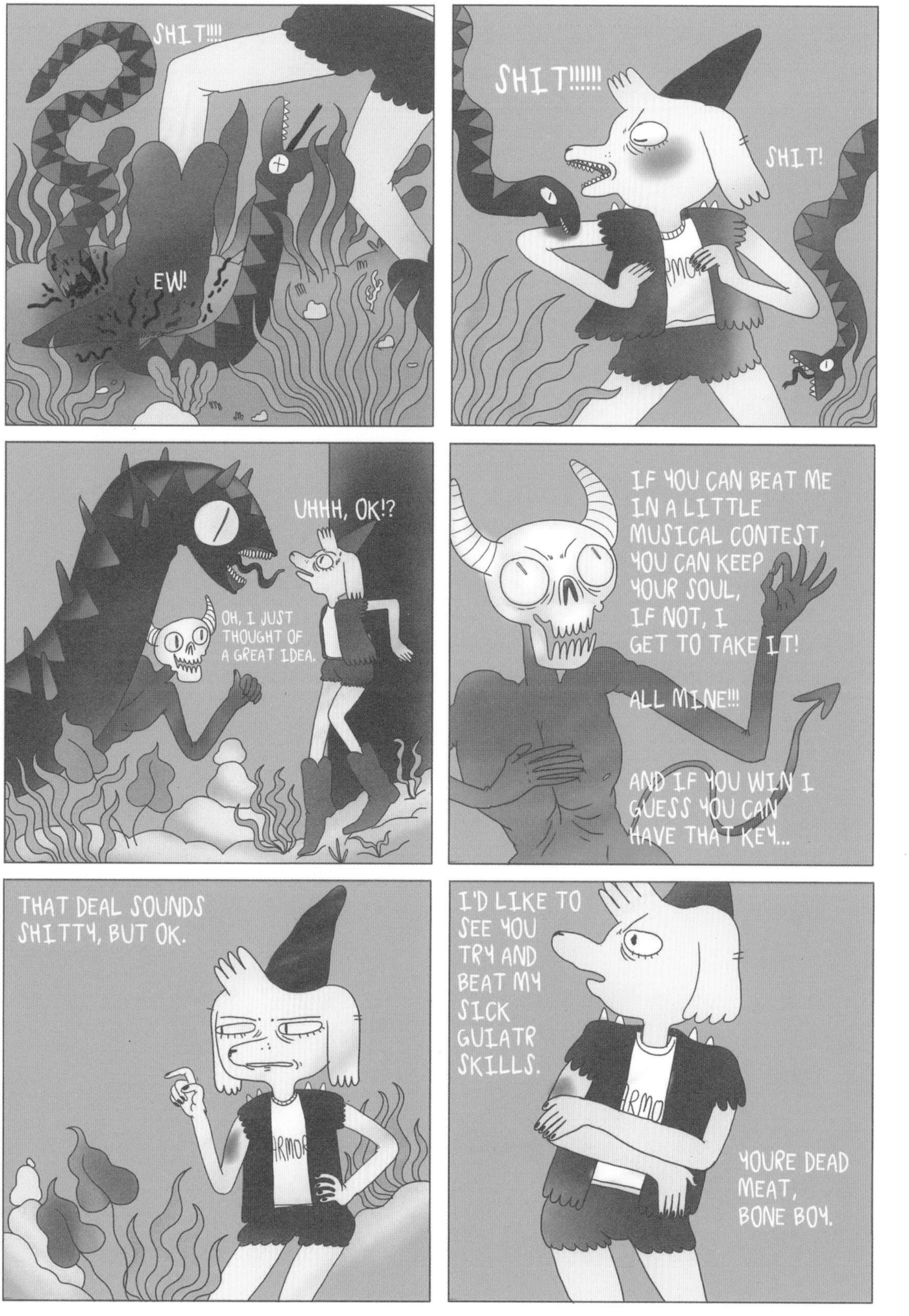
SHIT!!!!
EW!
SHIT!!!!!!
SHIT!
ARMOR
UHHH, OK!?
OH, I JUST THOUGHT OF A GREAT IDEA.
IF YOU CAN BEAT ME IN A LITTLE MUSICAL CONTEST, YOU CAN KEEP YOUR SOUL, IF NOT, I GET TO TAKE IT!
ALL MINE!!!
AND IF YOU WIN I GUESS YOU CAN HAVE THAT KEY...
THAT DEAL SOUNDS SHITTY, BUT OK.
ARMOR
I'D LIKE TO SEE YOU TRY AND BEAT MY SICK GUIATR SKILLS.
ARMO
YOURE DEAD MEAT, BONE BOY.

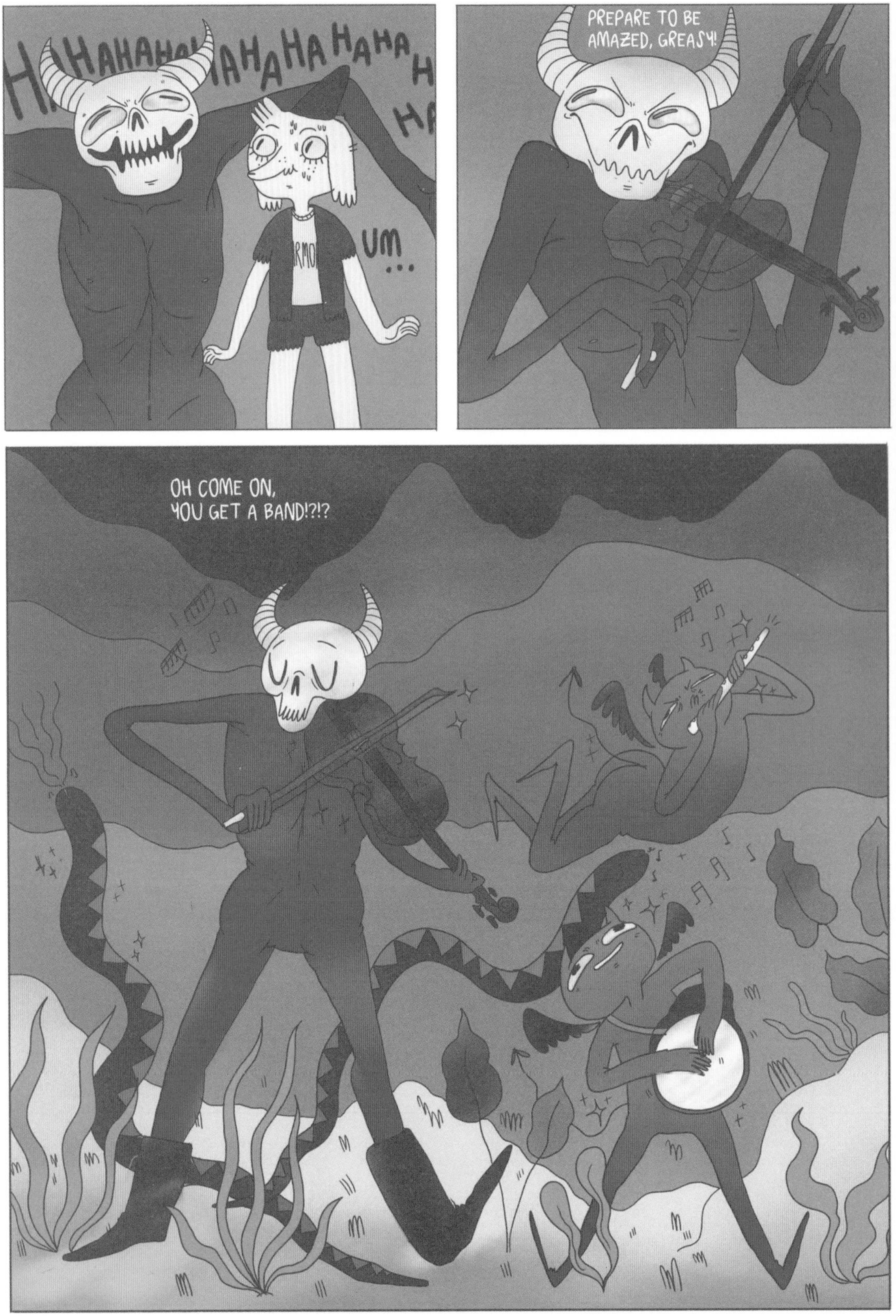
HAHAHAHAHAHAHA HAHA HA HA
UM ...
PREPARE TO BE AMAZED, GREASY!
OH COME ON, YOU GET A BAND!?!?

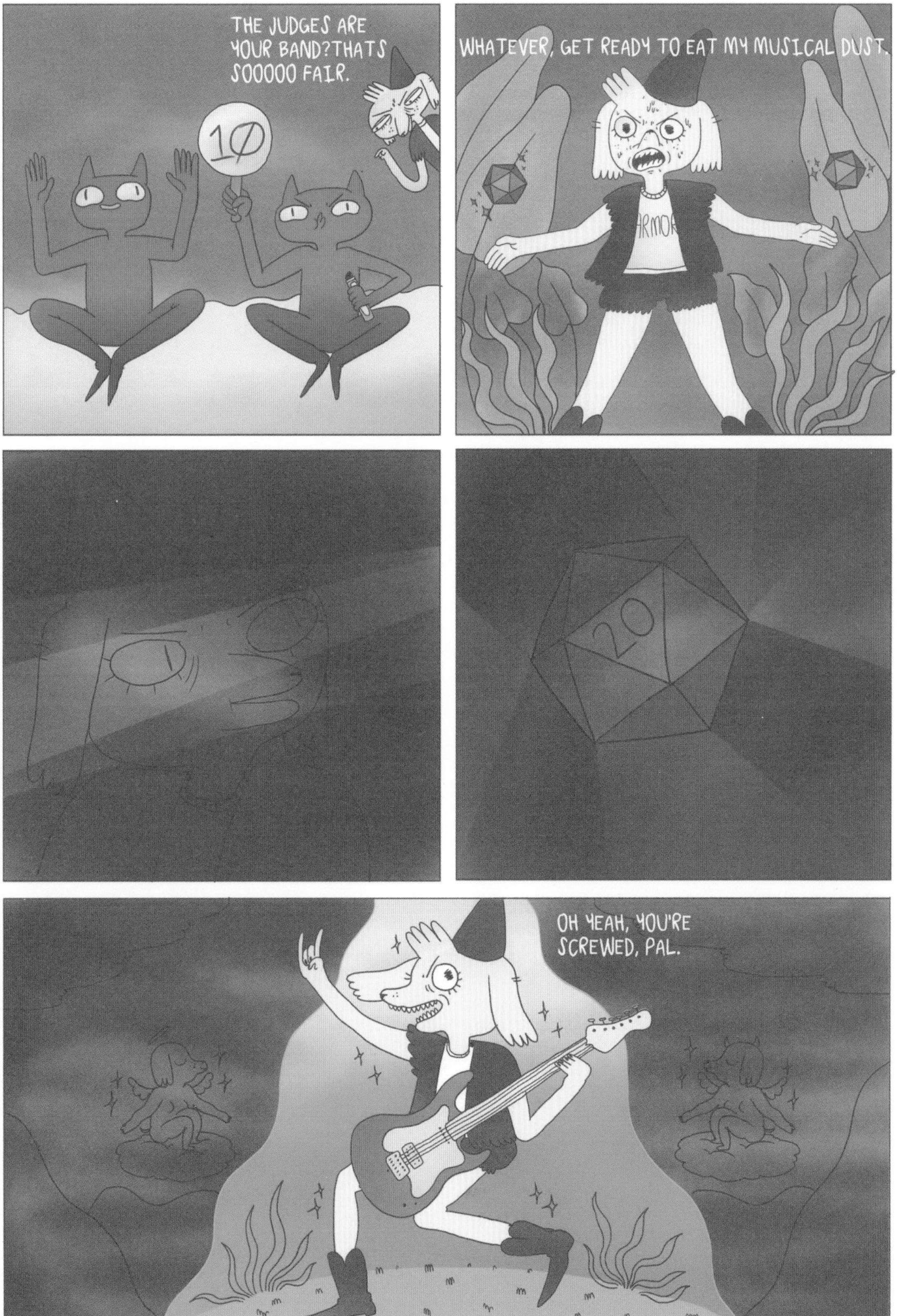
THE JUDGES ARE YOUR BAND? THATS SOOOOO FAIR.
10
WHATEVER, GET READY TO EAT MY MUSICAL DUST.
ARMOR
20
OH YEAH, YOU'RE SCREWED, PAL.

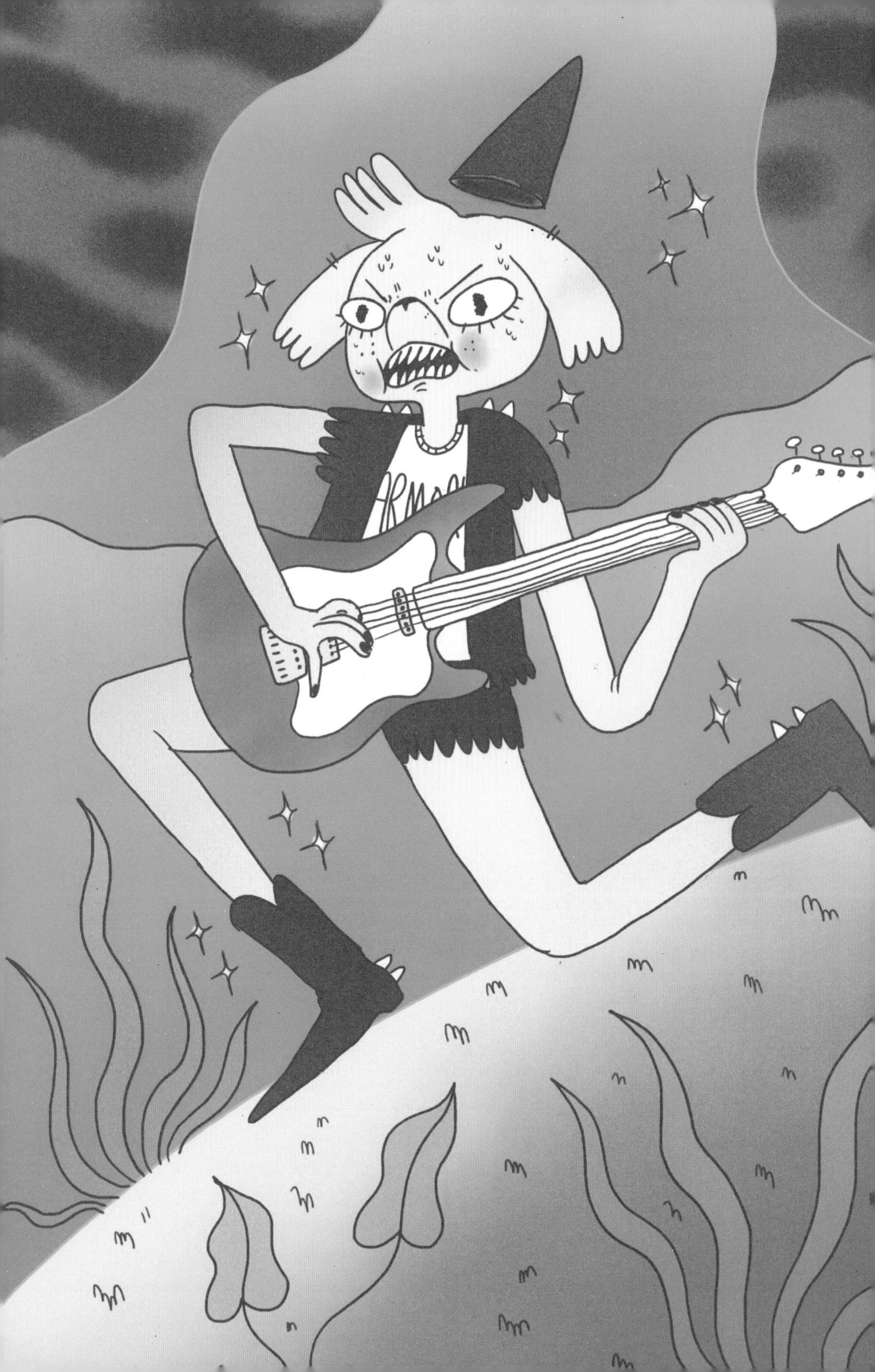

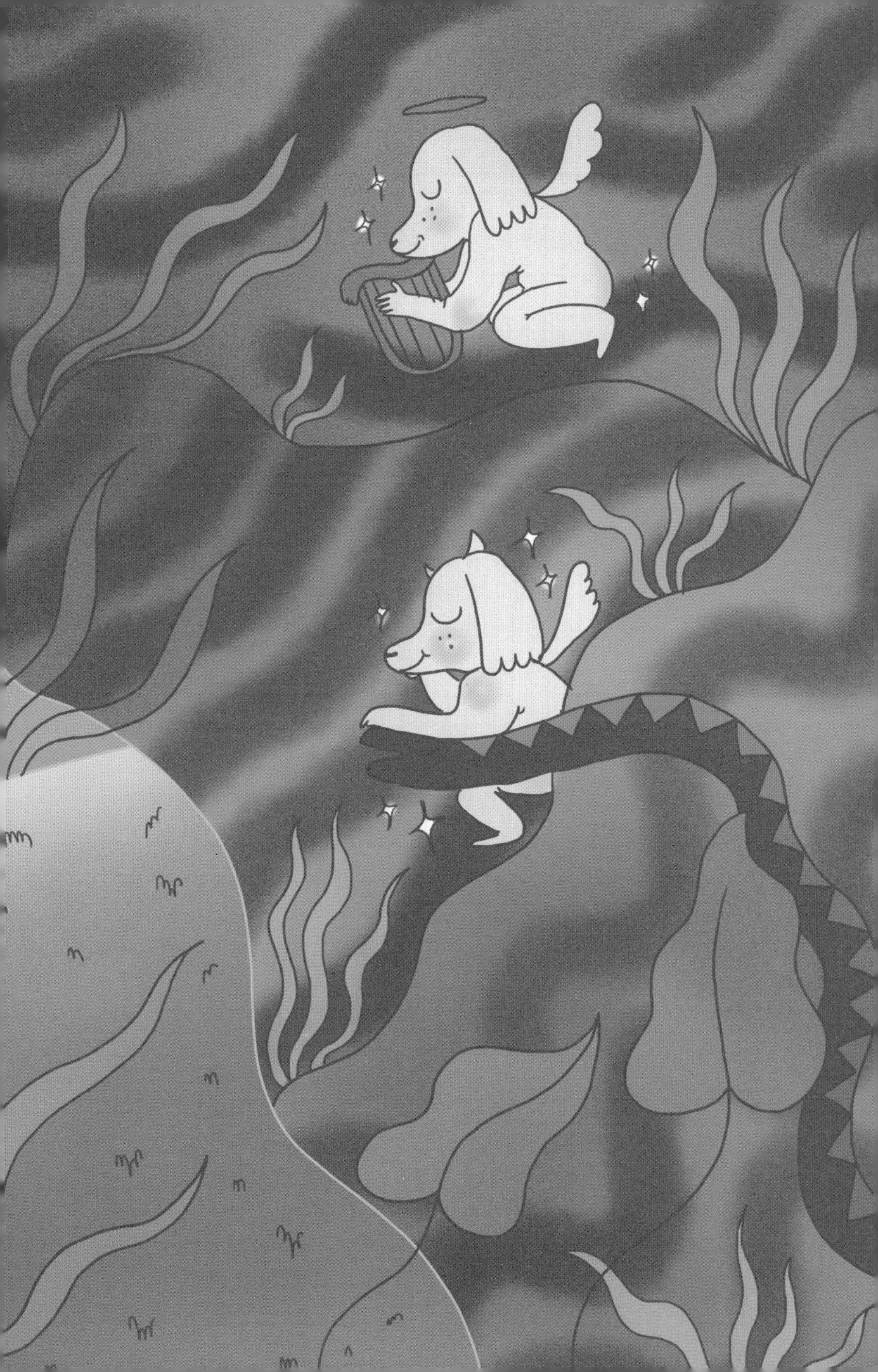

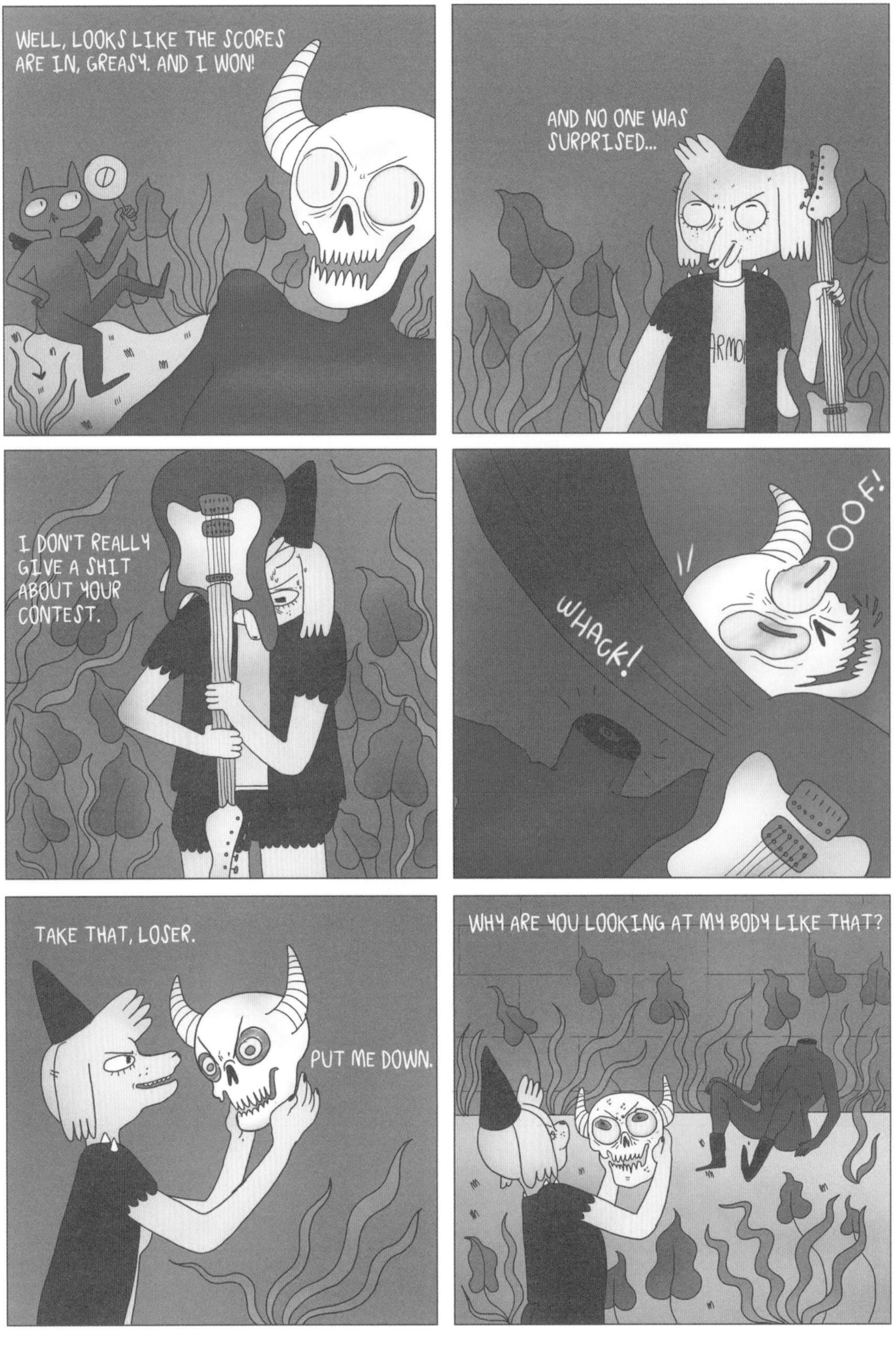
WELL, LOOKS LIKE THE SCORES ARE IN, GREASY. AND I WON!
AND NO ONE WAS SURPRISED...
ARMOR
I DON'T REALLY GIVE A SHIT ABOUT YOUR CONTEST.
OOF!
WHACK!
TAKE THAT, LOSER.
PUT ME DOWN.
WHY ARE YOU LOOKING AT MY BODY LIKE THAT?

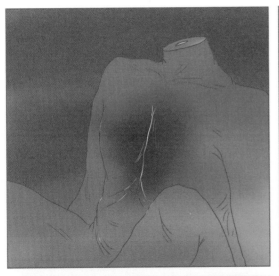

EW.

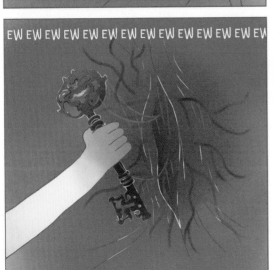

EW EW EW EW EW EW EW EW EW EW EW EW EW EW EW

ONWARD!!!

SEE YOU LATER, BONE HEAD!

SHIT.

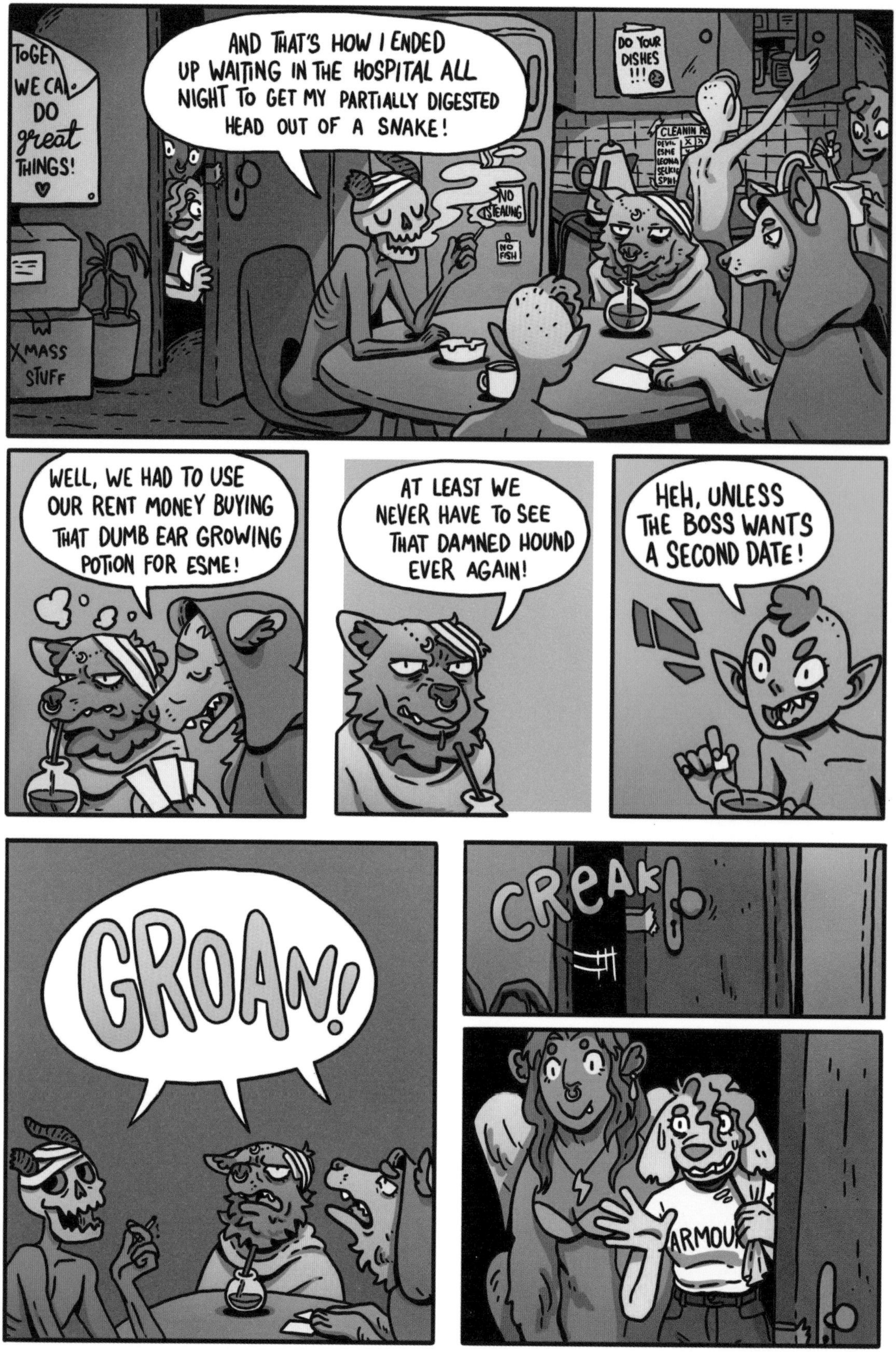
TOGET
WE CA
DO
great
THINGS!
AND THAT'S HOW I ENDED UP WAITING IN THE HOSPITAL ALL NIGHT TO GET MY PARTIALLY DIGESTED HEAD OUT OF A SNAKE!
DO YOUR DISHES !!!
NO STEALING
NO FISH
XMASS STUFF
WELL, WE HAD TO USE OUR RENT MONEY BUYING THAT DUMB EAR GROWING POTION FOR ESME!
AT LEAST WE NEVER HAVE TO SEE THAT DAMNED HOUND EVER AGAIN!
HEH, UNLESS THE BOSS WANTS A SECOND DATE!
GROAN!
CREAK
ARMOU

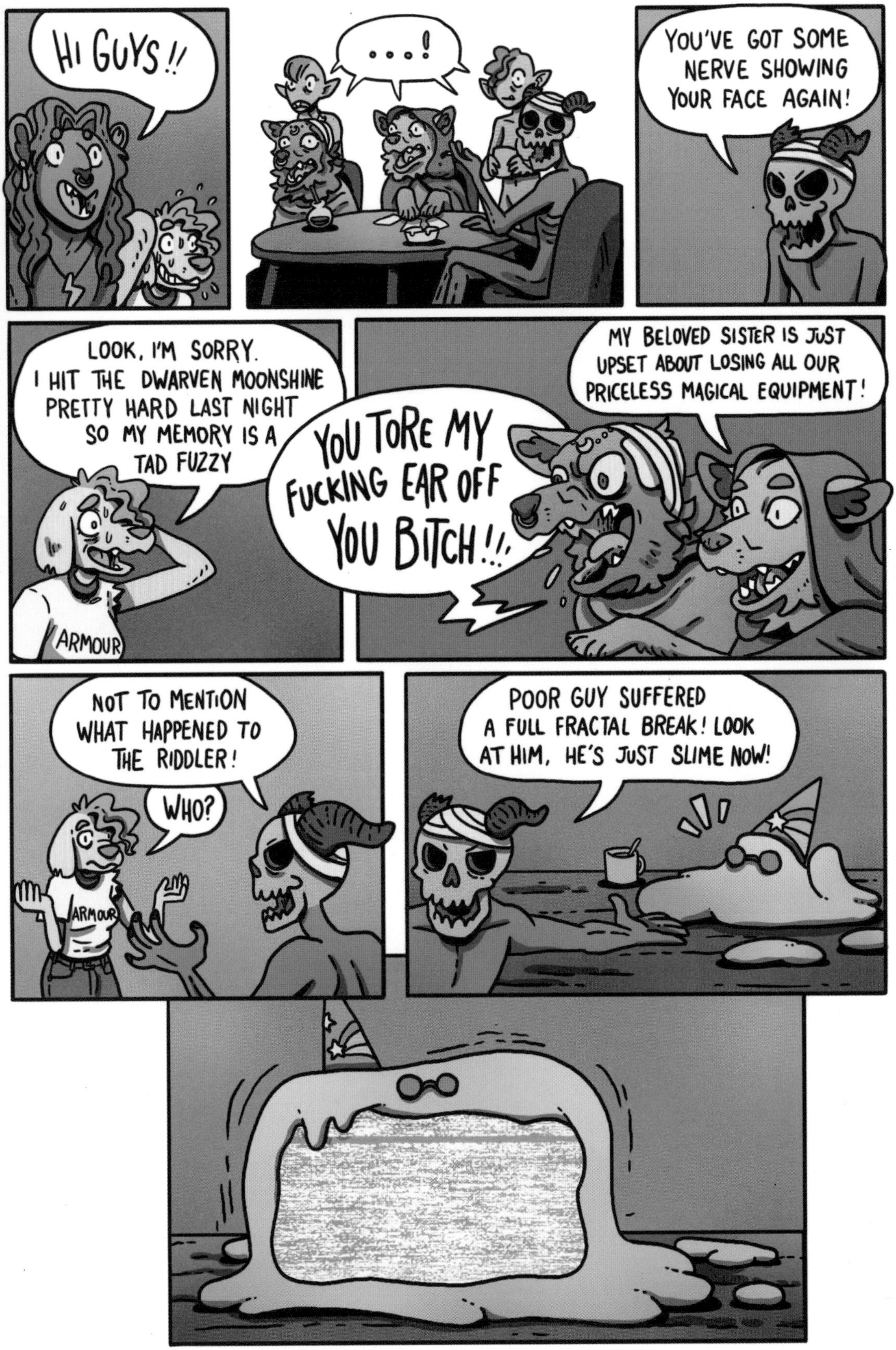
HI GUYS!!
...!
YOU'VE GOT SOME NERVE SHOWING YOUR FACE AGAIN!
LOOK, I'M SORRY. I HIT THE DWARVEN MOONSHINE PRETTY HARD LAST NIGHT SO MY MEMORY IS A TAD FUZZY
ARMOUR
YOU TORE MY FUCKING EAR OFF YOU BITCH!!!
MY BELOVED SISTER IS JUST UPSET ABOUT LOSING ALL OUR PRICELESS MAGICAL EQUIPMENT!
NOT TO MENTION WHAT HAPPENED TO THE RIDDLER!
WHO?
ARMOUR
POOR GUY SUFFERED A FULL FRACTAL BREAK! LOOK AT HIM, HE'S JUST SLIME NOW!

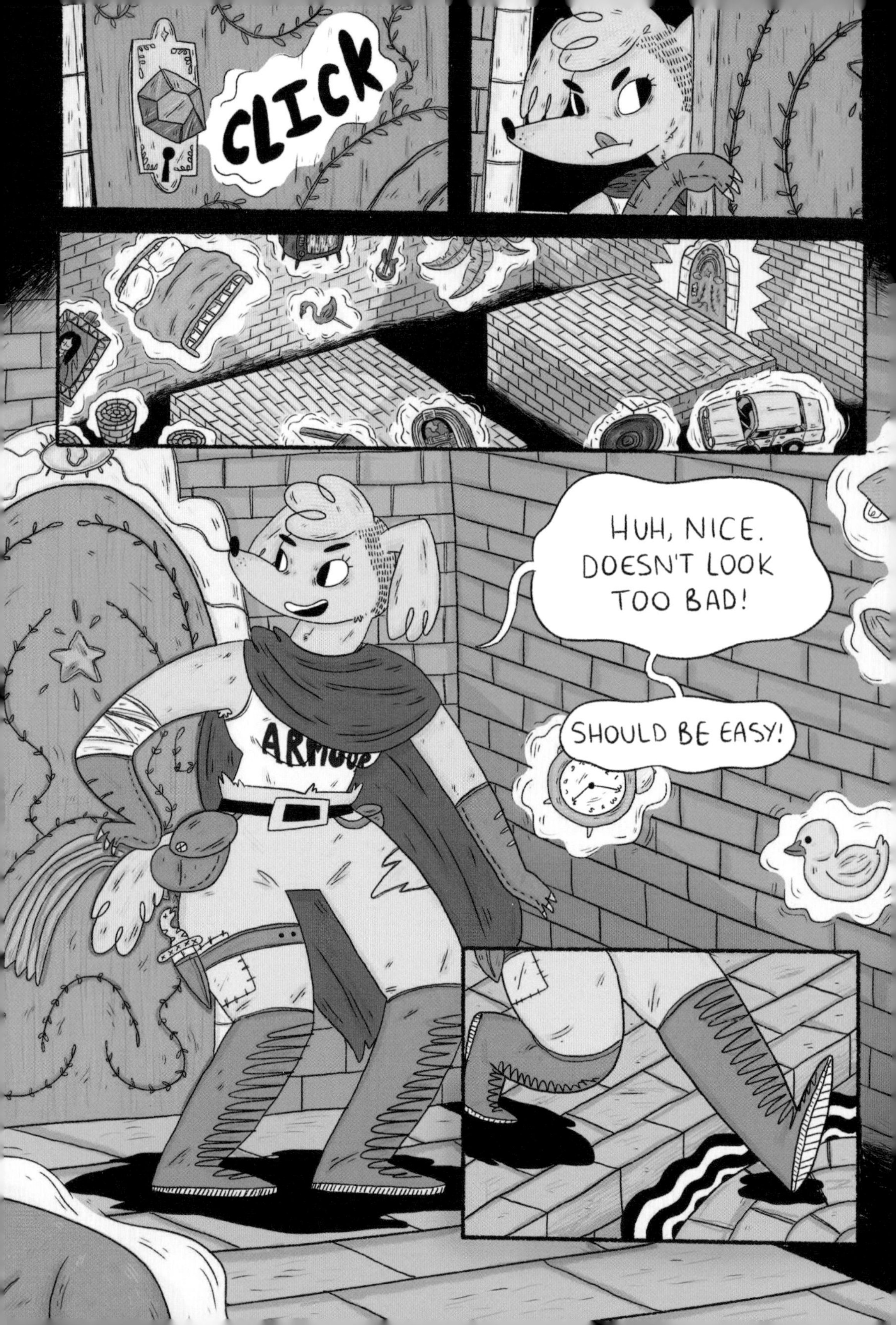
CLICK
HUH, NICE. DOESN'T LOOK TOO BAD!
SHOULD BE EASY!

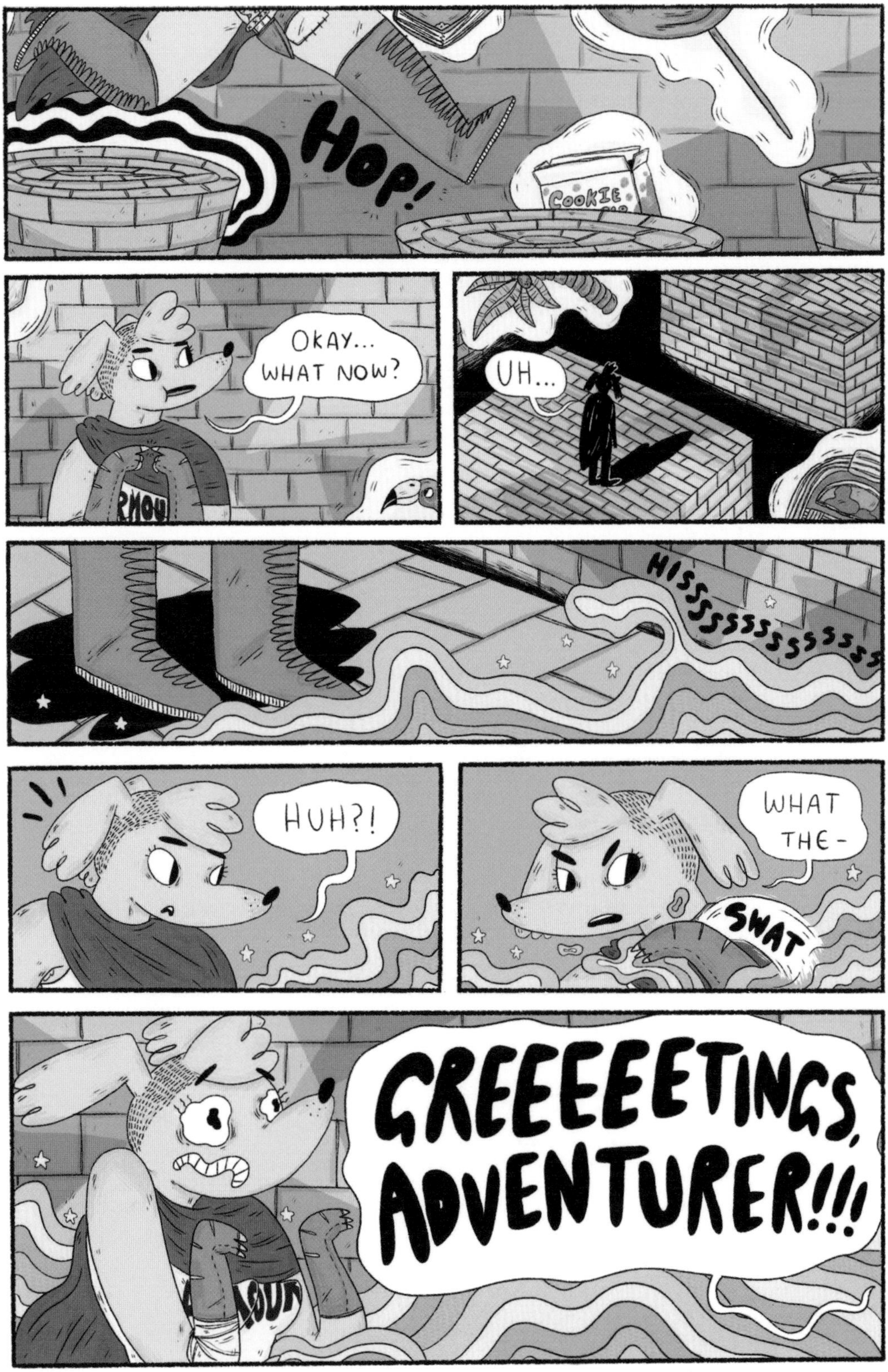

HOP!
COOKIE
OKAY... WHAT NOW?
UH...
HISSSSSSSSSSSSS
HUH?!
WHAT THE-
SWAT
GREEEEETINGS, ADVENTURER!!!

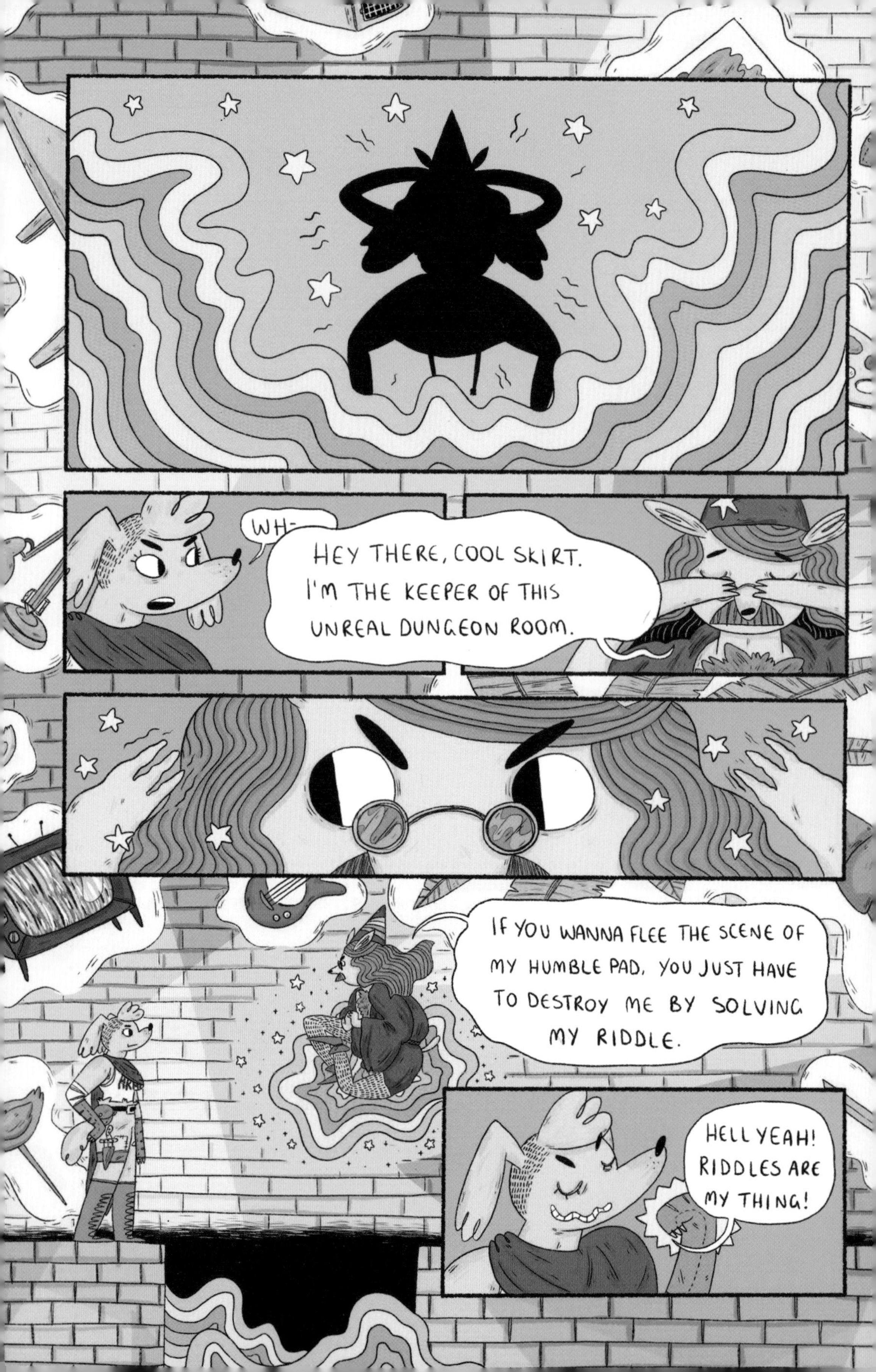
WH-
HEY THERE, COOL SKIRT. I'M THE KEEPER OF THIS UNREAL DUNGEON ROOM.
IF YOU WANNA FLEE THE SCENE OF MY HUMBLE PAD, YOU JUST HAVE TO DESTROY ME BY SOLVING MY RIDDLE.
HELL YEAH! RIDDLES ARE MY THING!

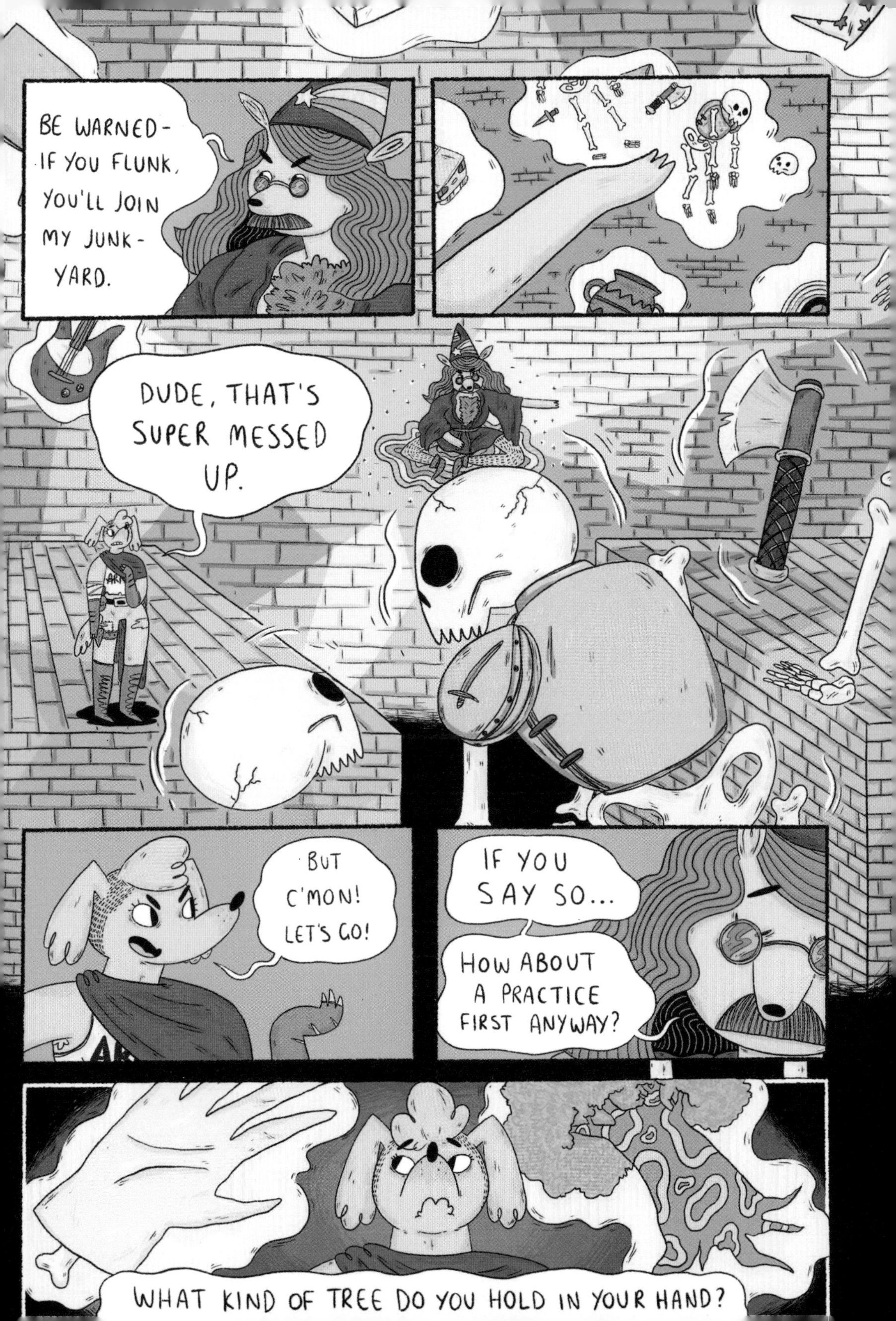
BE WARNED- IF YOU FLUNK, YOU'LL JOIN MY JUNK-YARD.
DUDE, THAT'S SUPER MESSED UP.
BUT C'MON! LET'S GO!
IF YOU SAY SO...
HOW ABOUT A PRACTICE FIRST ANYWAY?
WHAT KIND OF TREE DO YOU HOLD IN YOUR HAND?

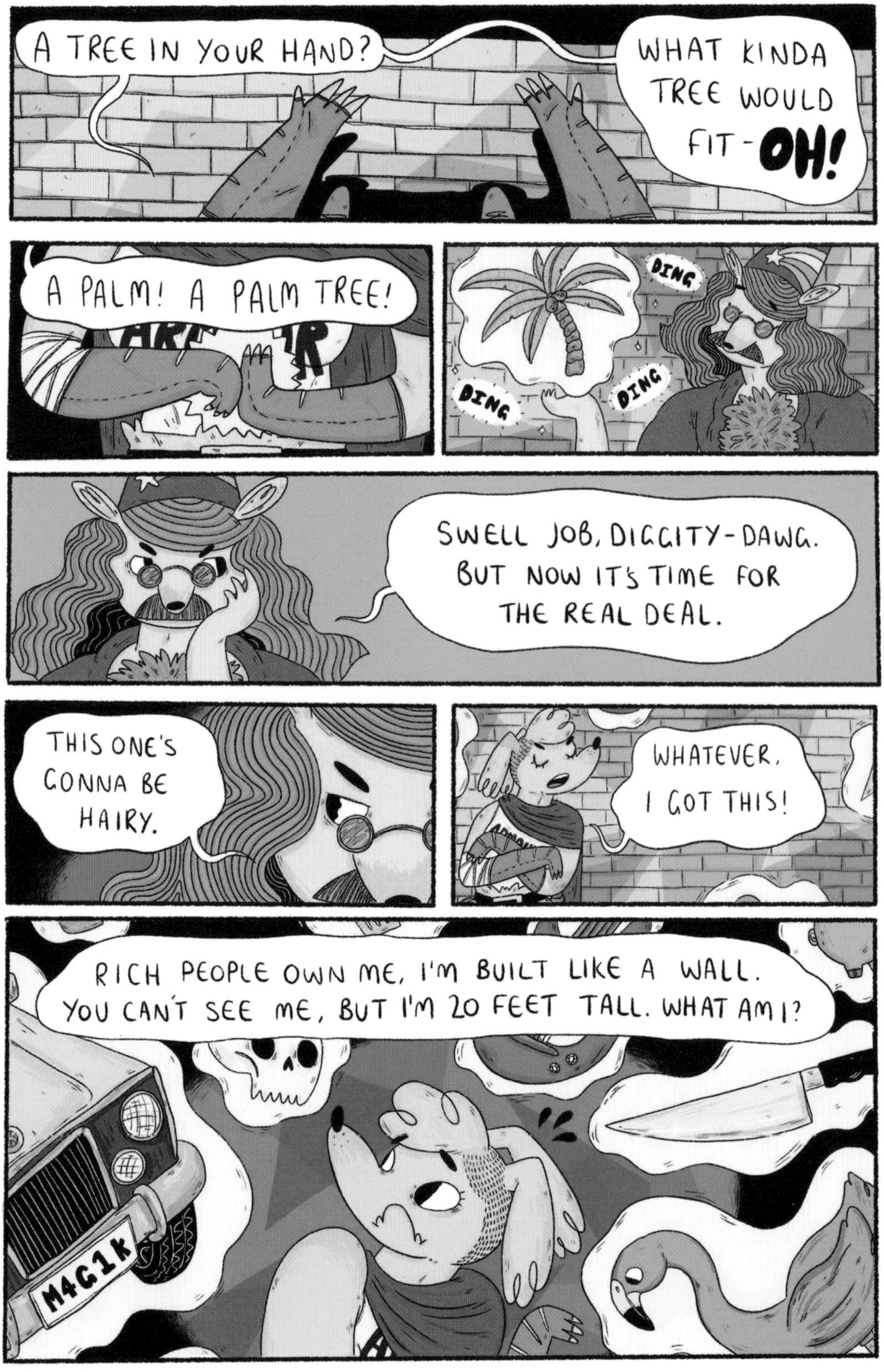
A TREE IN YOUR HAND?
WHAT KINDA TREE WOULD FIT-OH!
A PALM! A PALM TREE!
DING
DING
DING
SWELL JOB, DIGGITY-DAWG. BUT NOW IT'S TIME FOR THE REAL DEAL.
THIS ONE'S GONNA BE HAIRY.
WHATEVER, I GOT THIS!
RICH PEOPLE OWN ME, I'M BUILT LIKE A WALL. YOU CAN'T SEE ME, BUT I'M 20 FEET TALL. WHAT AM I?
M4G1K

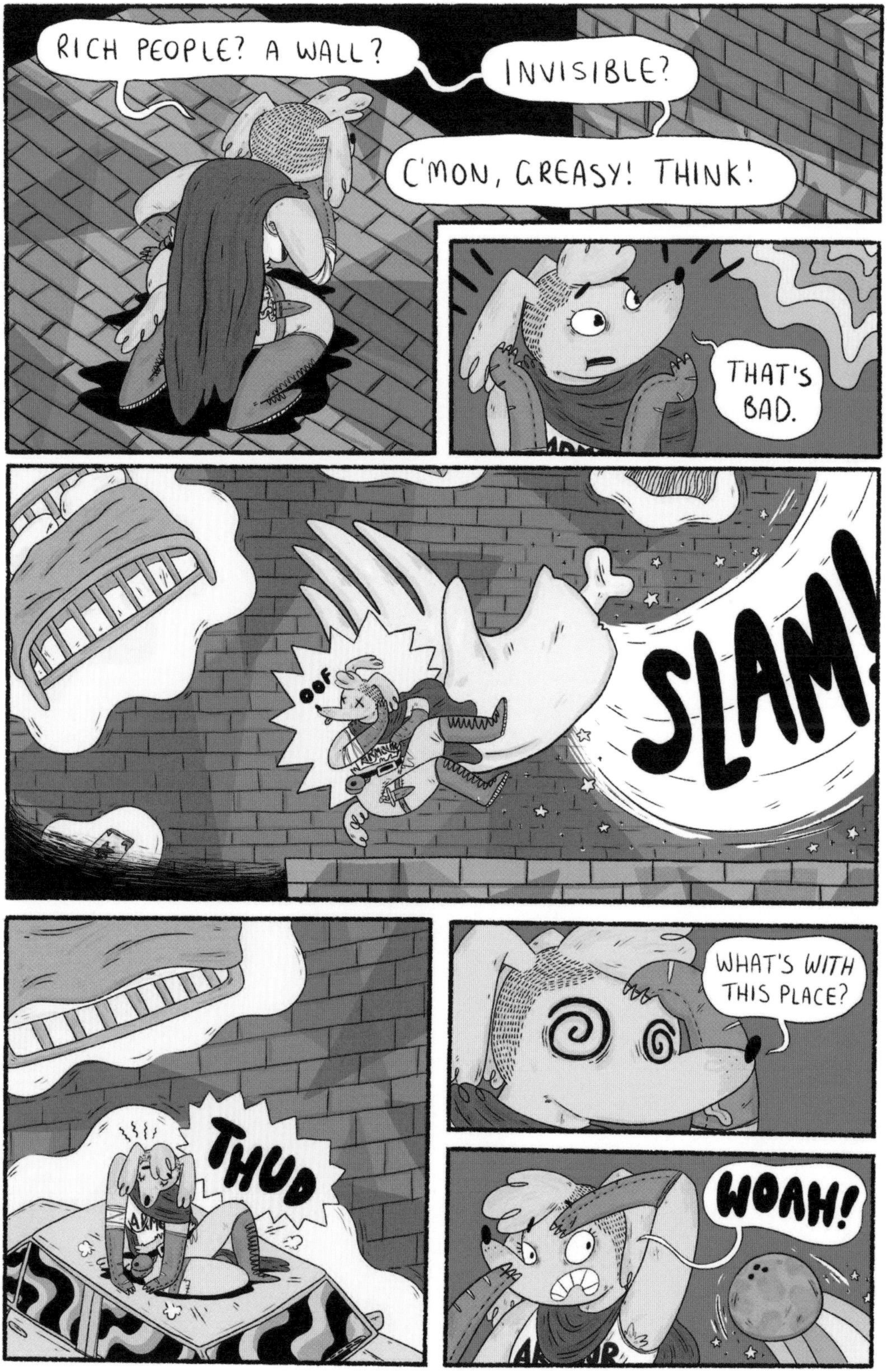
RICH PEOPLE? A WALL?
INVISIBLE?
C'MON, GREASY! THINK!
THAT'S BAD.
OOF
SLAM!
THUD
WHAT'S WITH THIS PLACE?
WOAH!

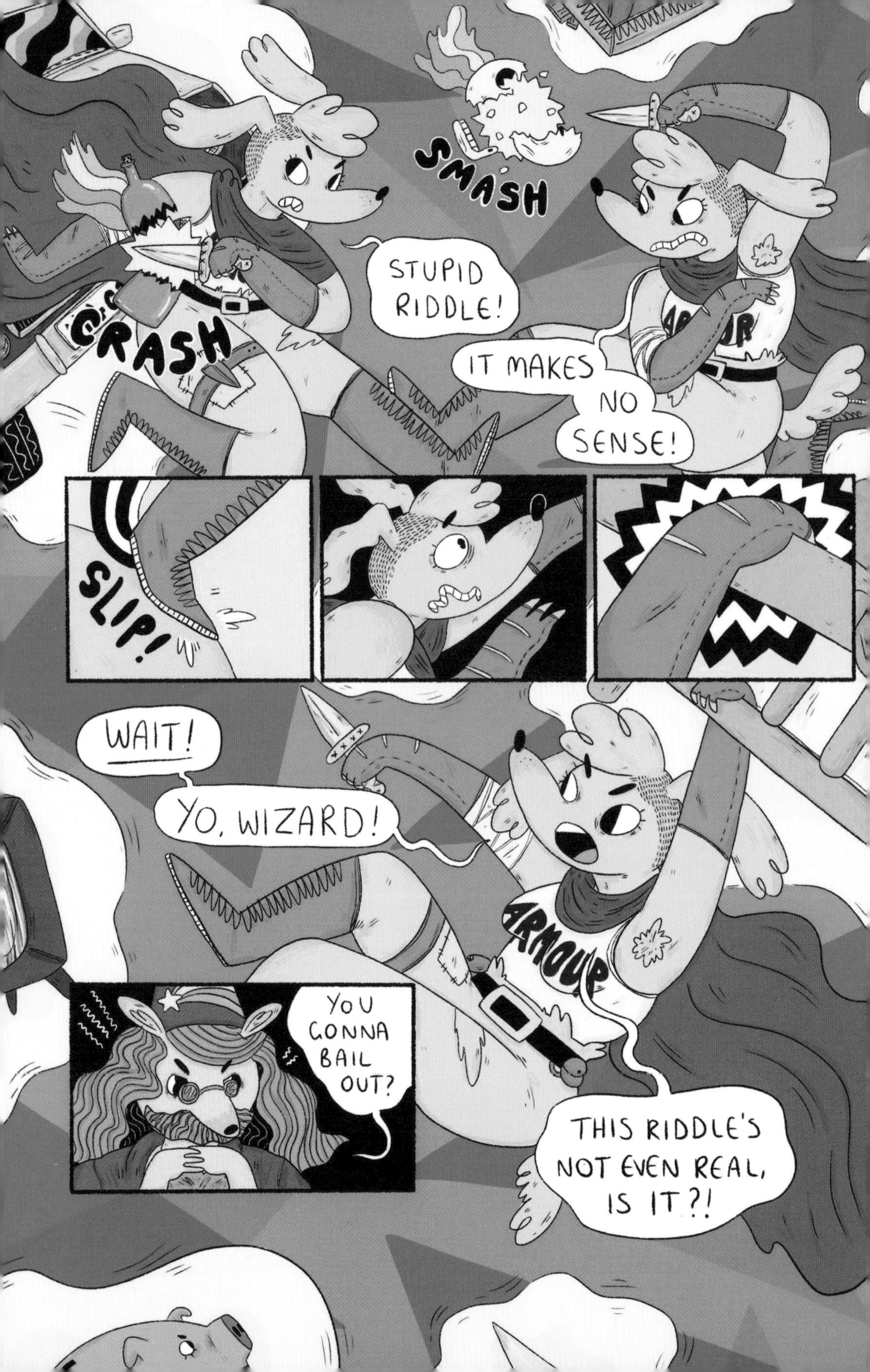
SMASH
CRASH
STUPID RIDDLE!
IT MAKES NO SENSE!
SLIP!
WAIT!
YO, WIZARD!
YOU GONNA BAIL OUT?
THIS RIDDLE'S NOT EVEN REAL, IS IT?!

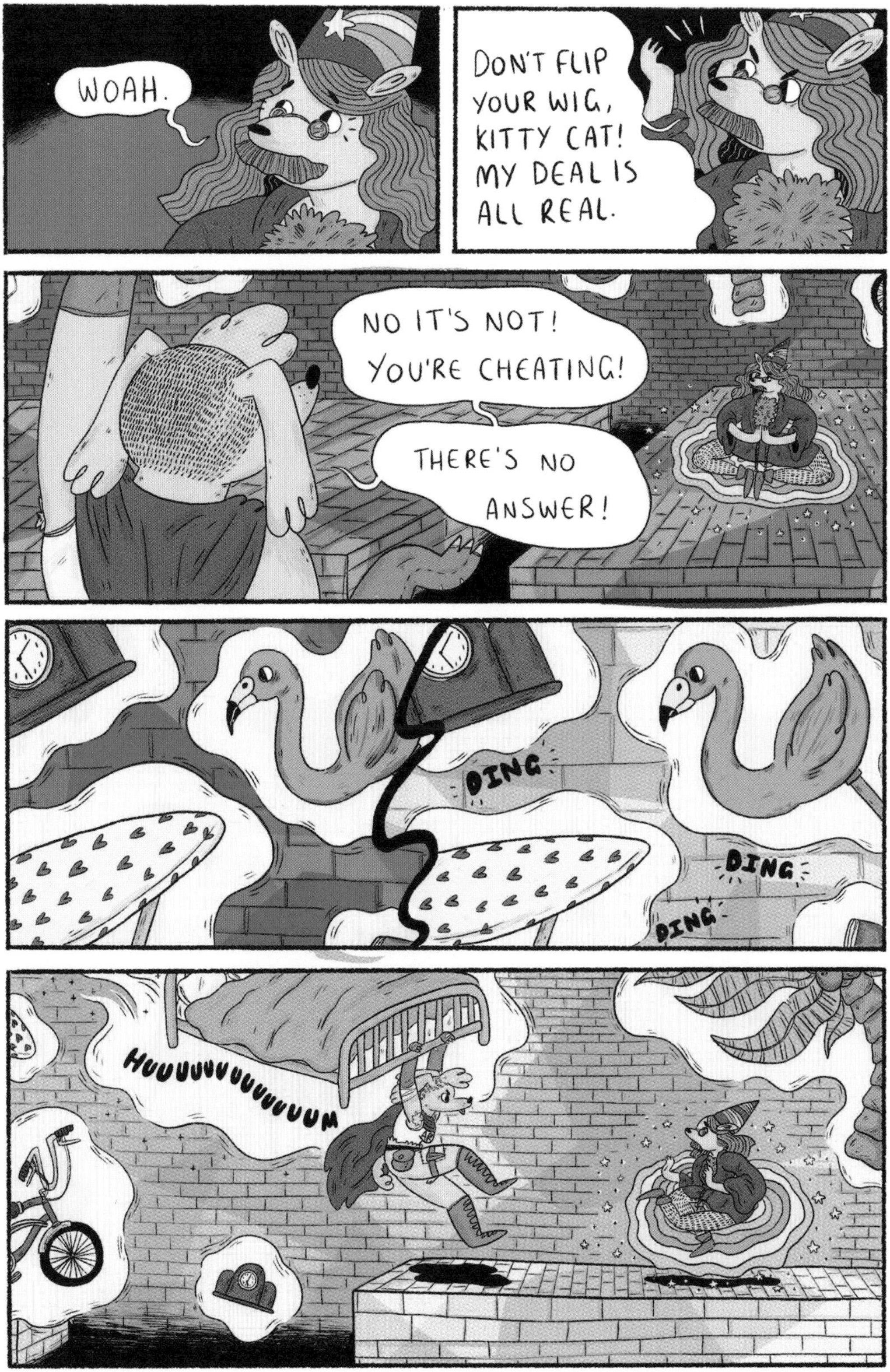

WOAH.
DON'T FLIP YOUR WIG, KITTY CAT! MY DEAL IS ALL REAL.
NO IT'S NOT! YOU'RE CHEATING!
THERE'S NO ANSWER!
DING
DING
DING
HUUUUUUUUUUUUUM

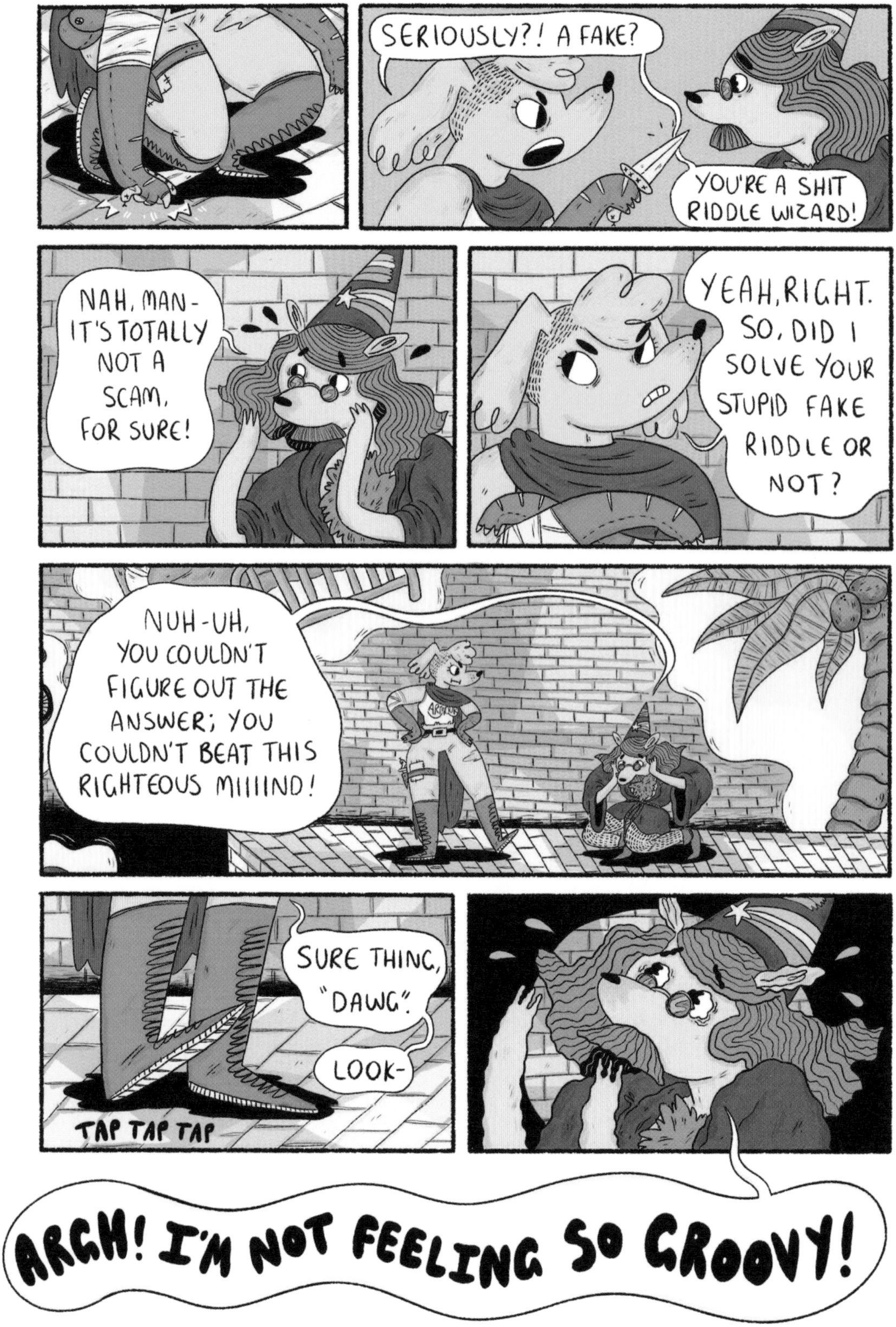
SERIOUSLY?! A FAKE?
YOU'RE A SHIT RIDDLE WIZARD!
NAH, MAN- IT'S TOTALLY NOT A SCAM, FOR SURE!
YEAH, RIGHT. SO, DID I SOLVE YOUR STUPID FAKE RIDDLE OR NOT?
NUH-UH, YOU COULDN'T FIGURE OUT THE ANSWER; YOU COULDN'T BEAT THIS RIGHTEOUS MIIIIND!
SURE THING, "DAWG".
LOOK-
TAP TAP TAP
ARGH! I'M NOT FEELING SO GROOVY!

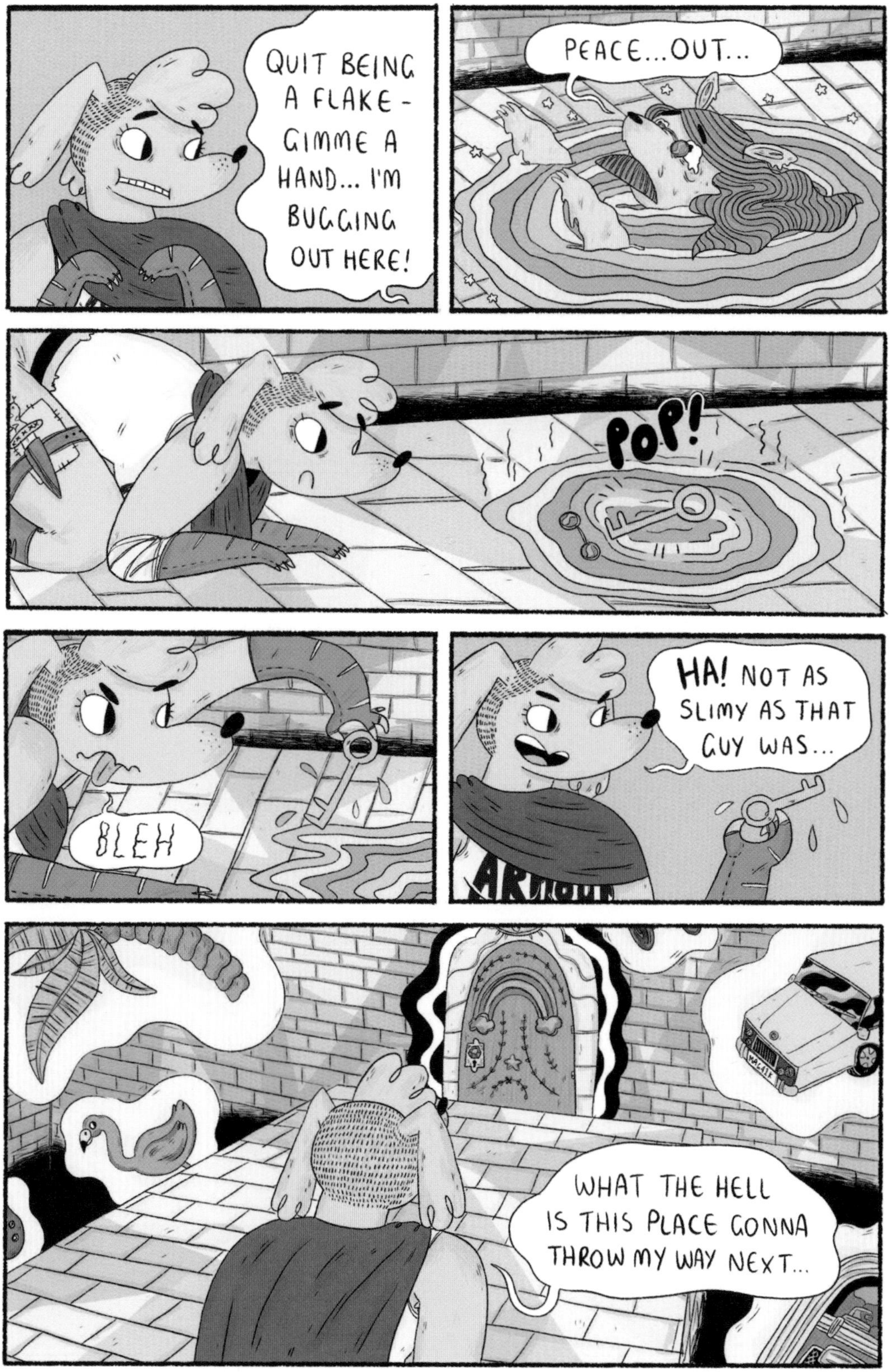
QUIT BEING A FLAKE - GIMME A HAND... I'M BUGGING OUT HERE!
PEACE...OUT...
POP!
BLEH
HA! NOT AS SLIMY AS THAT GUY WAS...
WHAT THE HELL IS THIS PLACE GONNA THROW MY WAY NEXT...

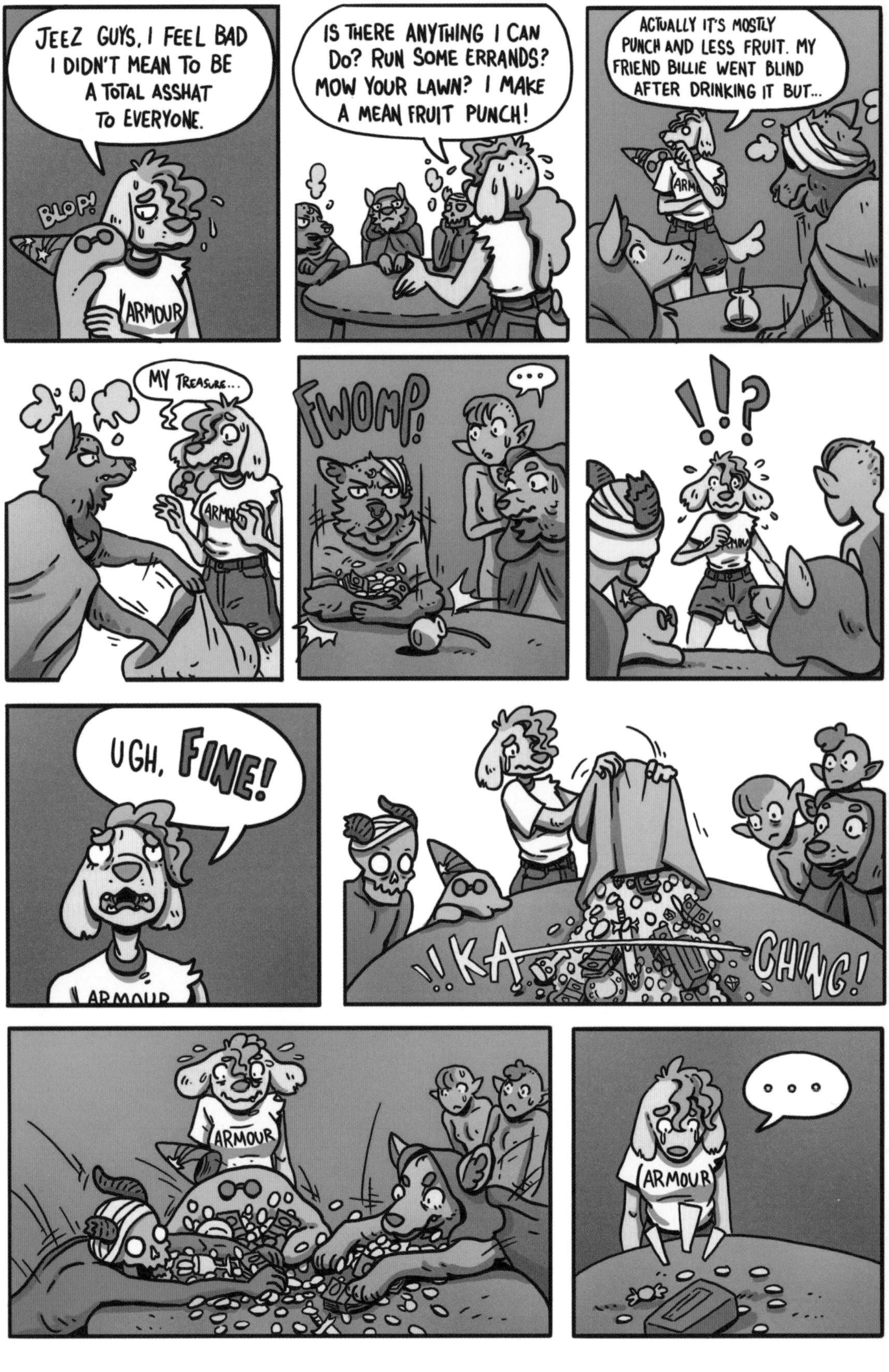
JEEZ GUYS, I FEEL BAD I DIDN'T MEAN TO BE A TOTAL ASSHAT TO EVERYONE.
BLOP!
IS THERE ANYTHING I CAN DO? RUN SOME ERRANDS? MOW YOUR LAWN? I MAKE A MEAN FRUIT PUNCH!
ACTUALLY IT'S MOSTLY PUNCH AND LESS FRUIT. MY FRIEND BILLIE WENT BLIND AFTER DRINKING IT BUT...
ARMOUR
MY TREASURE...
FWOMP!
...
!!?
UGH, FINE!
KA-CHING!
ARMOUR
...
ARMOUR

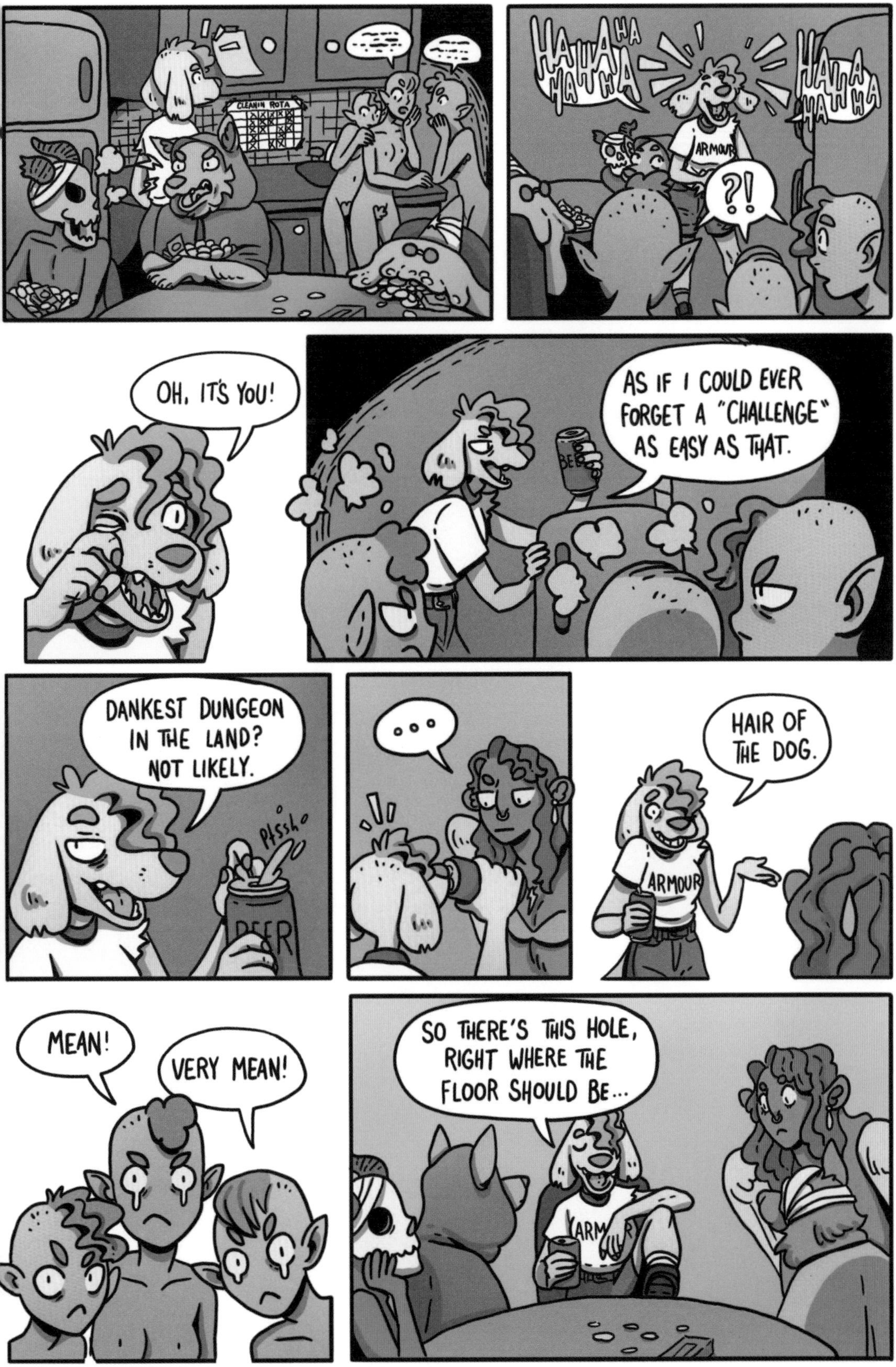

CLEANIN ROTA
HAHAHA HAHAHA
HAHA HAHAHA
ARMOUR
?!
OH, IT'S YOU!
AS IF I COULD EVER FORGET A "CHALLENGE" AS EASY AS THAT.
DANKEST DUNGEON IN THE LAND? NOT LIKELY.
Pfssh
BEER
...
HAIR OF THE DOG.
ARMOUR
MEAN!
VERY MEAN!
SO THERE'S THIS HOLE, RIGHT WHERE THE FLOOR SHOULD BE...

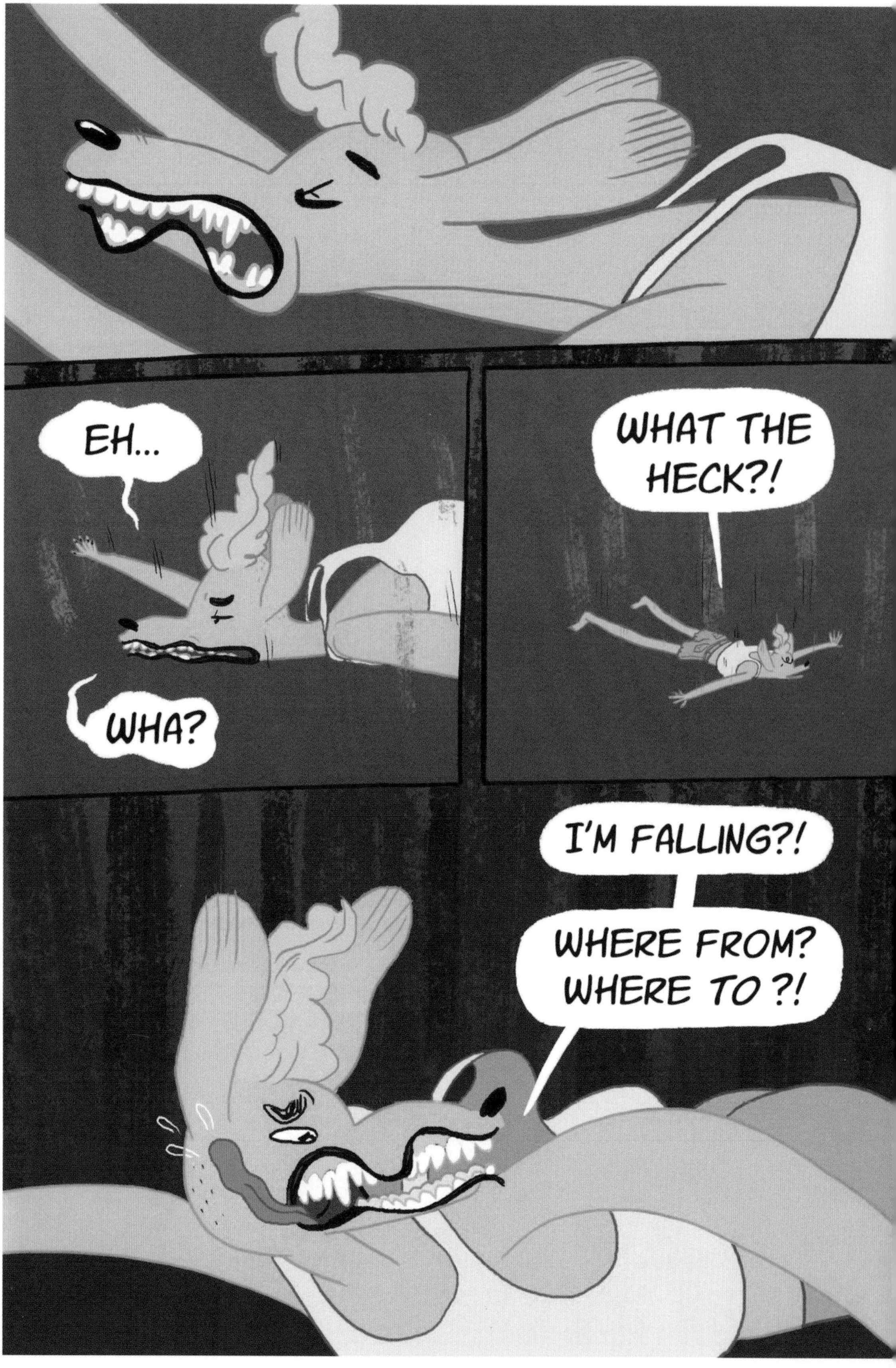
EH...
WHA?
WHAT THE HECK?!
I'M FALLING?!
WHERE FROM? WHERE TO?!

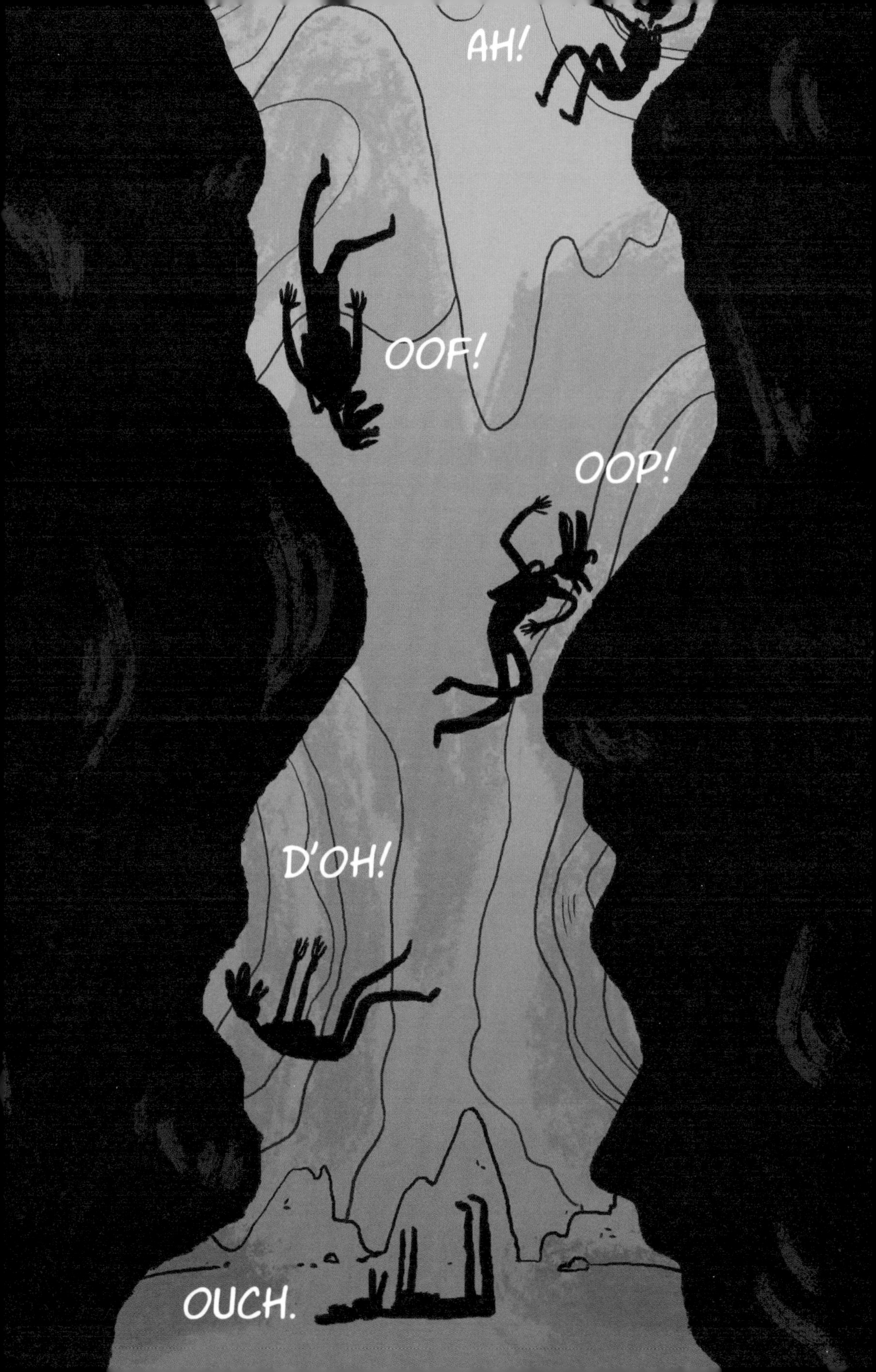
AH!
OOF!
OOP!
D'OH!
OUCH.

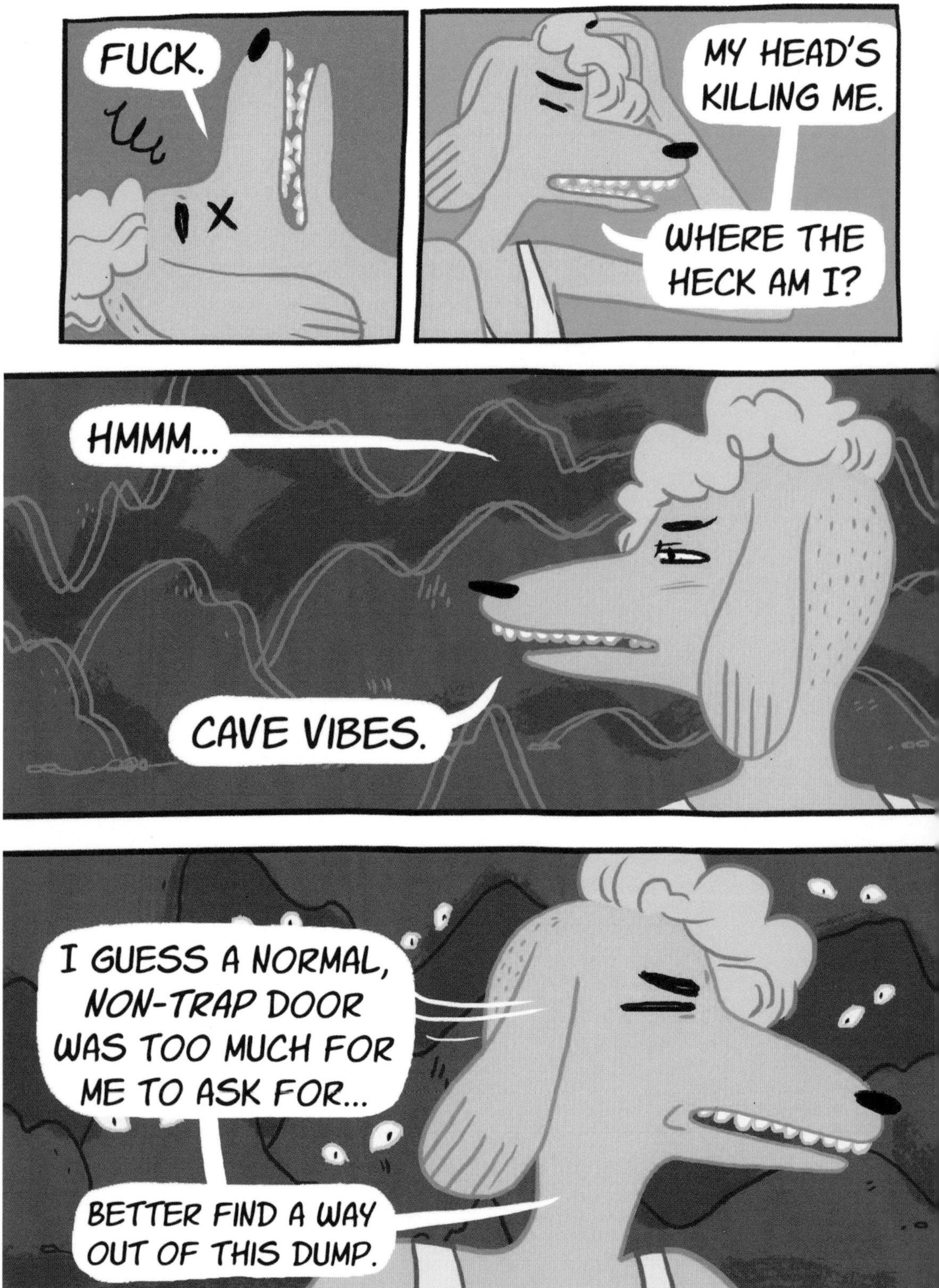

FUCK.
MY HEAD'S KILLING ME.
WHERE THE HECK AM I?
HMMM...
CAVE VIBES.
I GUESS A NORMAL, NON-TRAP DOOR WAS TOO MUCH FOR ME TO ASK FOR...
BETTER FIND A WAY OUT OF THIS DUMP.

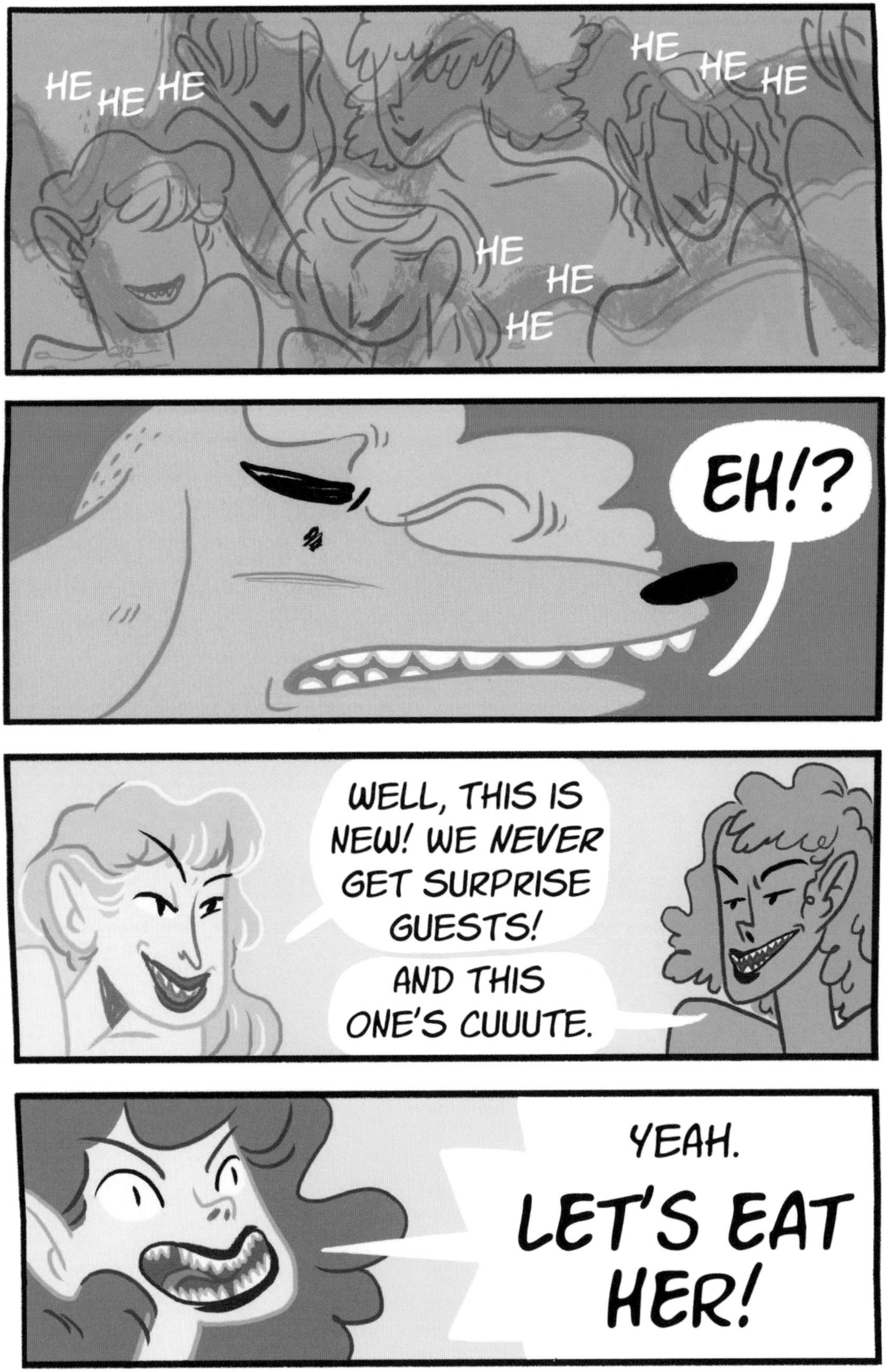
HE HE HE
HE HE HE
HE
HE
HE
EH!?
WELL, THIS IS NEW! WE NEVER GET SURPRISE GUESTS!
AND THIS ONE'S CUUUTE.
YEAH.
LET'S EAT HER!

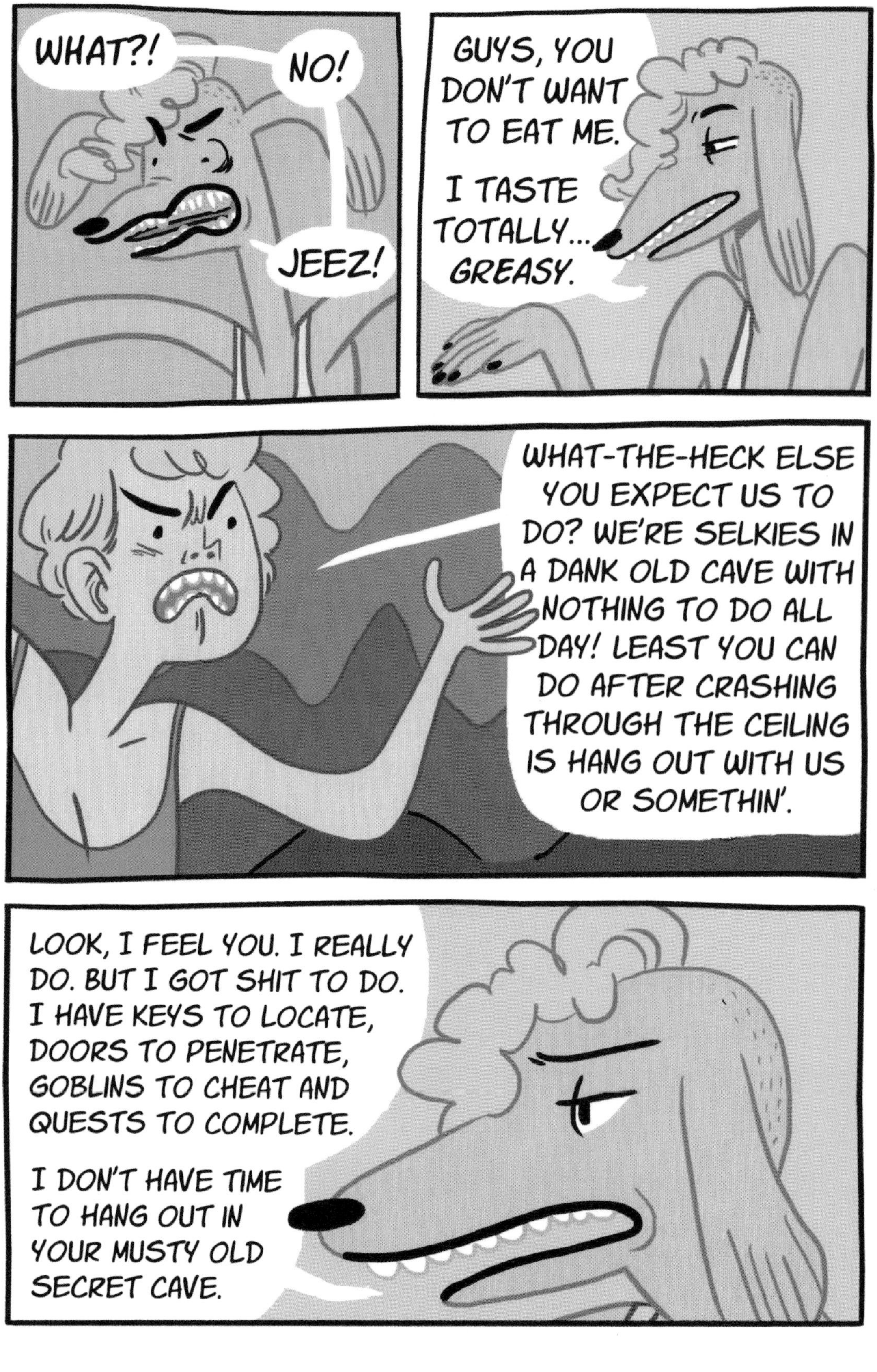
WHAT?!
NO!
JEEZ!
GUYS, YOU DON'T WANT TO EAT ME.
I TASTE TOTALLY... GREASY.
WHAT-THE-HECK ELSE YOU EXPECT US TO DO? WE'RE SELKIES IN A DANK OLD CAVE WITH NOTHING TO DO ALL DAY! LEAST YOU CAN DO AFTER CRASHING THROUGH THE CEILING IS HANG OUT WITH US OR SOMETHIN'.
LOOK, I FEEL YOU. I REALLY DO. BUT I GOT SHIT TO DO. I HAVE KEYS TO LOCATE, DOORS TO PENETRATE, GOBLINS TO CHEAT AND QUESTS TO COMPLETE.
I DON'T HAVE TIME TO HANG OUT IN YOUR MUSTY OLD SECRET CAVE.

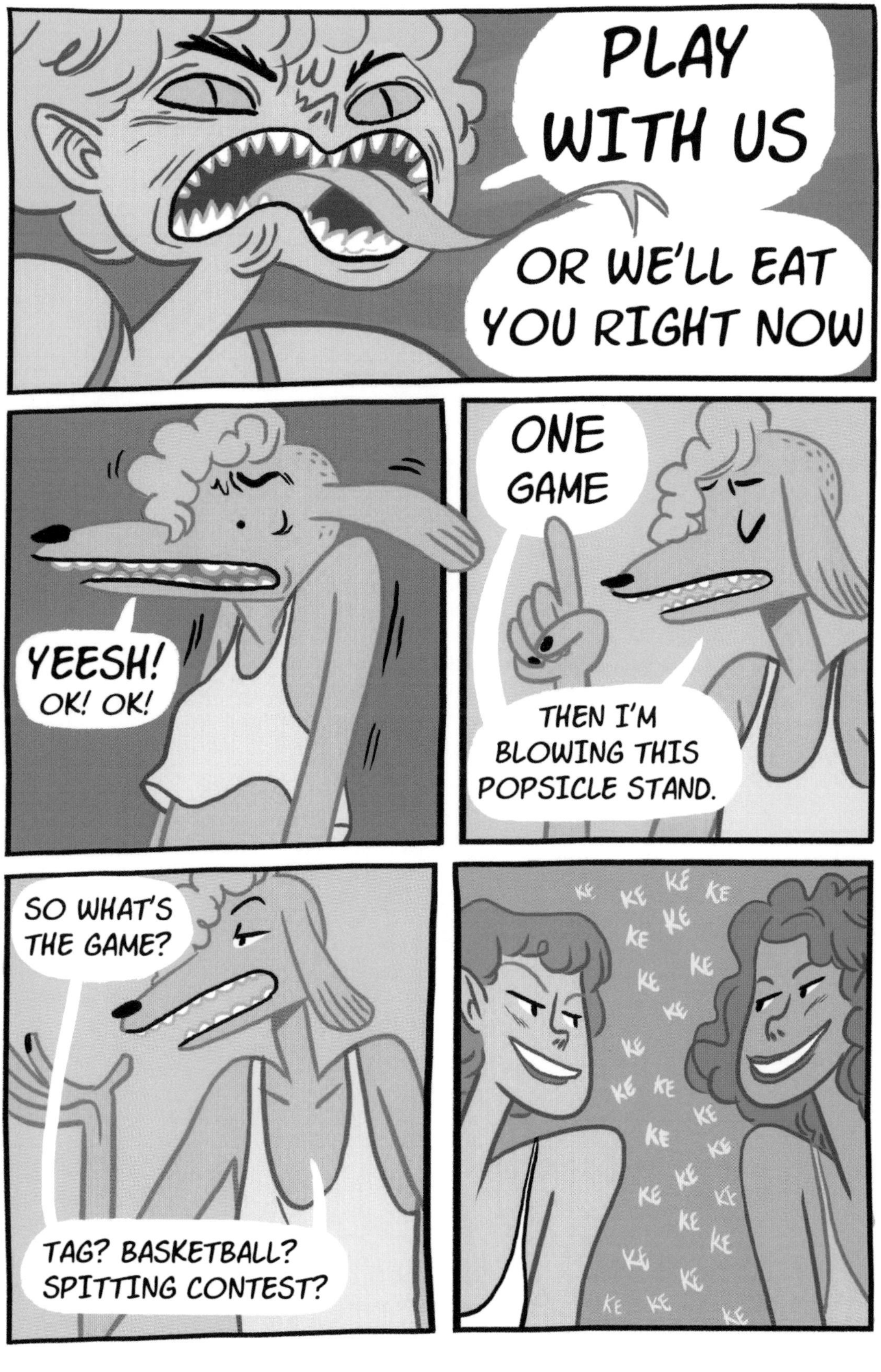
PLAY WITH US
OR WE'LL EAT YOU RIGHT NOW
YEESH! OK! OK!
ONE GAME
THEN I'M BLOWING THIS POPSICLE STAND.
SO WHAT'S THE GAME?
TAG? BASKETBALL? SPITTING CONTEST?
KE KE KE KE KE KE KE KE KE KE KE KE KE KE KE KE KE KE KE KE KE KE KE KE KE KE KE

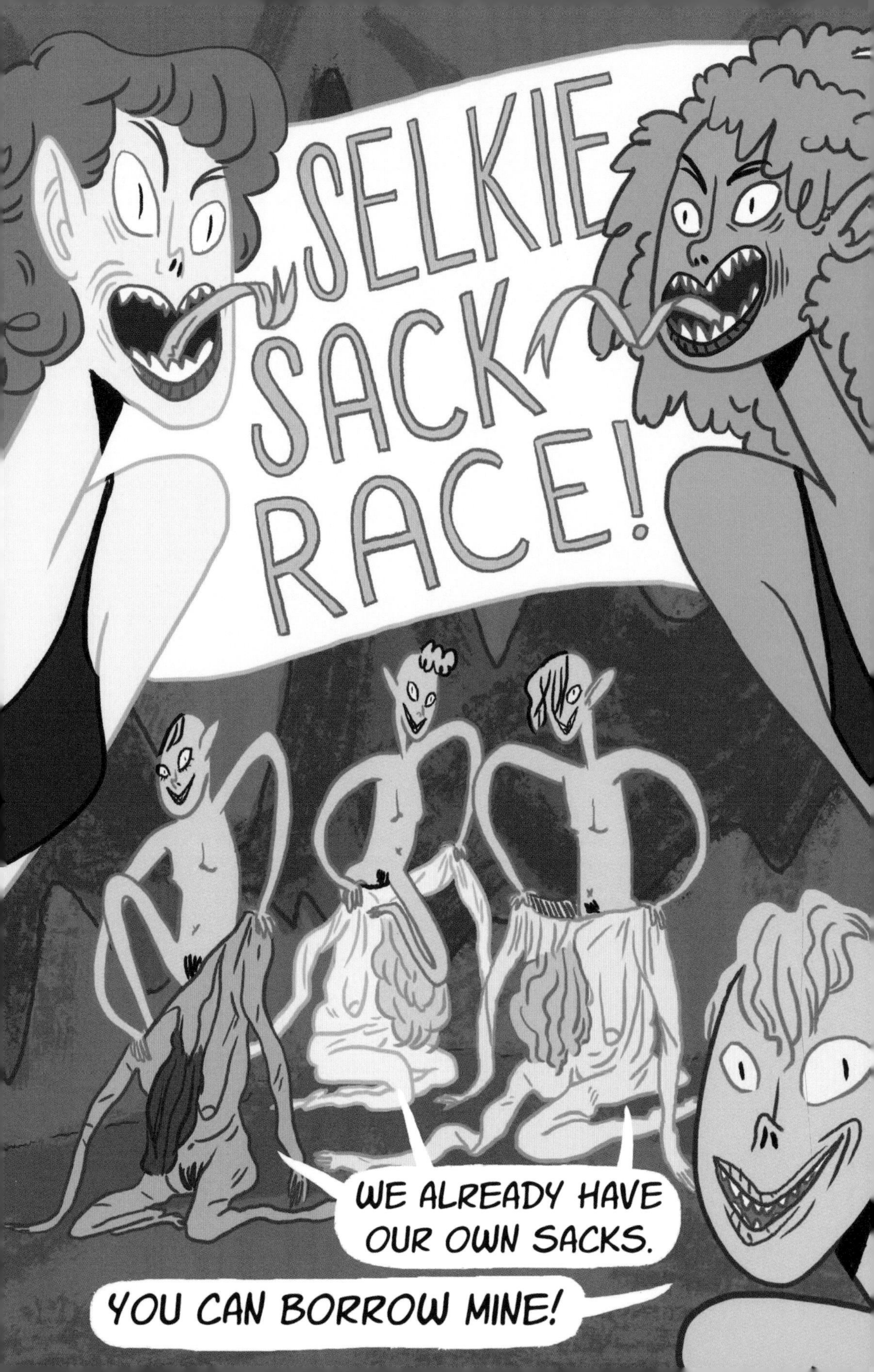
SELKIE SACK RACE!
WE ALREADY HAVE OUR OWN SACKS.
YOU CAN BORROW MINE!

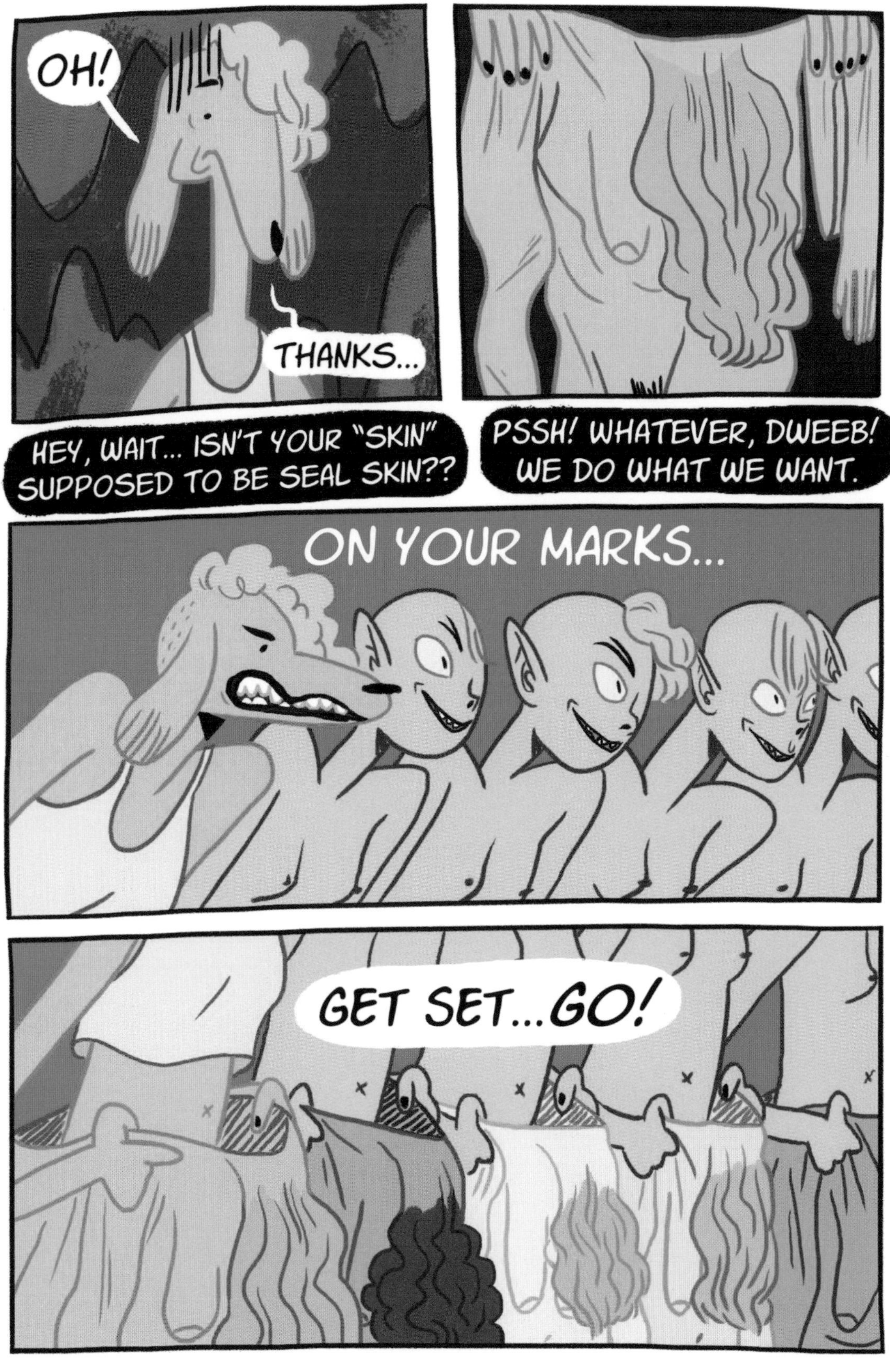
OH!
THANKS...
HEY, WAIT... ISN'T YOUR "SKIN" SUPPOSED TO BE SEAL SKIN??
PSSH! WHATEVER, DWEEB! WE DO WHAT WE WANT.
ON YOUR MARKS...
GET SET...GO!

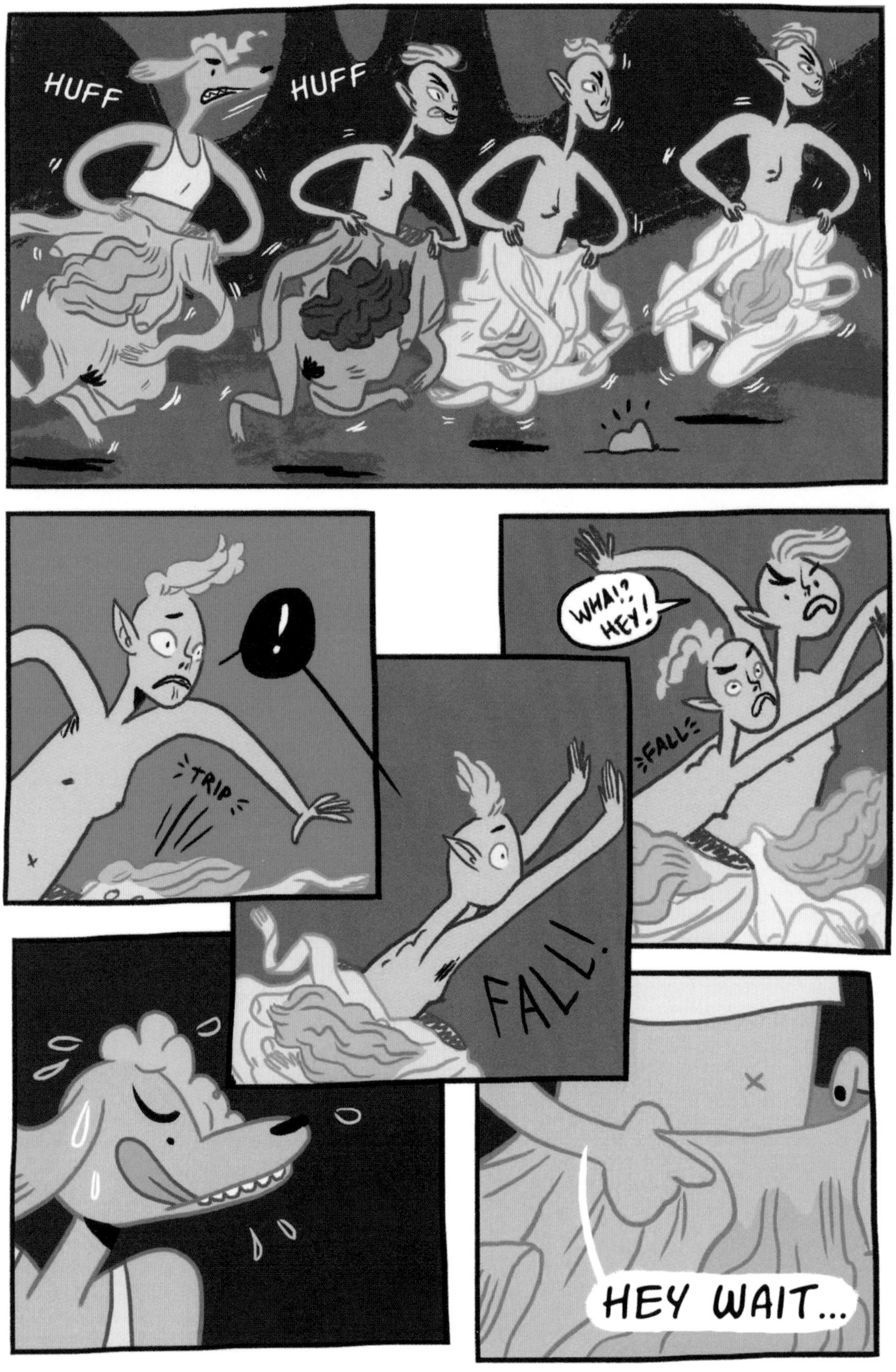
HUFF
HUFF
!
TRIP
FALL!
WHA!? HEY!
FALL
HEY WAIT...

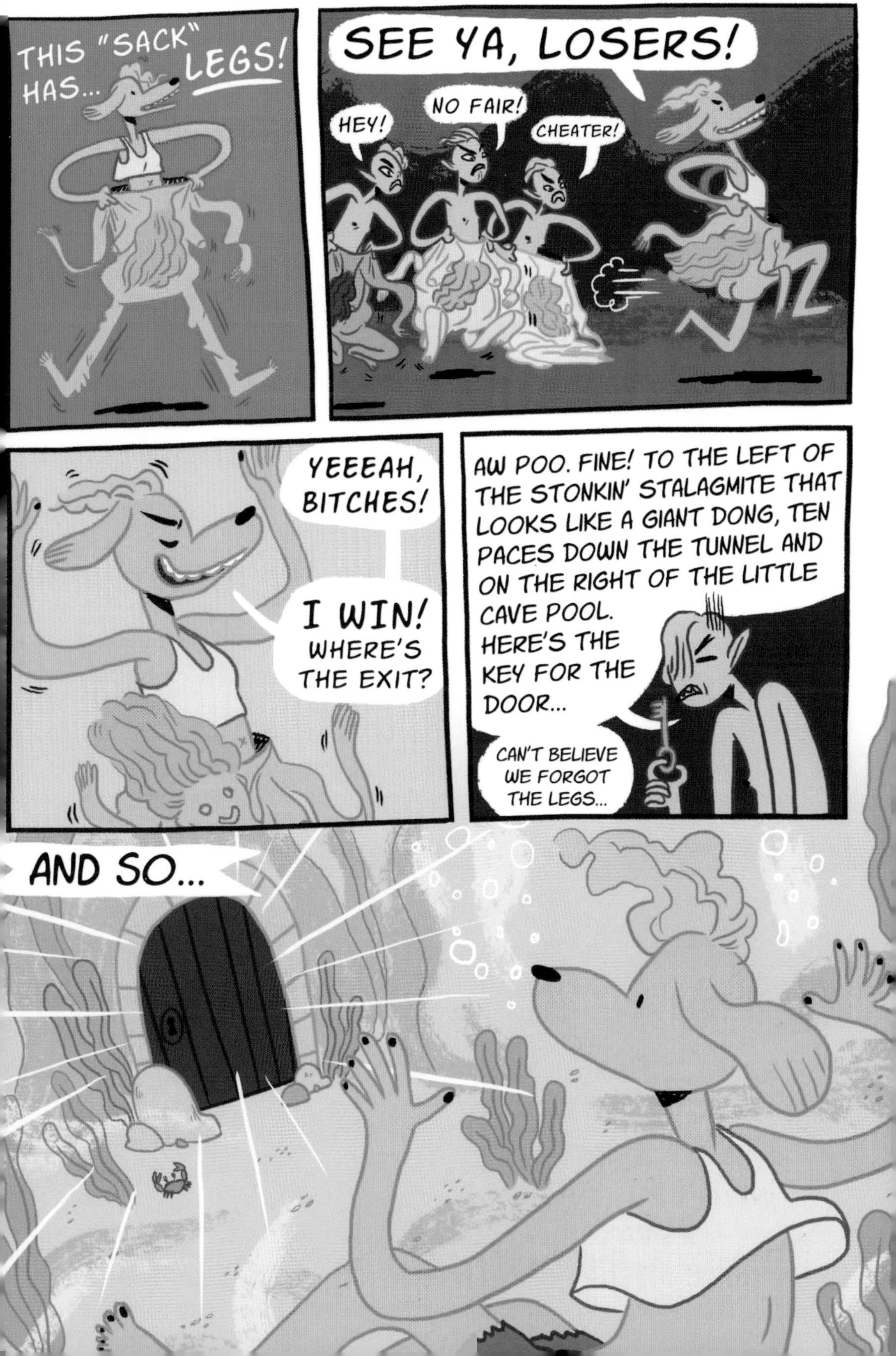

THIS "SACK" HAS... LEGS!
SEE YA, LOSERS!
HEY!
NO FAIR!
CHEATER!
YEEEAH, BITCHES!
I WIN! WHERE'S THE EXIT?
AW POO. FINE! TO THE LEFT OF THE STONKIN' STALAGMITE THAT LOOKS LIKE A GIANT DONG, TEN PACES DOWN THE TUNNEL AND ON THE RIGHT OF THE LITTLE CAVE POOL. HERE'S THE KEY FOR THE DOOR...
CAN'T BELIEVE WE FORGOT THE LEGS...
AND SO...

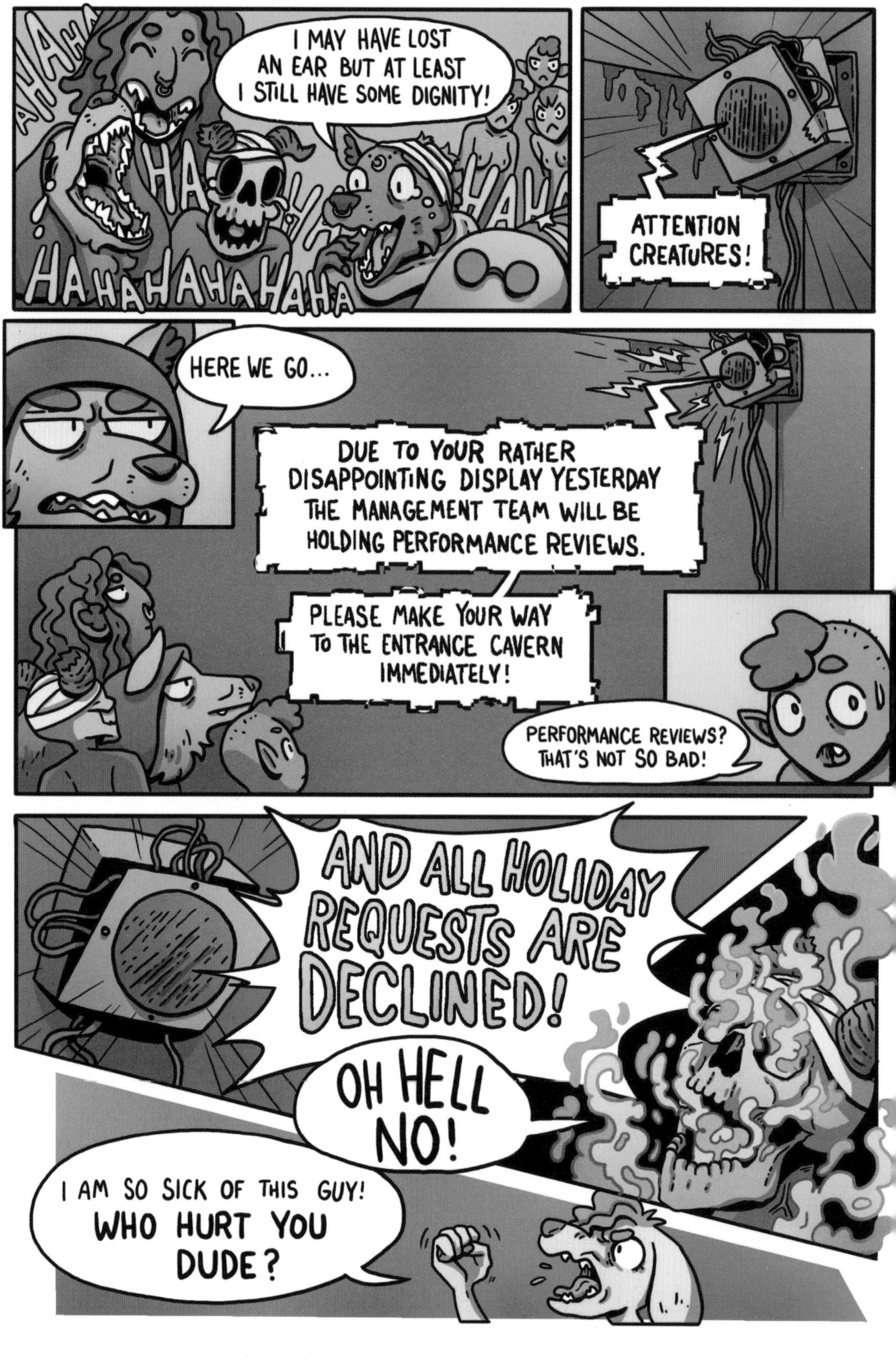

I MAY HAVE LOST AN EAR BUT AT LEAST I STILL HAVE SOME DIGNITY!
HAHAHAHAHAHAHA
ATTENTION CREATURES!
HERE WE GO...
DUE TO YOUR RATHER DISAPPOINTING DISPLAY YESTERDAY THE MANAGEMENT TEAM WILL BE HOLDING PERFORMANCE REVIEWS.
PLEASE MAKE YOUR WAY TO THE ENTRANCE CAVERN IMMEDIATELY!
PERFORMANCE REVIEWS? THAT'S NOT SO BAD!
AND ALL HOLIDAY REQUESTS ARE DECLINED!
OH HELL NO!
I AM SO SICK OF THIS GUY! WHO HURT YOU DUDE?

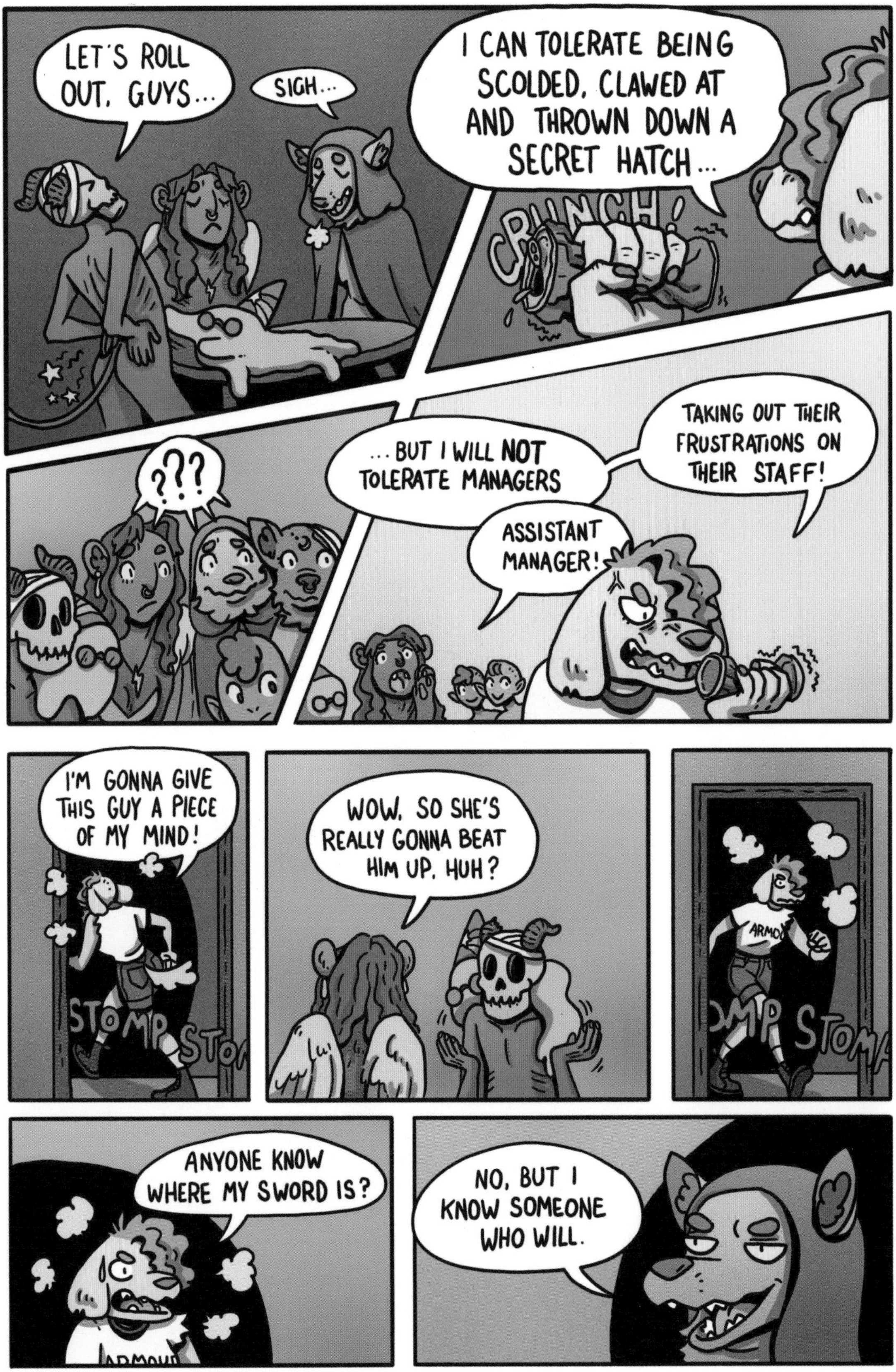

LET'S ROLL OUT, GUYS...
SIGH...
I CAN TOLERATE BEING SCOLDED, CLAWED AT AND THROWN DOWN A SECRET HATCH...
CRUNCH!
???
...BUT I WILL NOT TOLERATE MANAGERS
TAKING OUT THEIR FRUSTRATIONS ON THEIR STAFF!
ASSISTANT MANAGER!
I'M GONNA GIVE THIS GUY A PIECE OF MY MIND!
STOMP STOM
WOW, SO SHE'S REALLY GONNA BEAT HIM UP, HUH?
ARMOU
MP STOMP
ANYONE KNOW WHERE MY SWORD IS?
NO, BUT I KNOW SOMEONE WHO WILL.

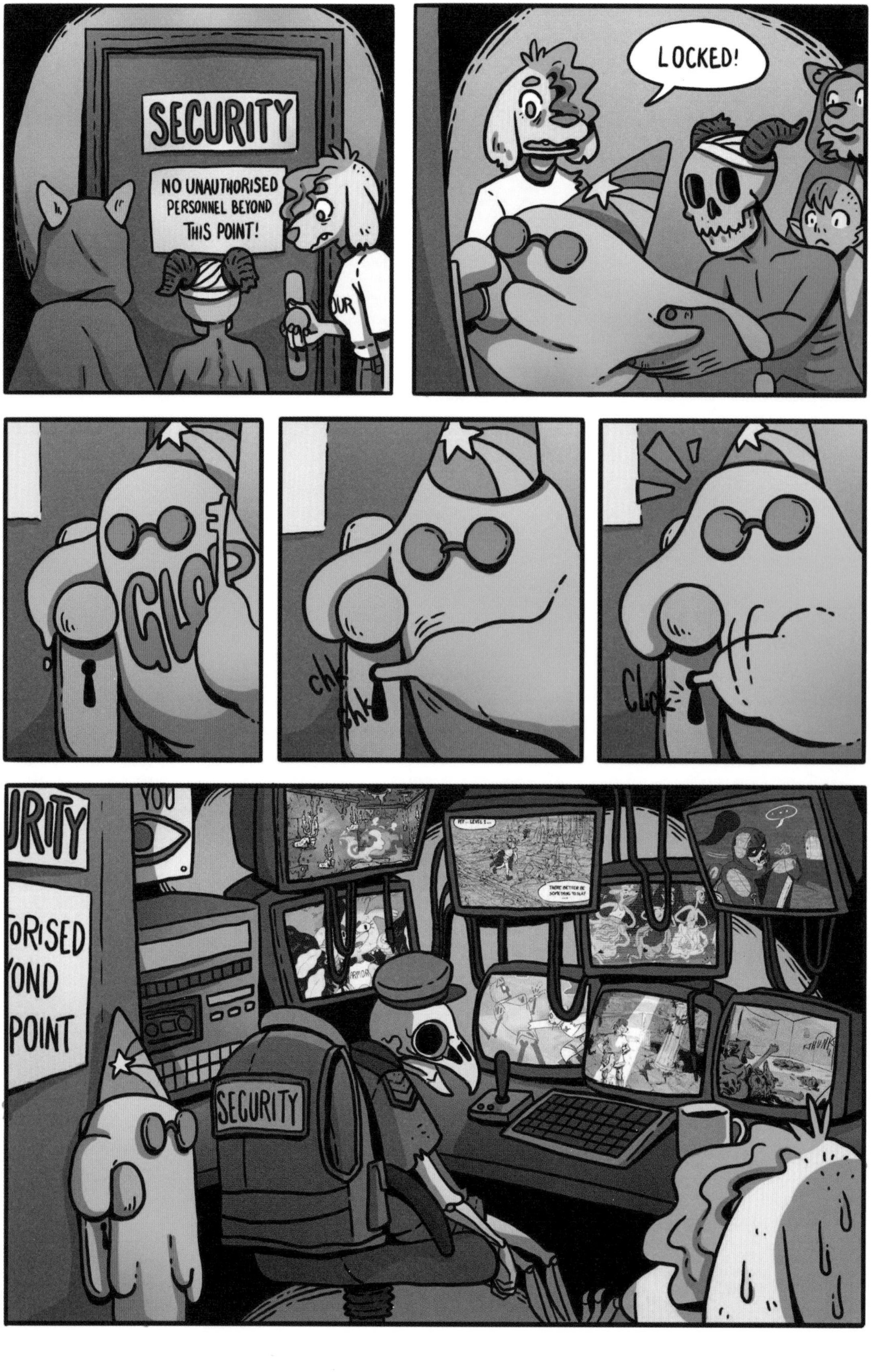
SECURITY
NO UNAUTHORISED PERSONNEL BEYOND THIS POINT!
LOCKED!
chk
chk
Click
YOU
URITY
TORISED
YOND
POINT
SECURITY

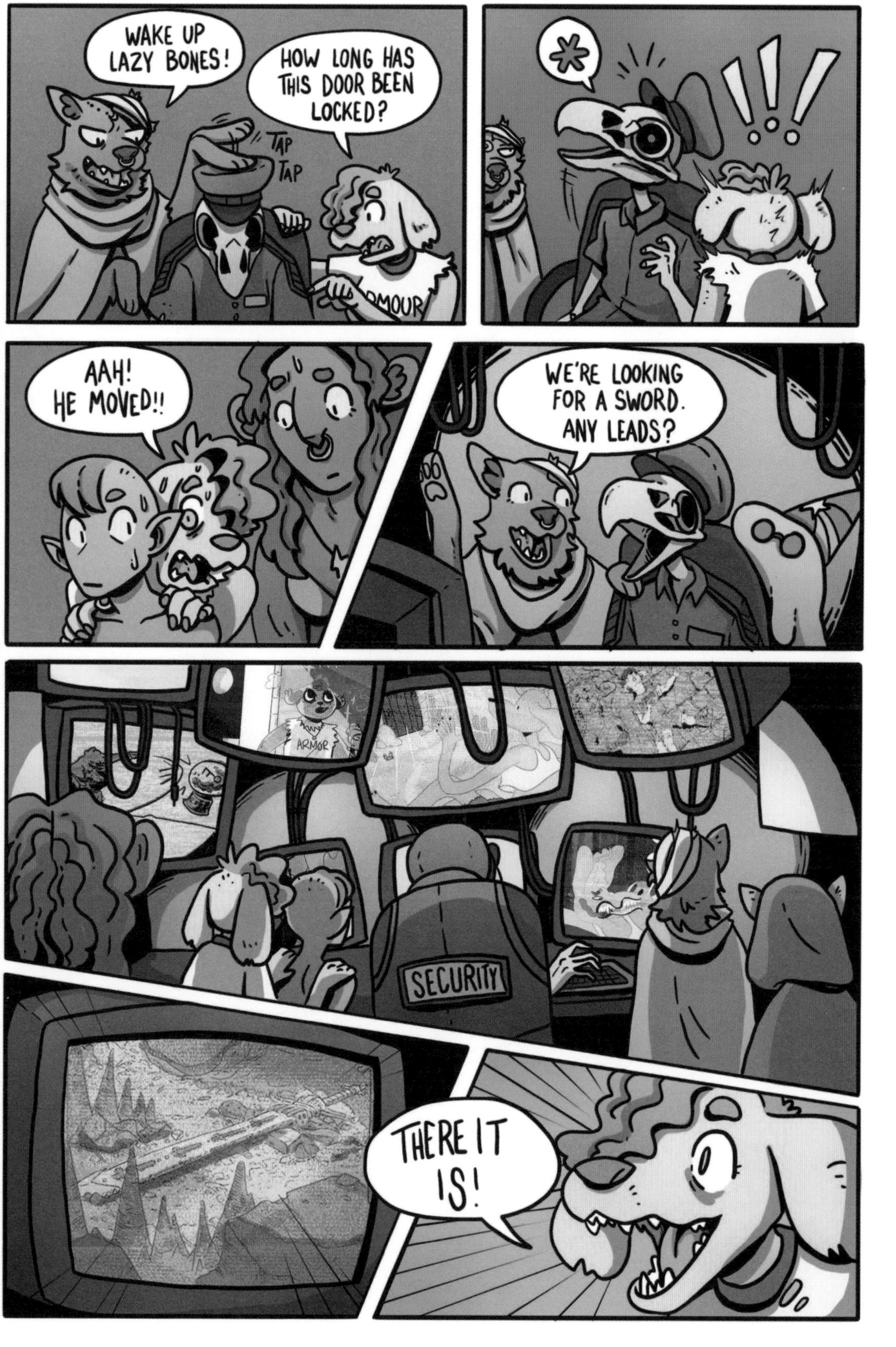
WAKE UP LAZY BONES!
HOW LONG HAS THIS DOOR BEEN LOCKED?
TAP TAP
RMOUR
*
!!!
AAH! HE MOVED!!
WE'RE LOOKING FOR A SWORD. ANY LEADS?
ARMOR
SECURITY
THERE IT IS!

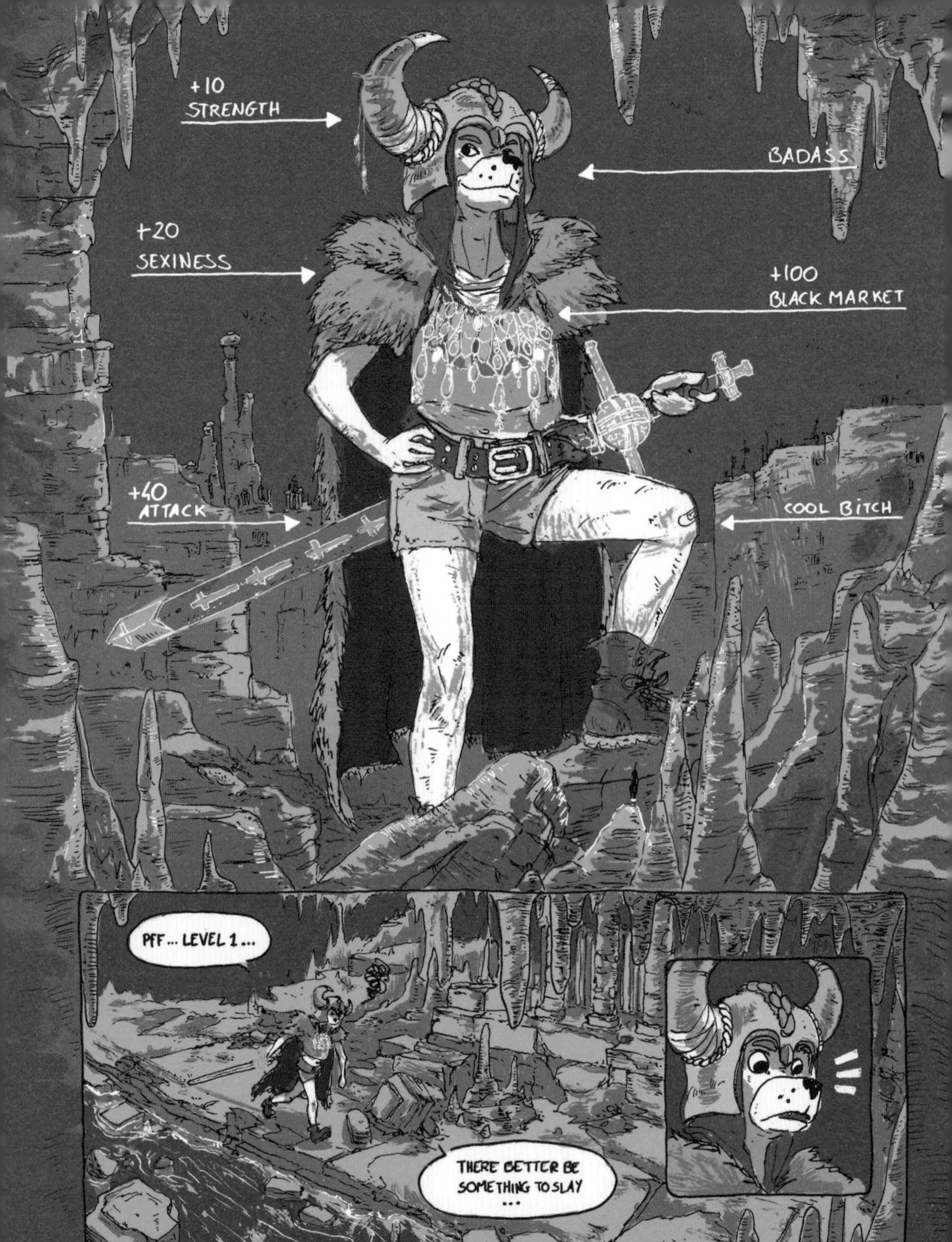

+10
STRENGTH
BADASS
+20
SEXINESS
+100
BLACK MARKET
+40
ATTACK
COOL BITCH
PFF... LEVEL 1...
THERE BETTER BE SOMETHING TO SLAY ...

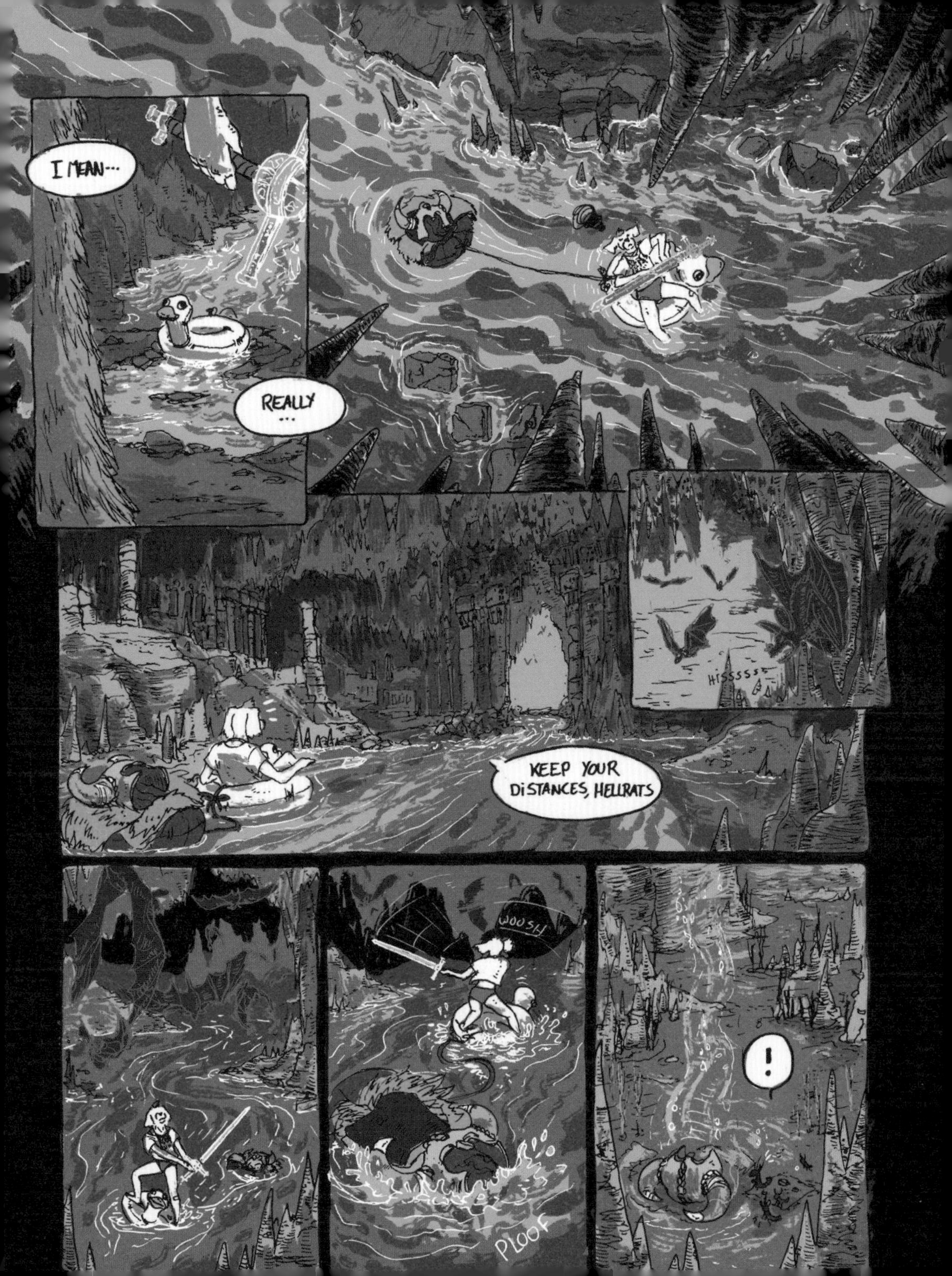
I MEAN...
REALLY ...
HISSSSSS
KEEP YOUR DISTANCES, HELLRATS
WOOSH
PLOOF
!

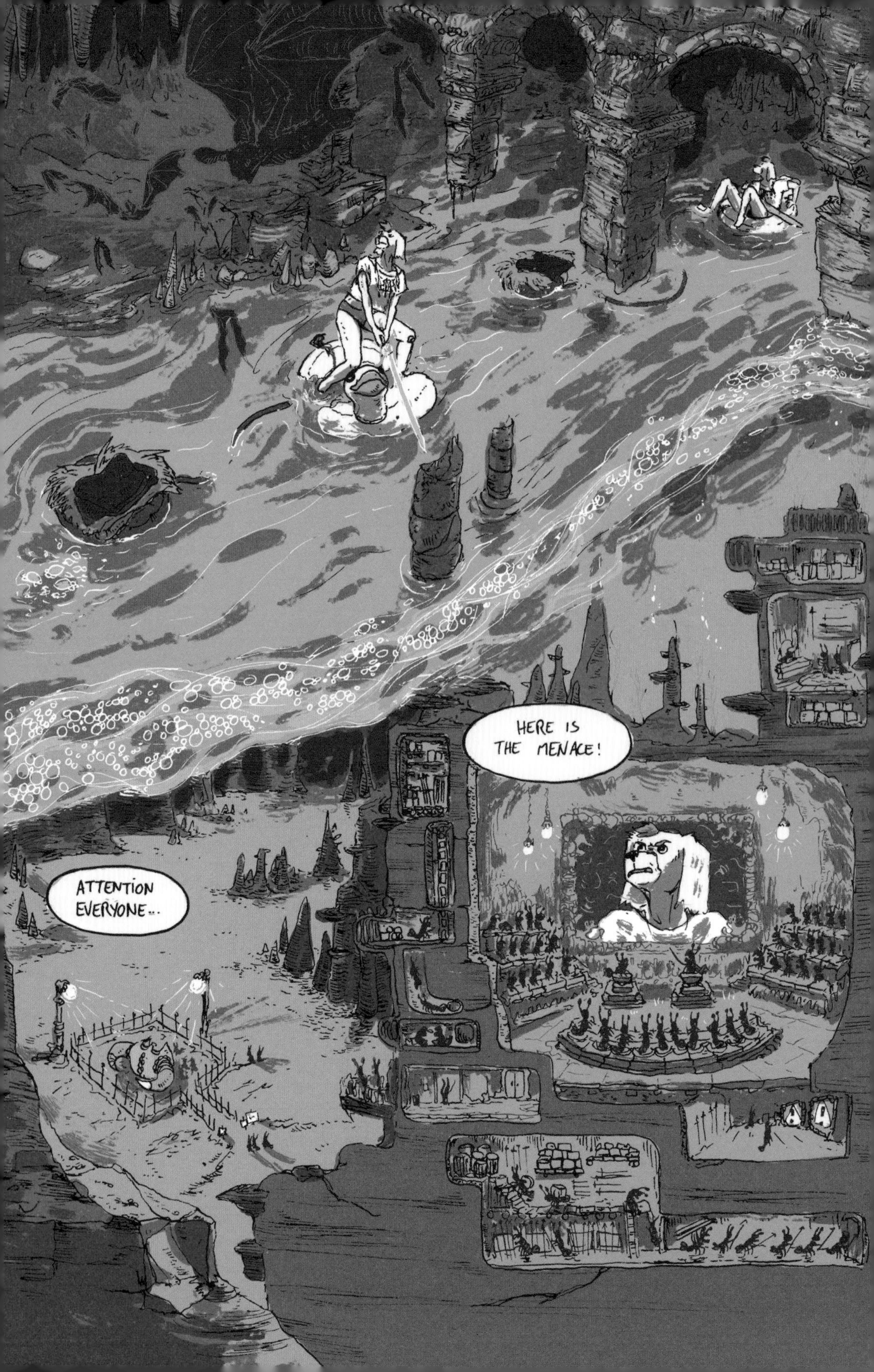
ATTENTION EVERYONE..
HERE IS THE MENACE!

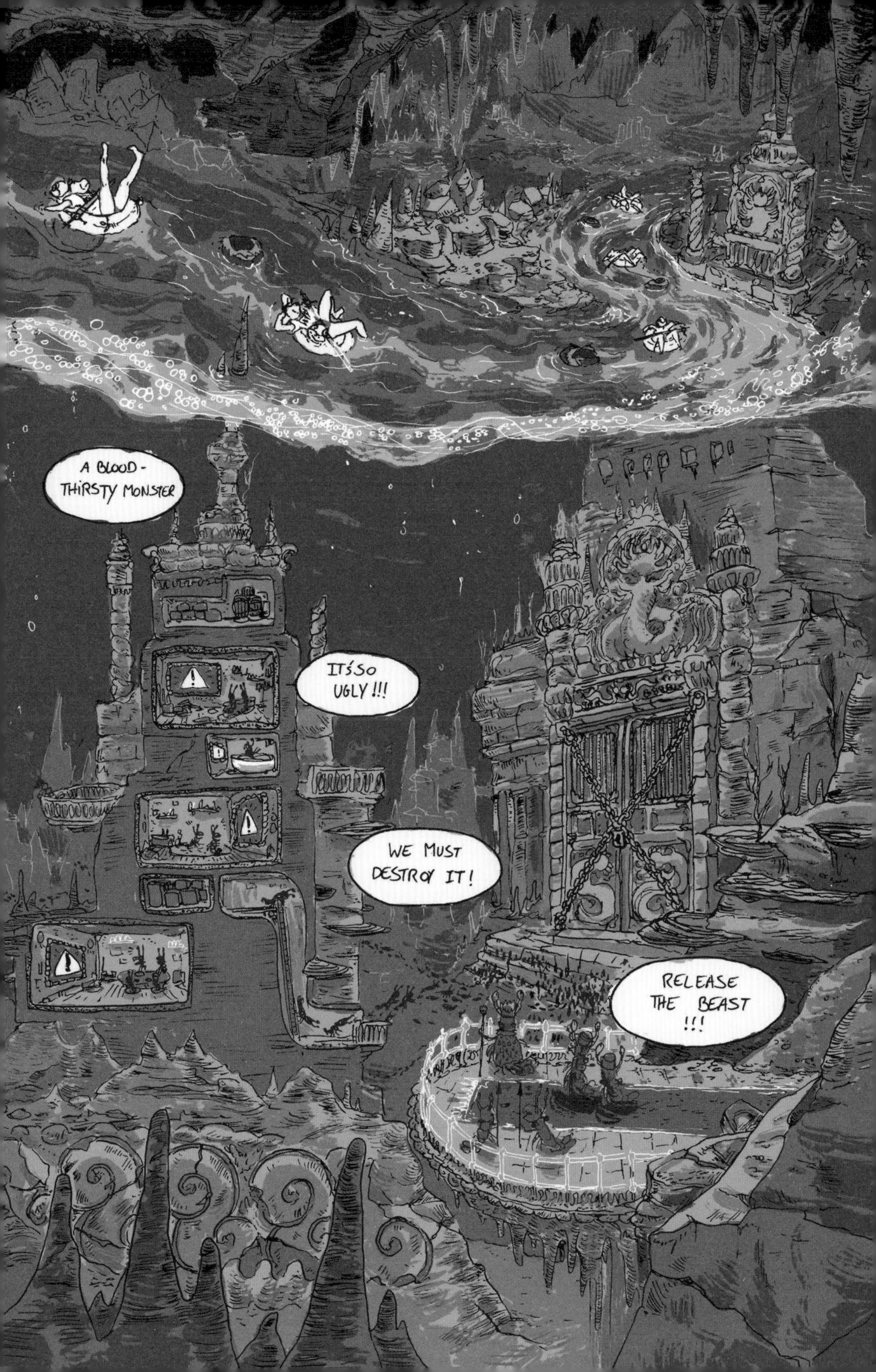
A BLOOD-THIRSTY MONSTER
IT'S SO UGLY!!!
WE MUST DESTROY IT!
RELEASE THE BEAST !!!

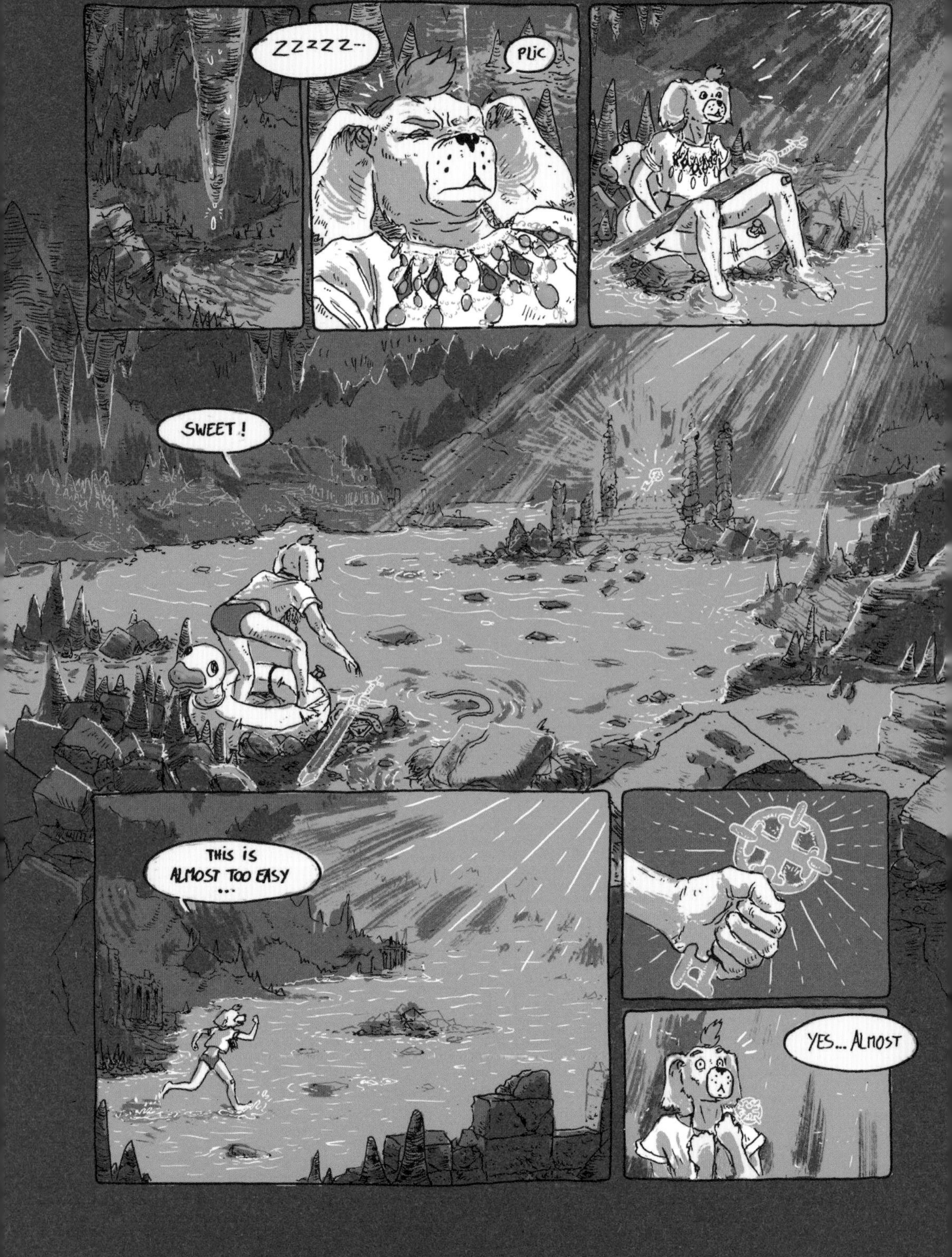
ZZZZZ...
PLIC
SWEET !
THIS IS ALMOST TOO EASY ...
YES... ALMOST

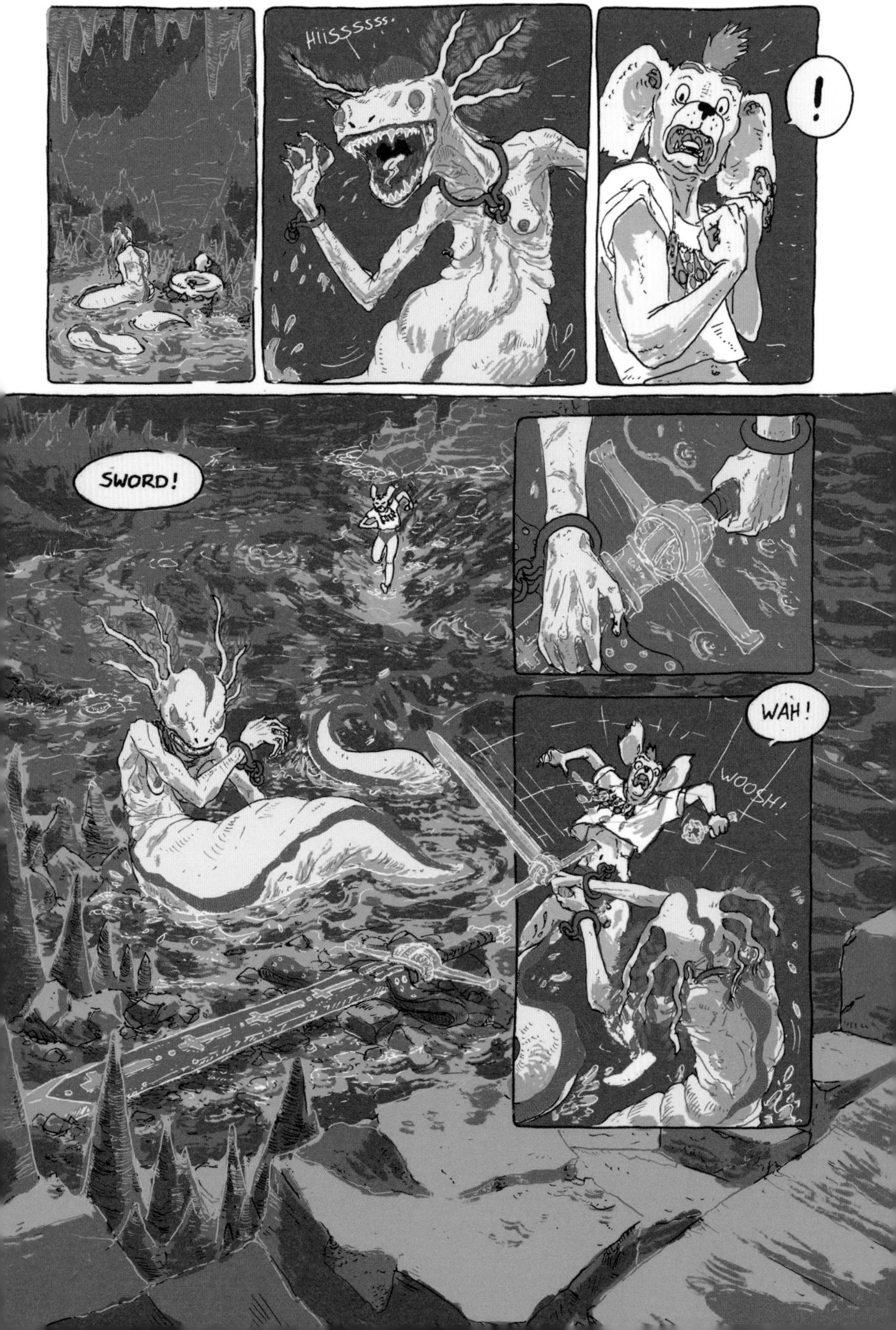
HIISSSSSS.
!
SWORD!
WAH!
WOOSH!

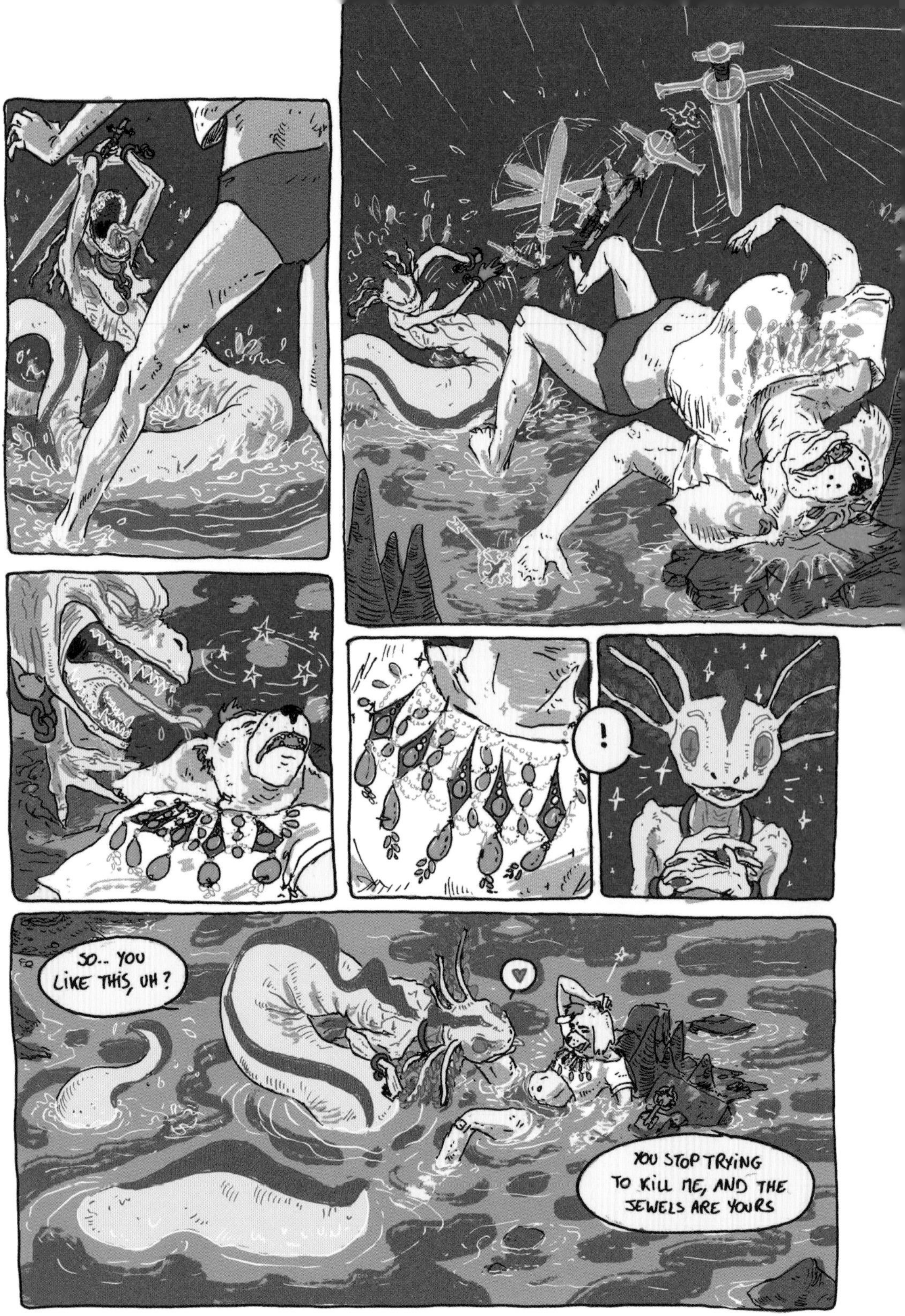
!
SO.. YOU LIKE THIS, UH?
YOU STOP TRYING TO KILL ME, AND THE JEWELS ARE YOURS

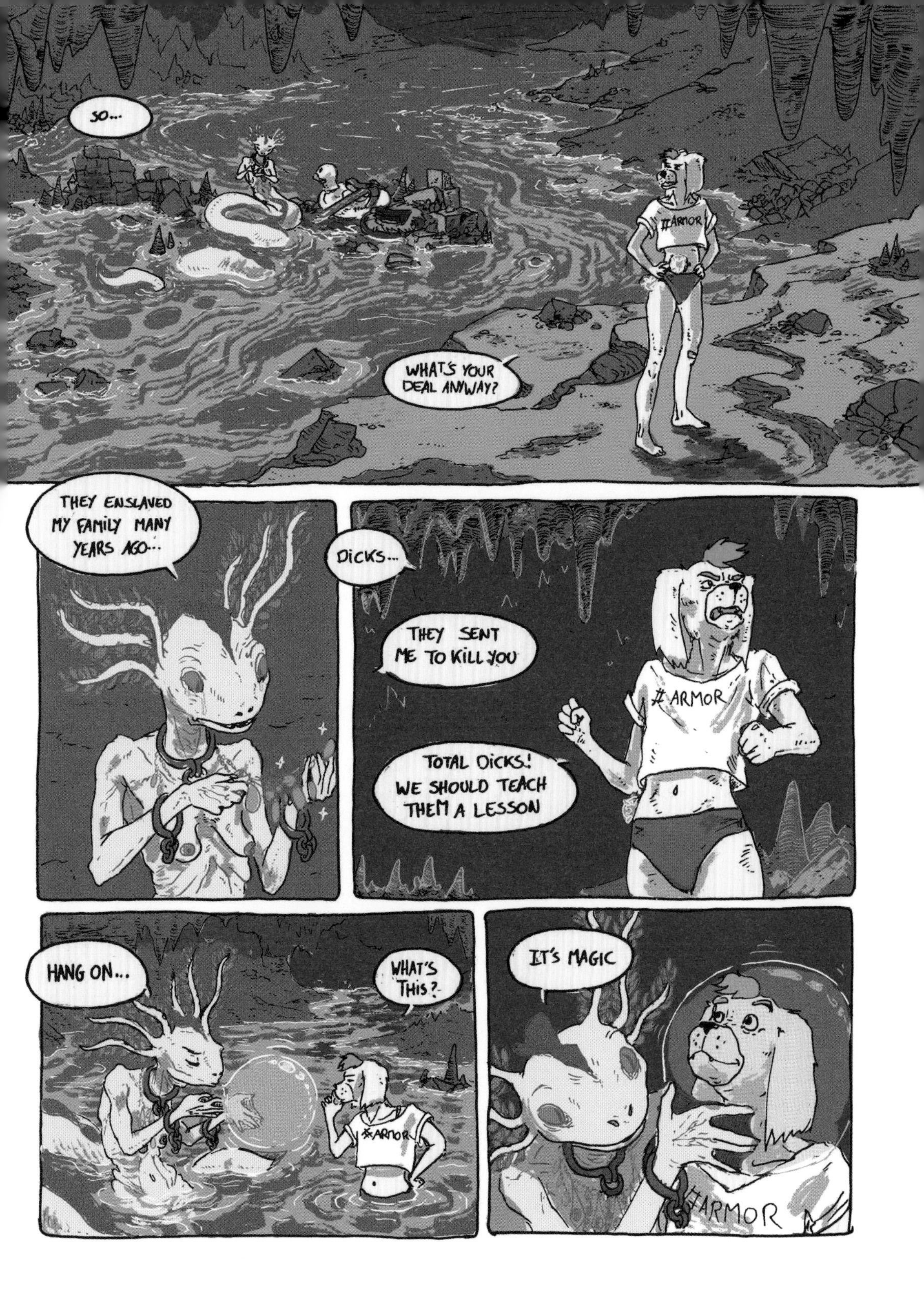
SO...
#ARMOR
WHAT'S YOUR DEAL ANYWAY?
THEY ENSLAVED MY FAMILY MANY YEARS AGO...
DICKS...
THEY SENT ME TO KILL YOU
#ARMOR
TOTAL DICKS! WE SHOULD TEACH THEM A LESSON
HANG ON...
WHAT'S THIS?
#ARMOR
IT'S MAGIC
#ARMOR

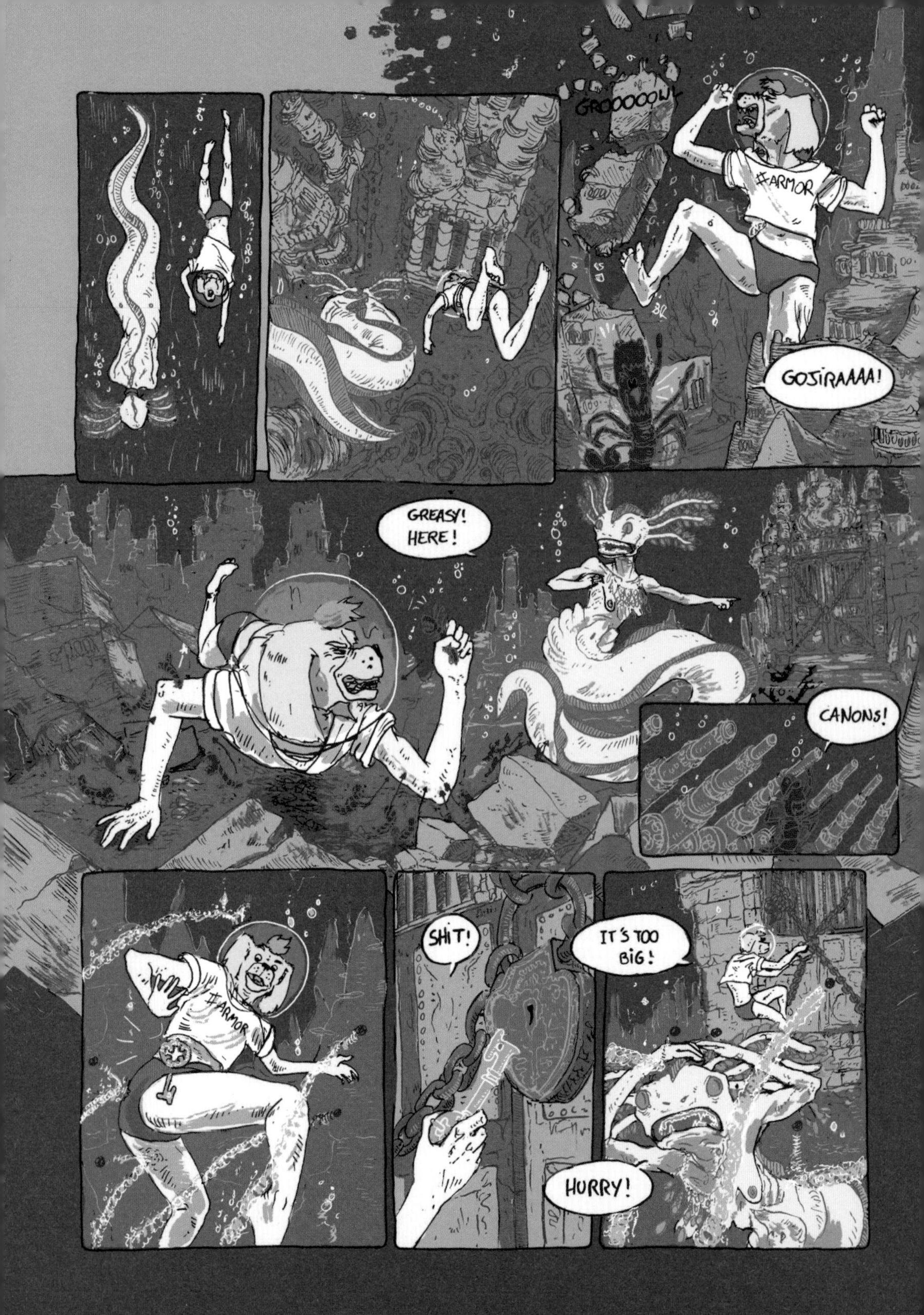
GROOOOOOW
GOJIRAAAA!
GREASY! HERE!
CANONS!
SHIT!
IT'S TOO BIG!
HURRY!

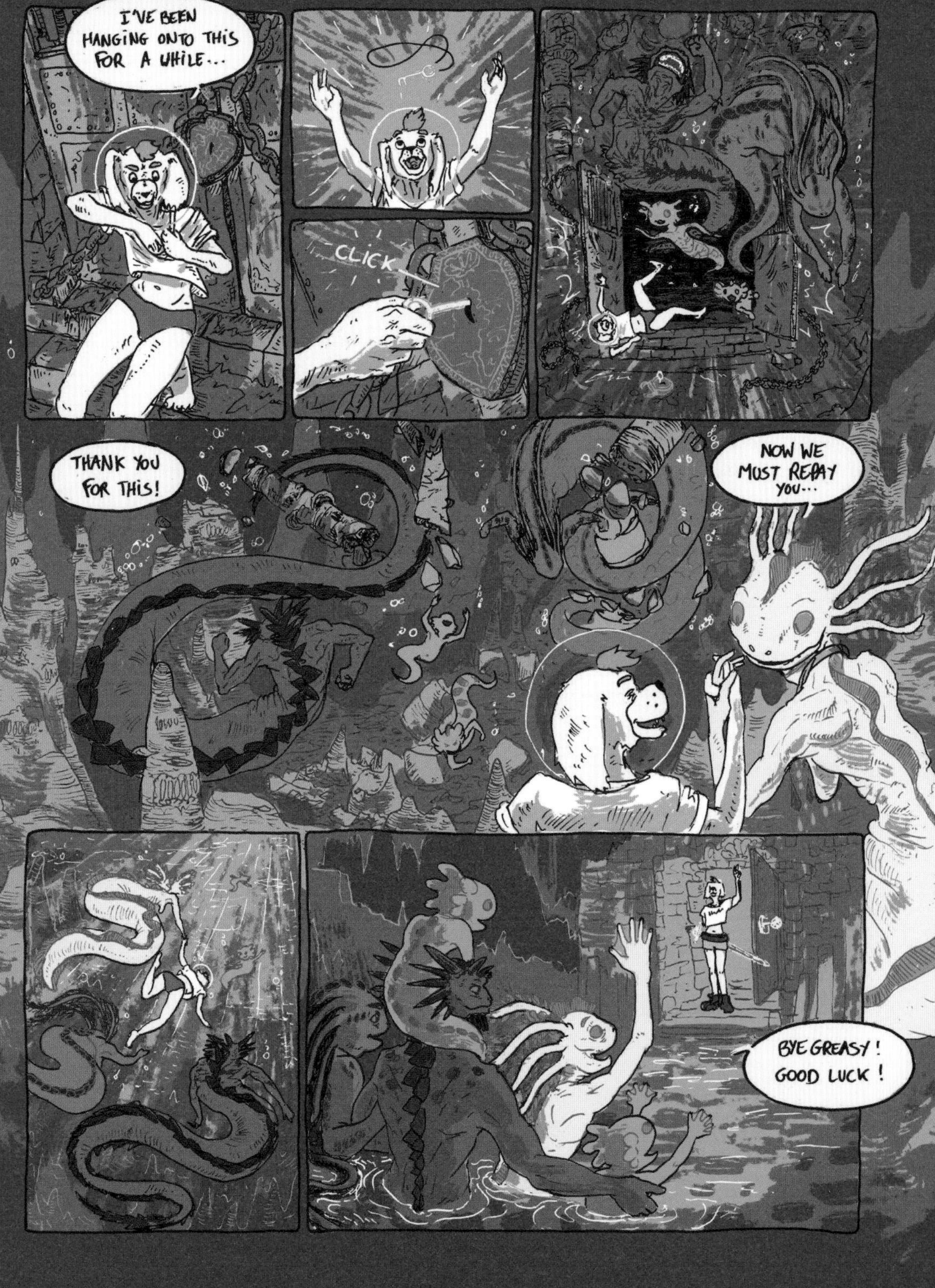
I'VE BEEN HANGING ONTO THIS FOR A WHILE...
CLICK
THANK YOU FOR THIS!
NOW WE MUST REPAY YOU...
BYE GREASY! GOOD LUCK!

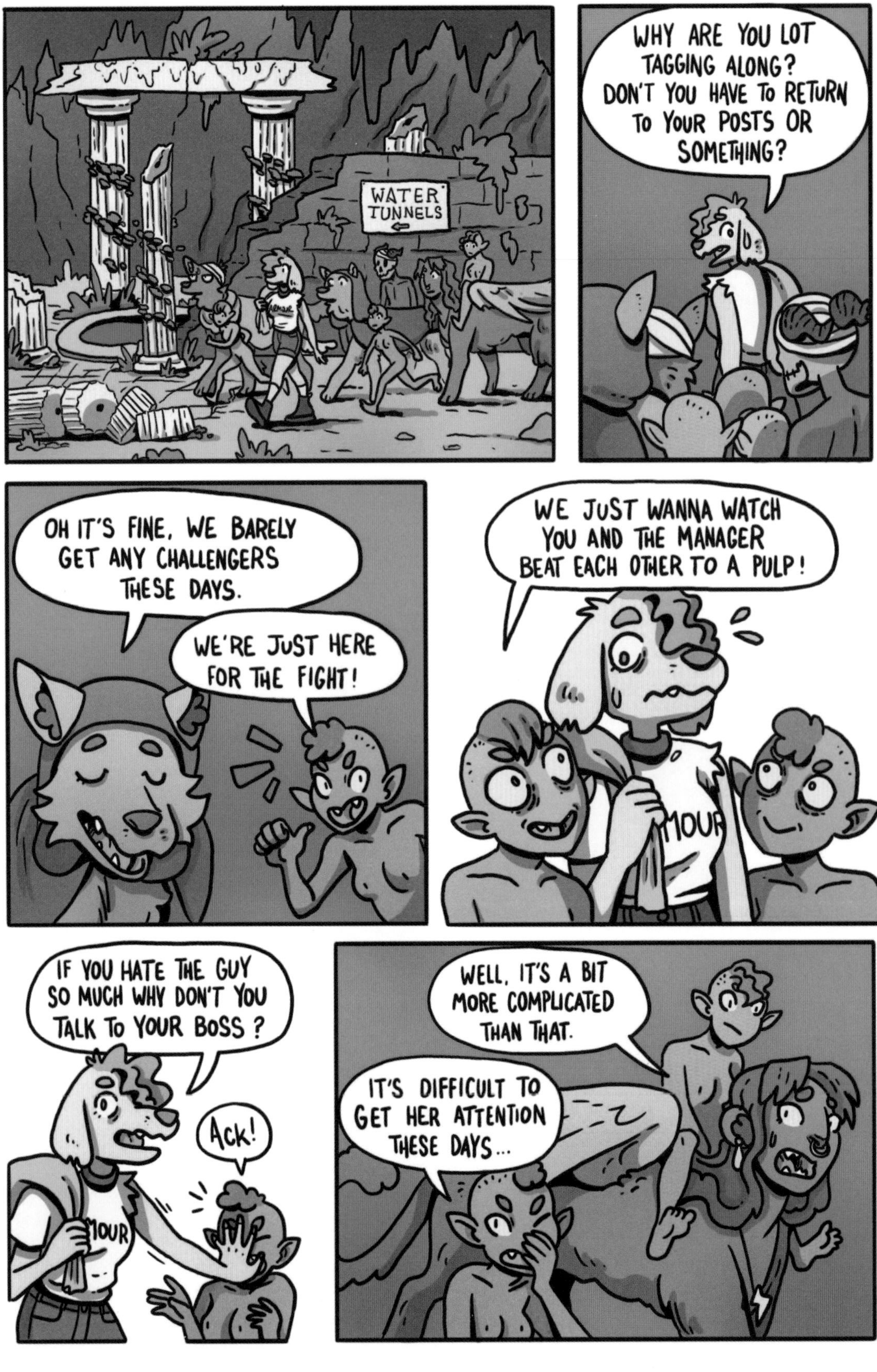
WATER TUNNELS
WHY ARE YOU LOT TAGGING ALONG? DON'T YOU HAVE TO RETURN TO YOUR POSTS OR SOMETHING?
OH IT'S FINE, WE BARELY GET ANY CHALLENGERS THESE DAYS.
WE'RE JUST HERE FOR THE FIGHT!
WE JUST WANNA WATCH YOU AND THE MANAGER BEAT EACH OTHER TO A PULP!
MOUR
IF YOU HATE THE GUY SO MUCH WHY DON'T YOU TALK TO YOUR BOSS?
Ack!
MOUR
WELL, IT'S A BIT MORE COMPLICATED THAN THAT.
IT'S DIFFICULT TO GET HER ATTENTION THESE DAYS...

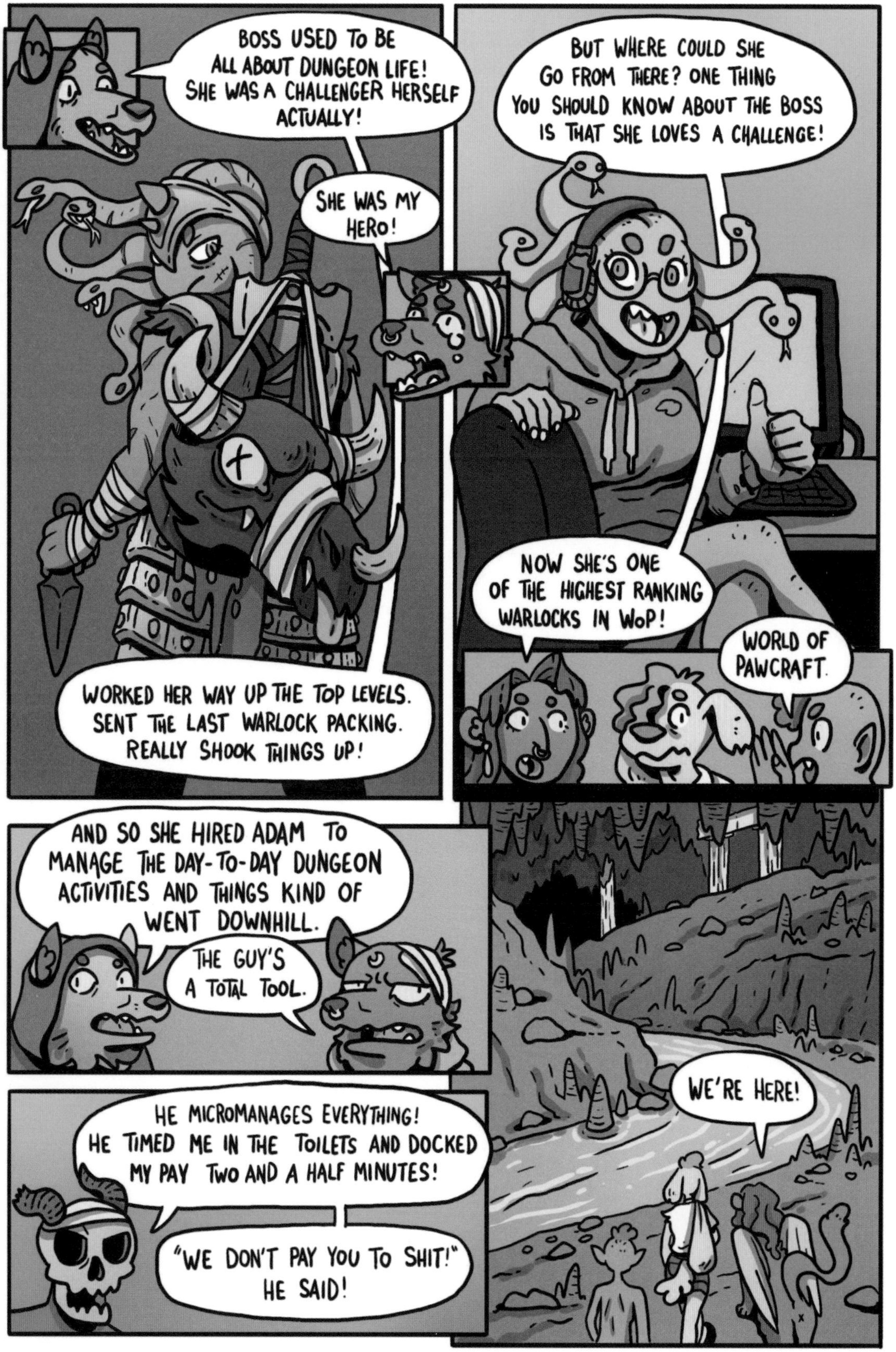
BOSS USED TO BE ALL ABOUT DUNGEON LIFE! SHE WAS A CHALLENGER HERSELF ACTUALLY!
SHE WAS MY HERO!
WORKED HER WAY UP THE TOP LEVELS. SENT THE LAST WARLOCK PACKING. REALLY SHOOK THINGS UP!
BUT WHERE COULD SHE GO FROM THERE? ONE THING YOU SHOULD KNOW ABOUT THE BOSS IS THAT SHE LOVES A CHALLENGE!
NOW SHE'S ONE OF THE HIGHEST RANKING WARLOCKS IN WoP!
WORLD OF PAWCRAFT.
AND SO SHE HIRED ADAM TO MANAGE THE DAY-TO-DAY DUNGEON ACTIVITIES AND THINGS KIND OF WENT DOWNHILL.
THE GUY'S A TOTAL TOOL.
HE MICROMANAGES EVERYTHING! HE TIMED ME IN THE TOILETS AND DOCKED MY PAY TWO AND A HALF MINUTES!
"WE DON'T PAY YOU TO SHIT!" HE SAID!
WE'RE HERE!

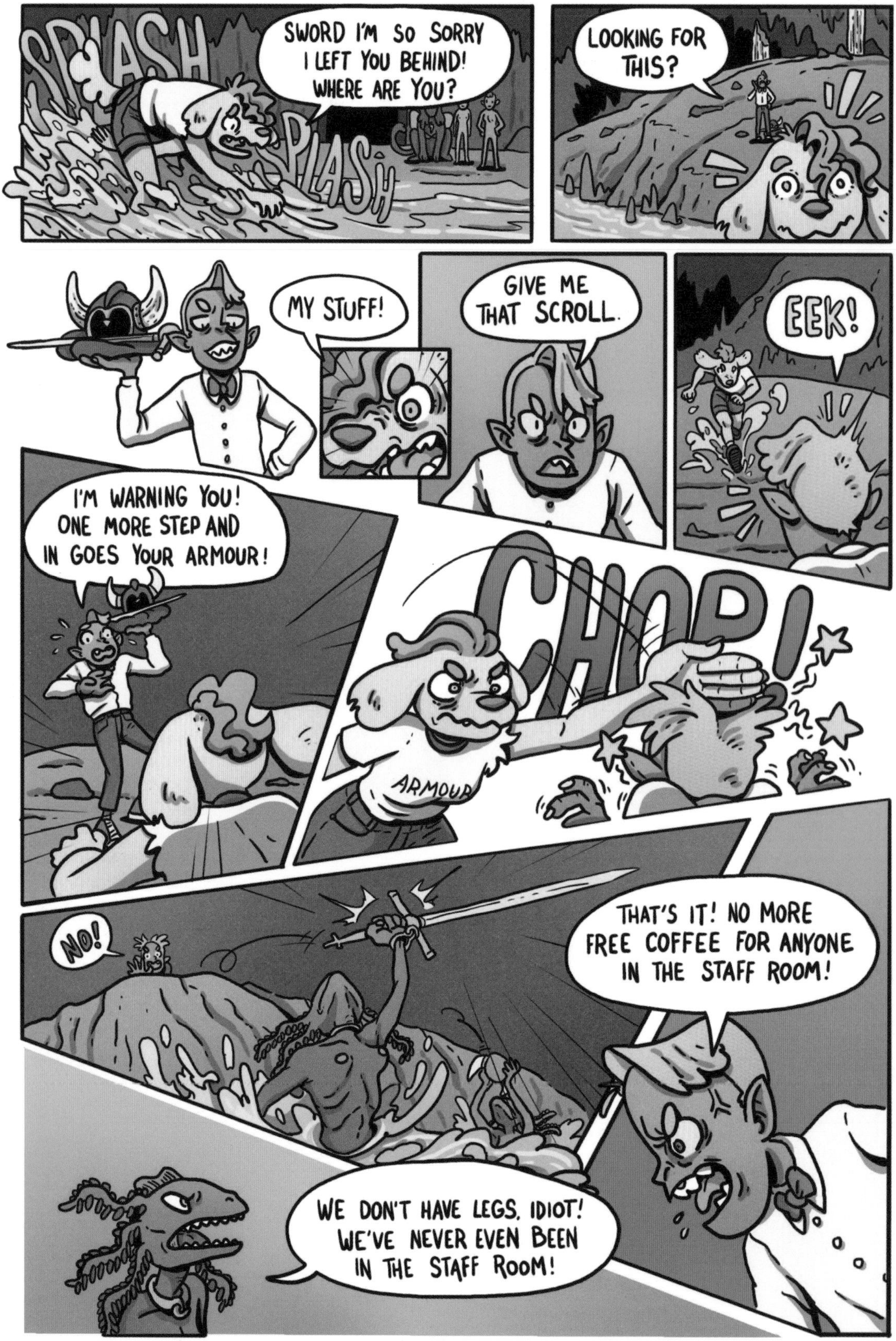
SPLASH
SWORD I'M SO SORRY I LEFT YOU BEHIND! WHERE ARE YOU?
SPLASH
LOOKING FOR THIS?
MY STUFF!
GIVE ME THAT SCROLL.
EEK!
I'M WARNING YOU! ONE MORE STEP AND IN GOES YOUR ARMOUR!
CHOP!
ARMOUR
NO!
THAT'S IT! NO MORE FREE COFFEE FOR ANYONE IN THE STAFF ROOM!
WE DON'T HAVE LEGS, IDIOT! WE'VE NEVER EVEN BEEN IN THE STAFF ROOM!

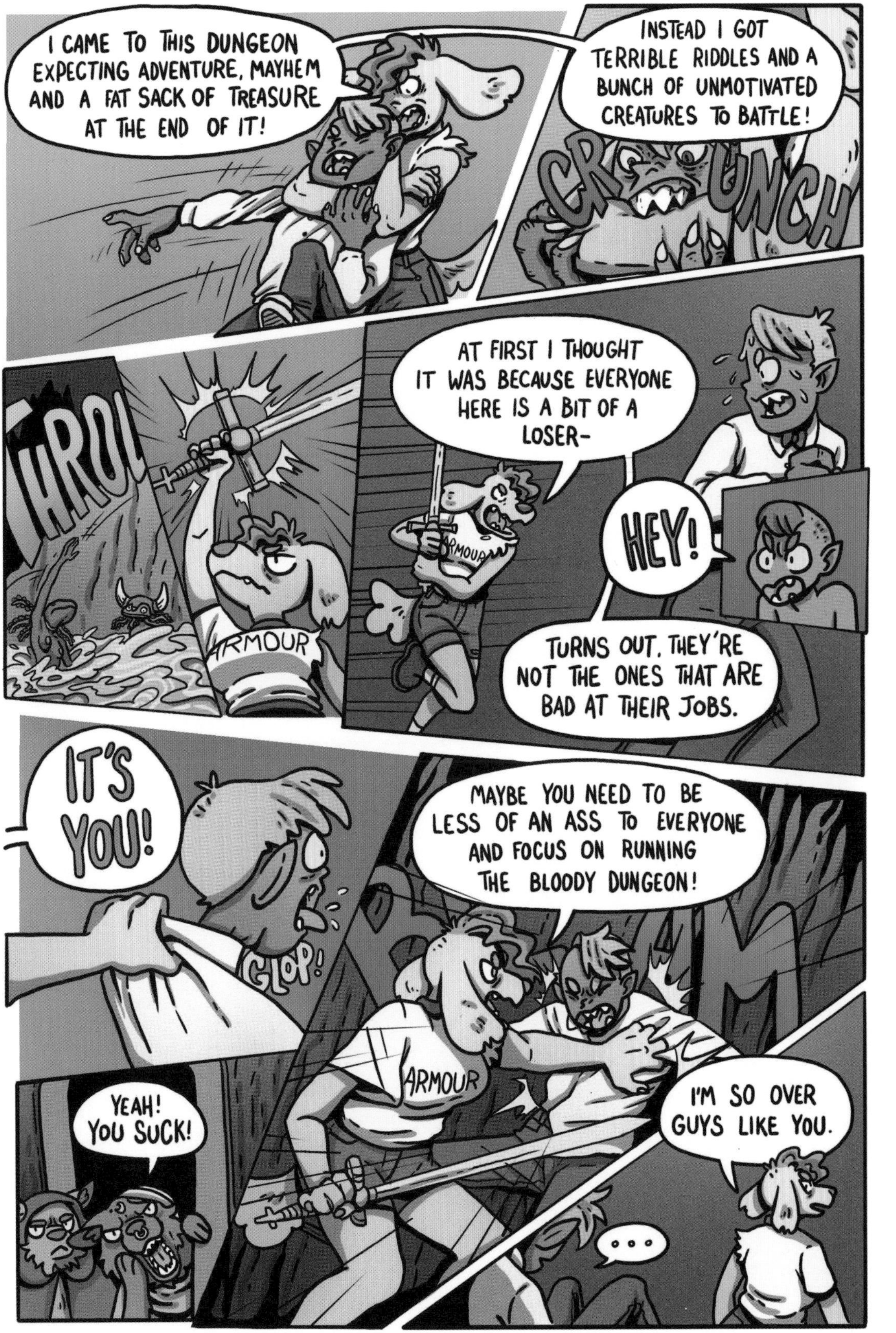
I CAME TO THIS DUNGEON EXPECTING ADVENTURE, MAYHEM AND A FAT SACK OF TREASURE AT THE END OF IT!
INSTEAD I GOT TERRIBLE RIDDLES AND A BUNCH OF UNMOTIVATED CREATURES TO BATTLE!
CRUNCH
ARMOUR
AT FIRST I THOUGHT IT WAS BECAUSE EVERYONE HERE IS A BIT OF A LOSER-
ARMOUR
HEY!
TURNS OUT, THEY'RE NOT THE ONES THAT ARE BAD AT THEIR JOBS.
IT'S YOU!
GLOP!
MAYBE YOU NEED TO BE LESS OF AN ASS TO EVERYONE AND FOCUS ON RUNNING THE BLOODY DUNGEON!
ARMOUR
YEAH! YOU SUCK!
I'M SO OVER GUYS LIKE YOU.
...

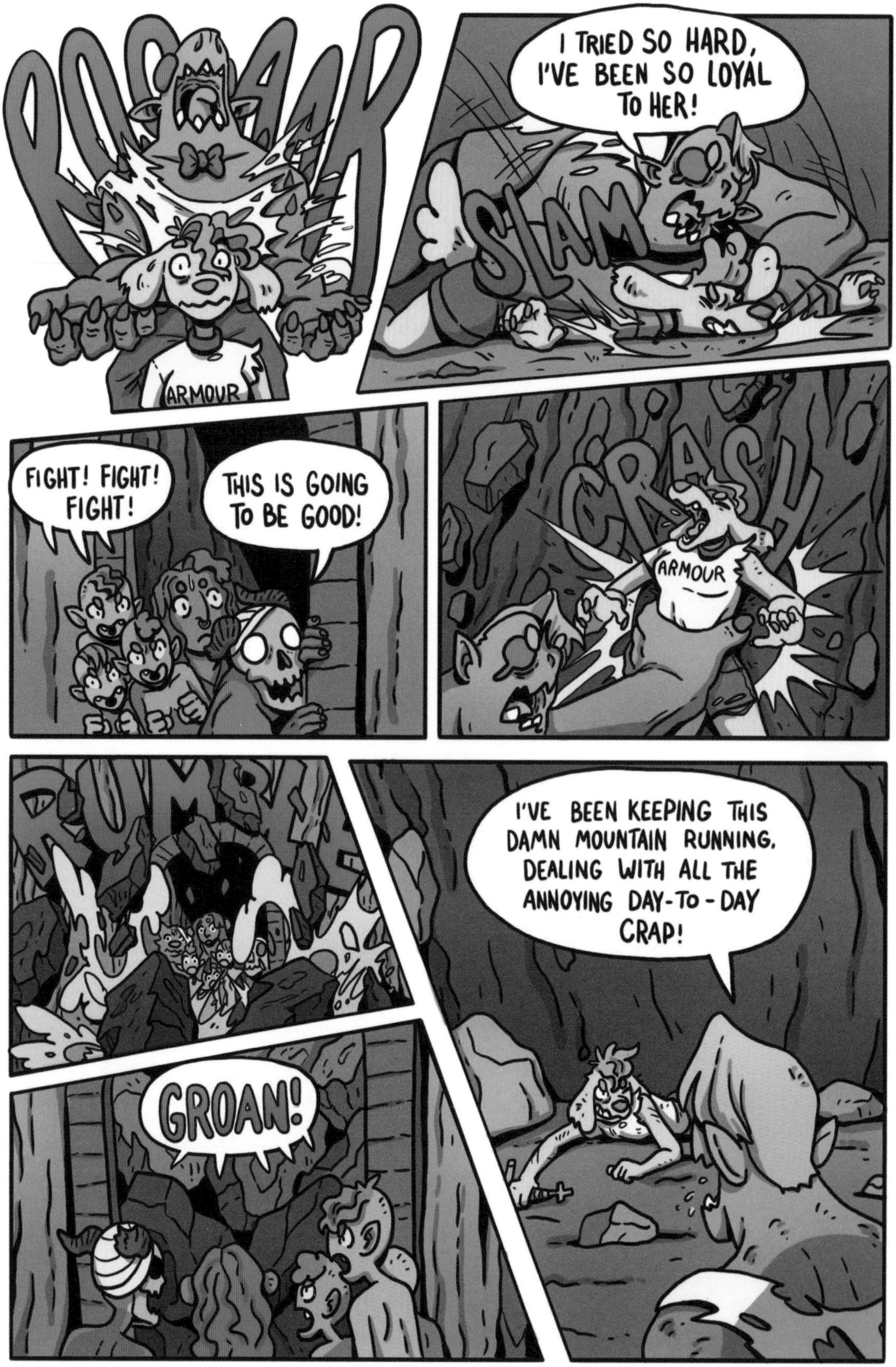
ROOAAAR
ARMOUR
I TRIED SO HARD, I'VE BEEN SO LOYAL TO HER!
SLAM
FIGHT! FIGHT! FIGHT!
THIS IS GOING TO BE GOOD!
CRASH
ARMOUR
I'VE BEEN KEEPING THIS DAMN MOUNTAIN RUNNING. DEALING WITH ALL THE ANNOYING DAY-TO-DAY CRAP!
GROAN!

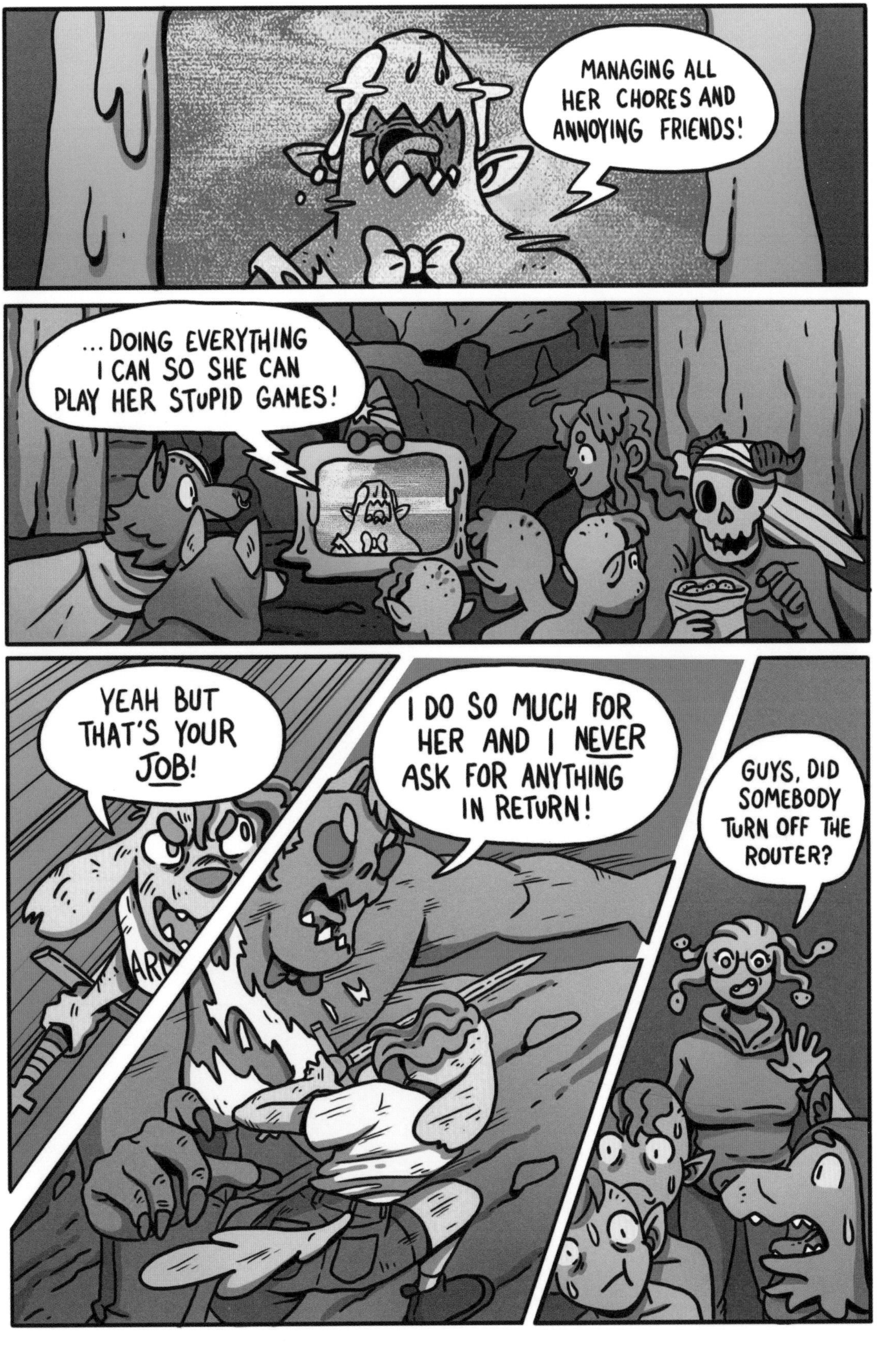
MANAGING ALL HER CHORES AND ANNOYING FRIENDS!
... DOING EVERYTHING I CAN SO SHE CAN PLAY HER STUPID GAMES!
YEAH BUT THAT'S YOUR JOB!
I DO SO MUCH FOR HER AND I NEVER ASK FOR ANYTHING IN RETURN!
GUYS, DID SOMEBODY TURN OFF THE ROUTER?

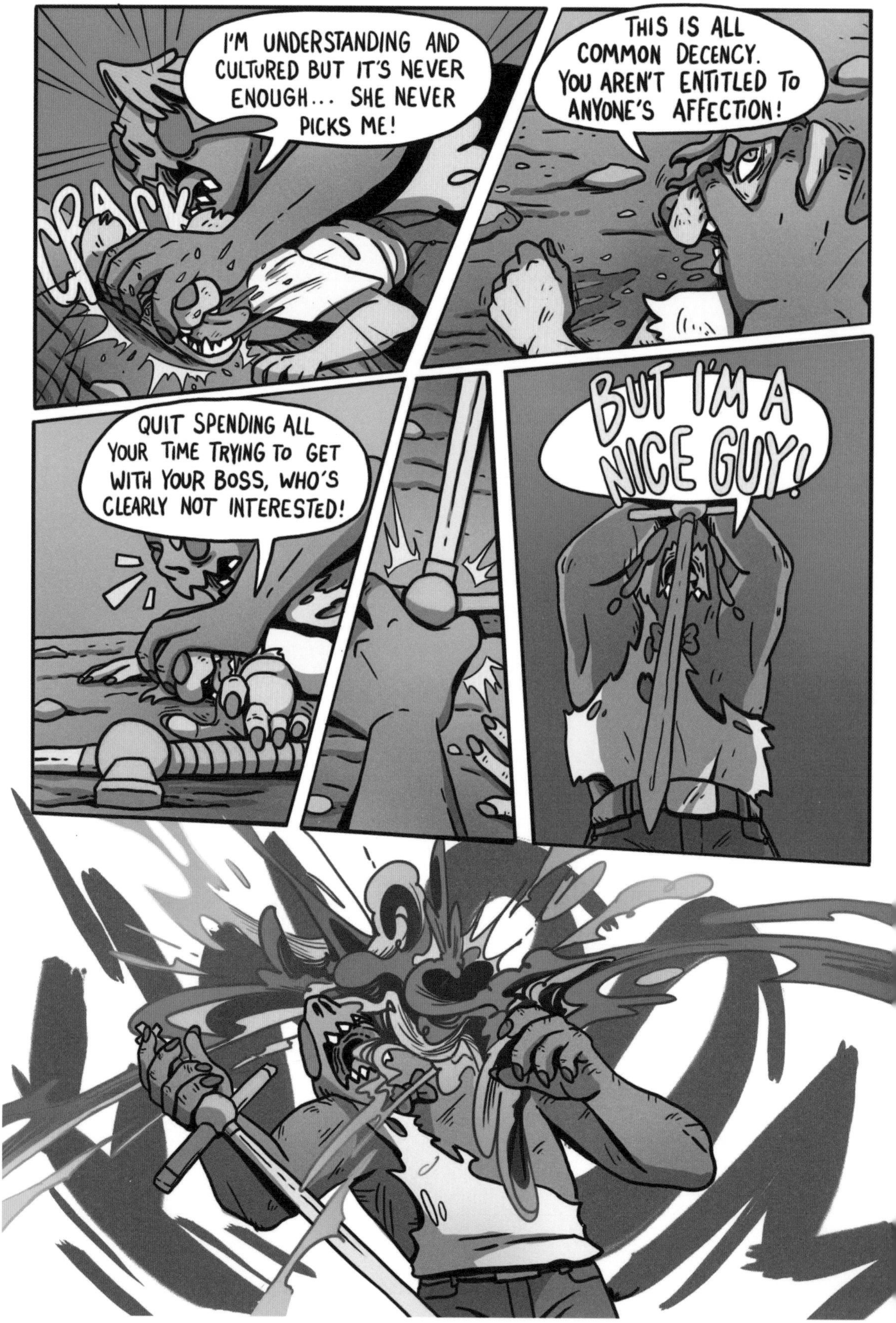
I'M UNDERSTANDING AND CULTURED BUT IT'S NEVER ENOUGH... SHE NEVER PICKS ME!
CRACK
THIS IS ALL COMMON DECENCY. YOU AREN'T ENTITLED TO ANYONE'S AFFECTION!
QUIT SPENDING ALL YOUR TIME TRYING TO GET WITH YOUR BOSS, WHO'S CLEARLY NOT INTERESTED!
BUT I'M A NICE GUY!

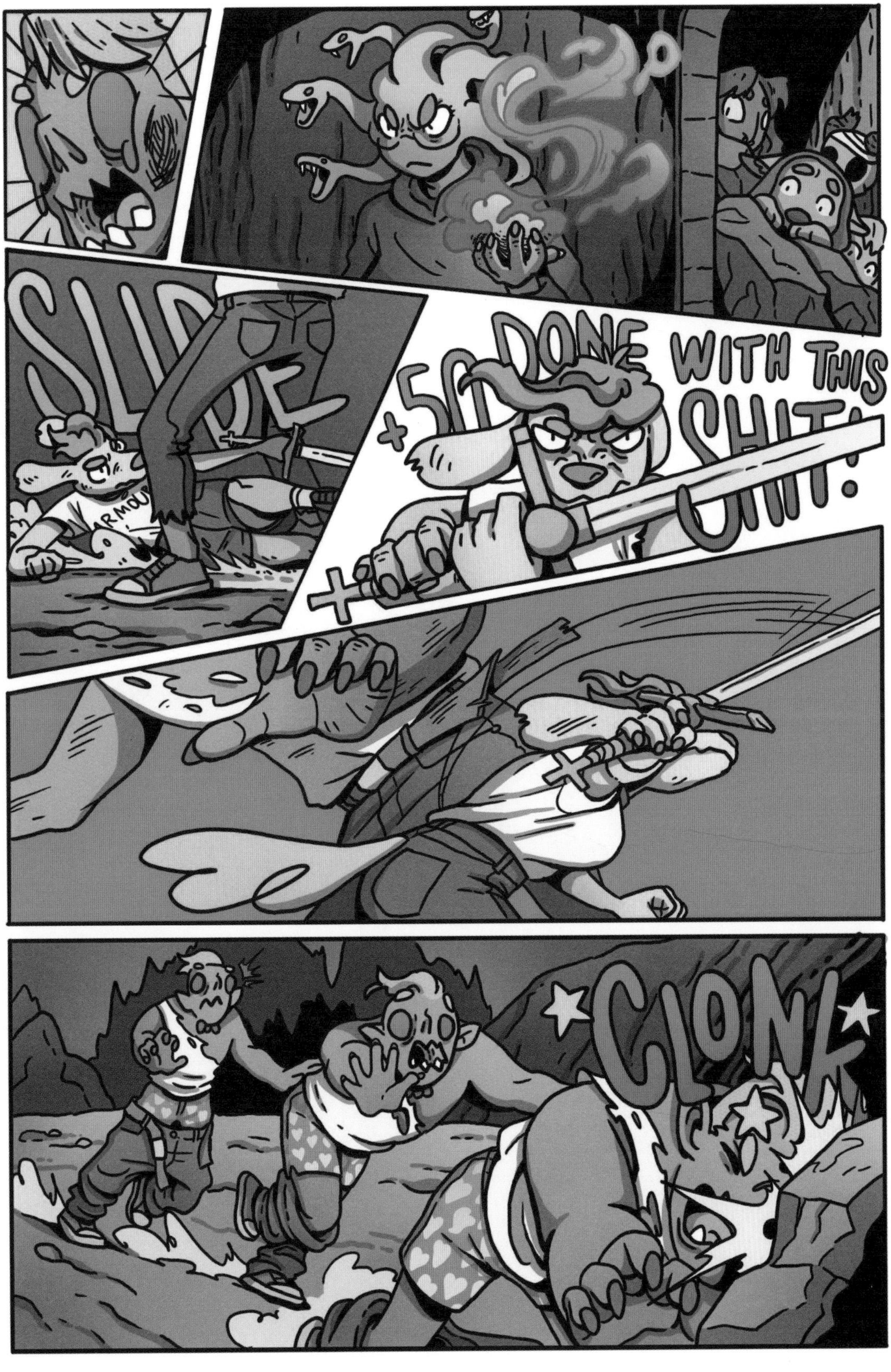

SLIDE
+50 DONE WITH THIS SHIT!
CLONK

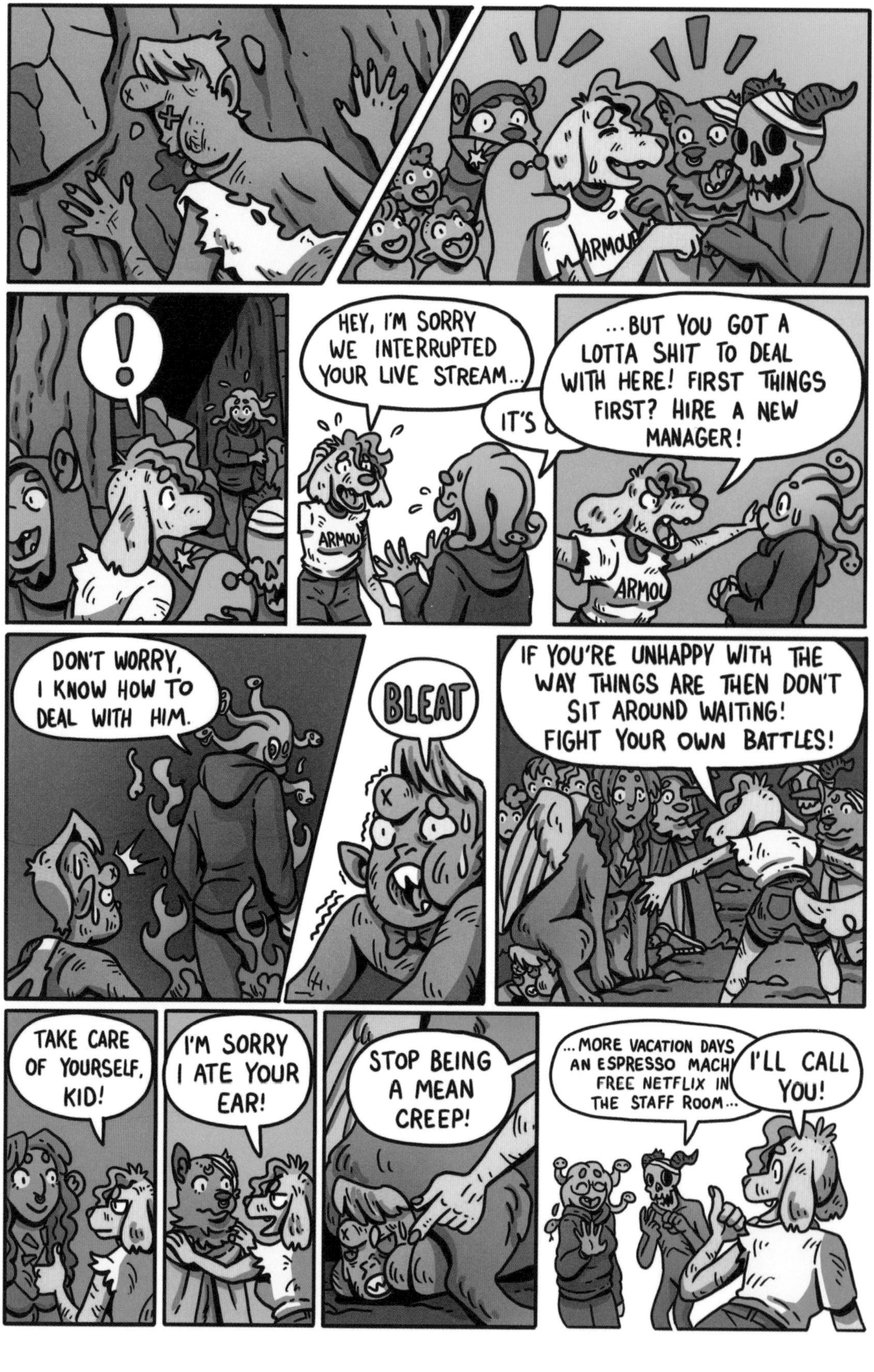
!
HEY, I'M SORRY WE INTERRUPTED YOUR LIVE STREAM...
IT'S
...BUT YOU GOT A LOTTA SHIT TO DEAL WITH HERE! FIRST THINGS FIRST? HIRE A NEW MANAGER!
ARMOU
DON'T WORRY, I KNOW HOW TO DEAL WITH HIM.
BLEAT
IF YOU'RE UNHAPPY WITH THE WAY THINGS ARE THEN DON'T SIT AROUND WAITING! FIGHT YOUR OWN BATTLES!
TAKE CARE OF YOURSELF, KID!
I'M SORRY I ATE YOUR EAR!
STOP BEING A MEAN CREEP!
...MORE VACATION DAYS AN ESPRESSO MACH FREE NETFLIX IN THE STAFF ROOM...
I'LL CALL YOU!

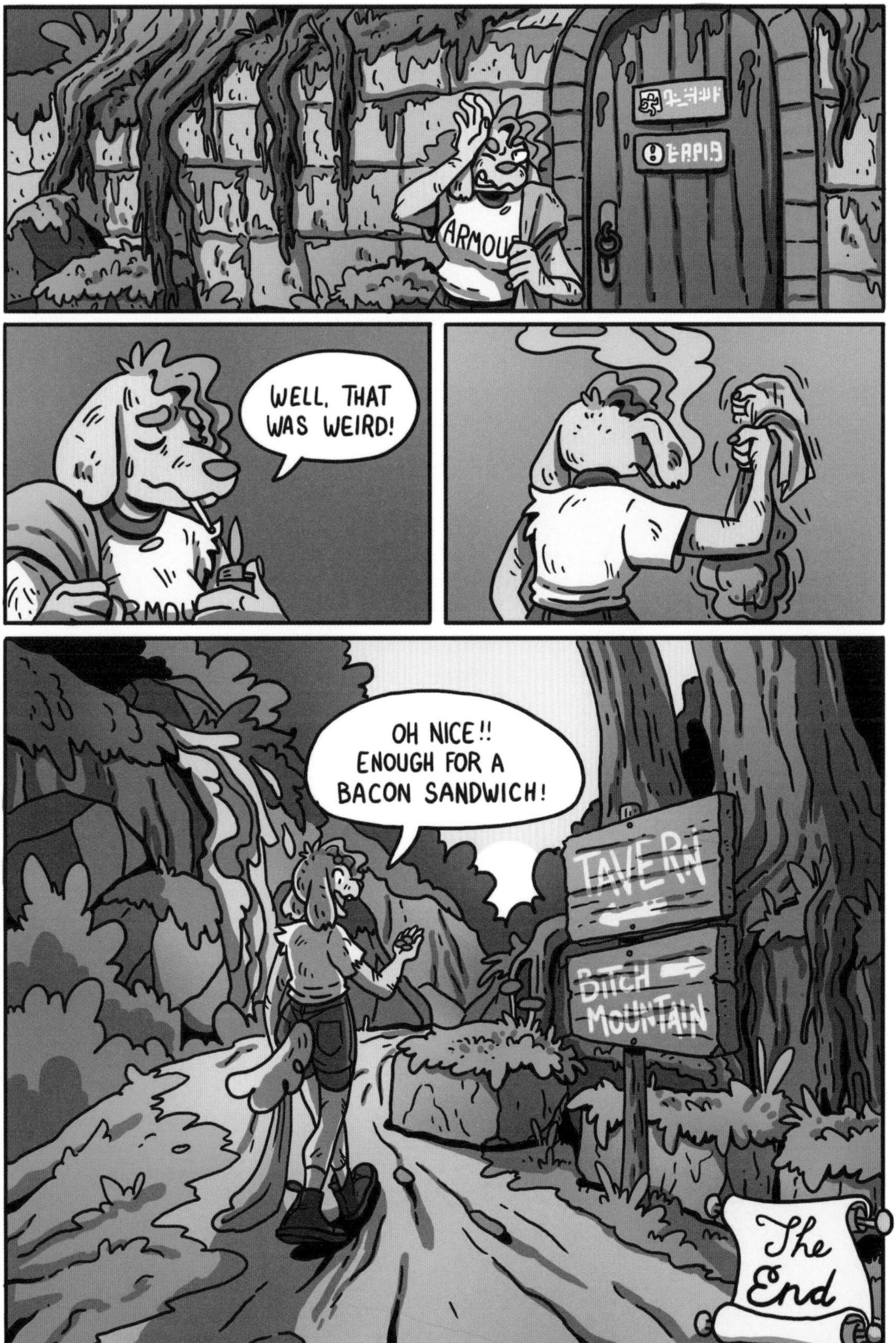
ARMOU
WELL, THAT WAS WEIRD!
OH NICE!! ENOUGH FOR A BACON SANDWICH!
TAVERN
BITCH MOUNTAIN
The End

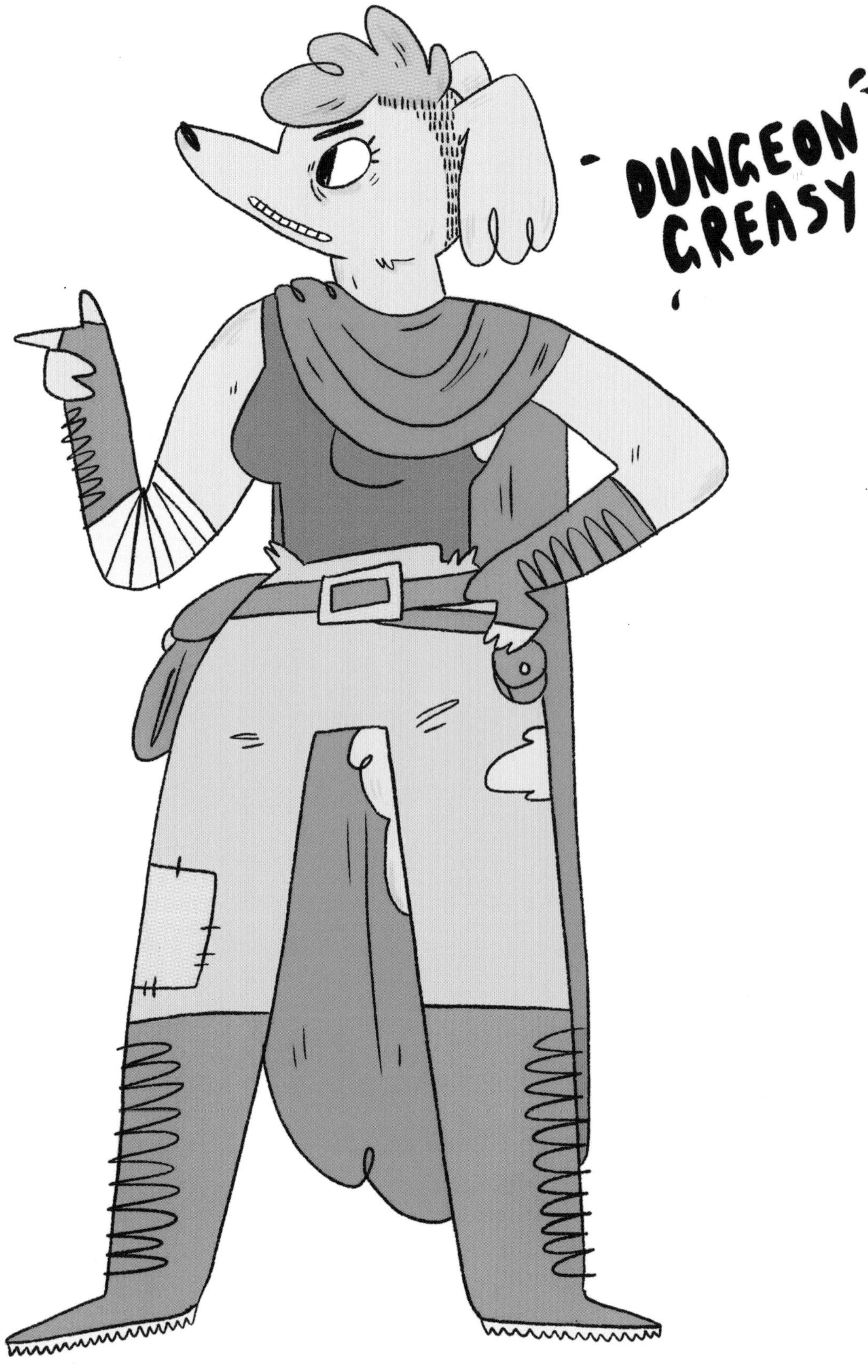
DUNGEON
GREASY

EARLY CONCEPT ART
by BARBAWK

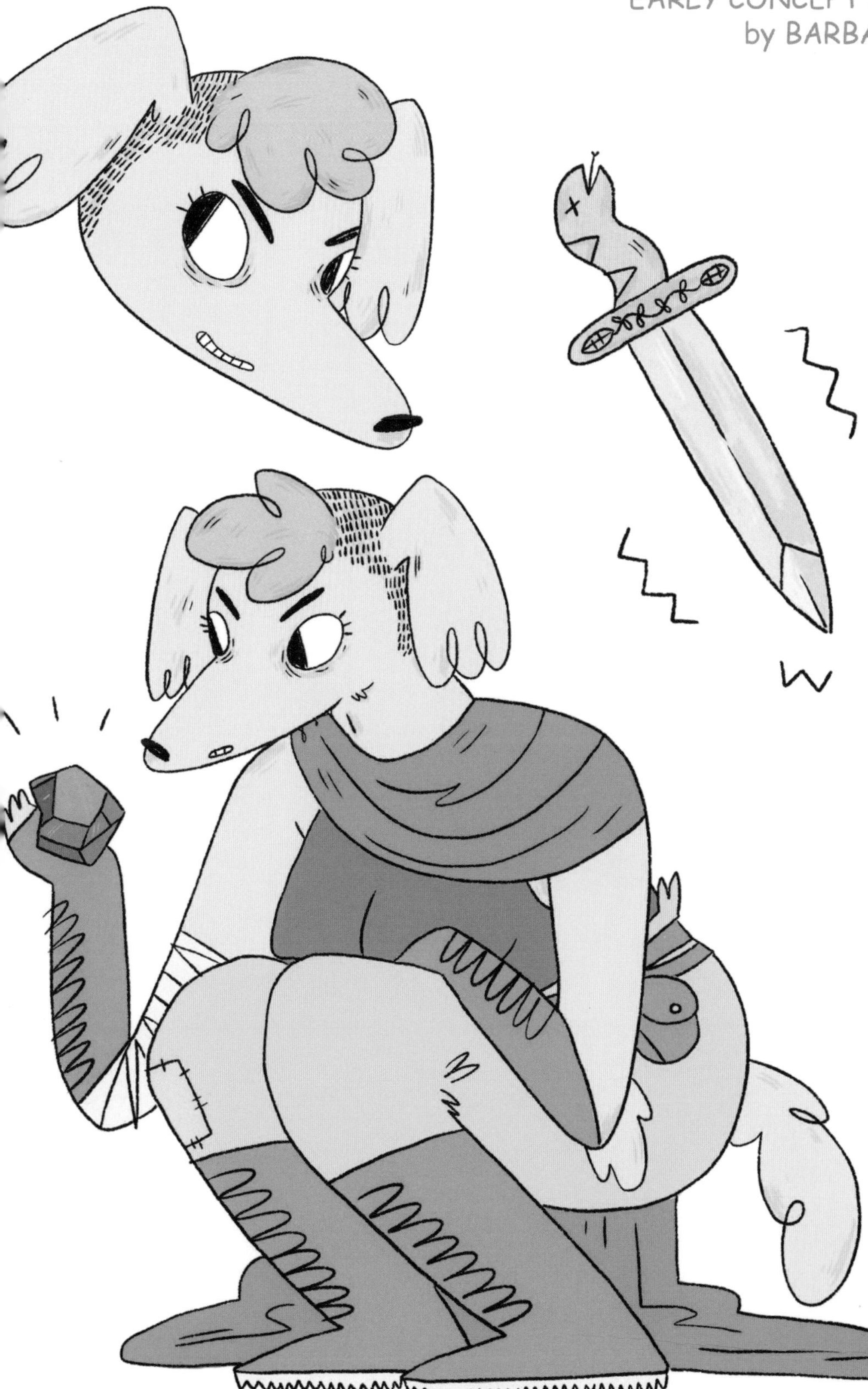

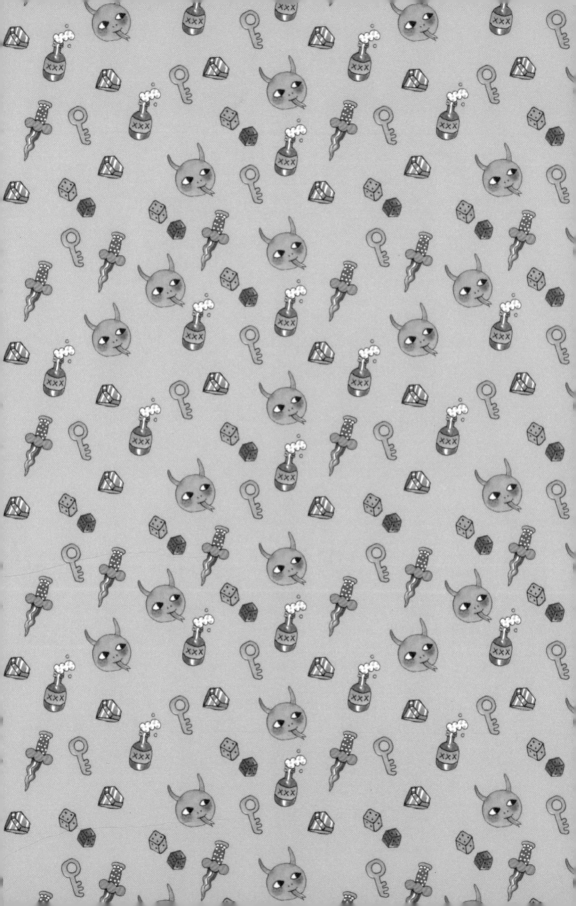